MW00947826

HOMELESS TO THE WHITE HOUSE

Tess Cacciatore

Homeless to the Whitehouse: Copyright © 2018

www.GWEN.Live

All rights reserved. Printed in the United States of America & the UK. No part of this book may be used or reproduced in any manner what so ever without written permission by the author, except in the case of brief quotations within critical articles or reviews.

Although the author and publisher have made every effort to ensure that the information in this book was correct at press time, the author and publisher do not assume and hereby disclaim any liability to any party due to these words coming from the author's own opinion based on their experiences.

Every word in this book is based on the author's own personal experience of their personal development journey and the outcomes with clients that they may have witnessed. Although we have made every reasonable attempt to achieve complete accuracy in the content of this book, we assume no responsibility for errors or omissions in the information in this book.

You should only use this information as you see fit at your own risk. Your life and circumstances may not be suited to these examples with what we share within these pages. The author and publisher are neither doctors nor in the position of registered authorities to give you expert advice. All we can share is what we have tested on ourselves and obtained through witnessing the changes in our lives or our clients' lives along the way.

How you choose to use this information in this book within your own life is completely your own responsibility and own risk.

For more information: **www.GWEN.Live**

GWEN Publishing House

ISBN-13:978-1720941668

ISBN-10:1720941661

This book is dedicated to first and foremost God and my parents, Louis and Carolynn, who are now part of my divine Angel God Squad.

To my dear brothers Mike and Rick who have been my champions and protectors along the way.

To my nephew Christopher, my nieces Jessica, Natalie, Savanah, Rebekka, and to my family: Ruth Conner, Jan and Doug Weimerman, Aunt Annie Costanzo, Aunt Phylis & Dick Cacciatore, John, Cathy, Jim, Joe Caron and their extended families, Denise Cacciatore, Brenda, Chris, Alex and Samantha Villers.

To Edie Fraser, for writing the forward to the book. Edie, cheers to you for your endless passion for all you do with the spirit of mentoring young women in the world.

To Mira Tresa Howard, who believed in me and my story to come on board for endless hours to edit my book. Mira, I thank you for your tenacity, wisdom, and most of all honoring my voice, which is a great quality to have in an editor and a dear friend.

To Pat Fultz and Jeff Huggins, for the endless hours of hard work and much laughter to get me launched in Iowa and beyond AND the new branding of GWEN. Both of you deserve a lifetime supply of the best Bourbon.

To Kate Batten, for your wisdom, spirit, love, and energy to launch my book with me and to bring GWEN Books Publishing to life.

To Brenda Brown, who has stayed with me at the helm during the transitions and hiccups of GWEN, dedicated to the core.

To Jacob Foko, photojournalist who captured the photos for the front and back cover at the White House.

To the divine introductions that brought me to the place of coming out of being homeless and to the birth of GWEN: Delbi Smart, Sue Smart, Anika Paris, Michael Littenberg, Lynn Fanelli. As all great things that are born at "kitchen tables" where the hearth of family and love are nourished.

To Kim Reed who has been an extraordinary person in my life, my protector throughout Congo and beyond. You have stayed with me all the way through the thick and thin of this GWEN journey, including coming up with our name GWEN.

To all the children from around the world who have changed me for the better, knowing that my personal journey was not to have biological children, but to be part of a global birthing. You all have touched my life forever.

To the Young Leaders of Ghana who are still part of the Mama Tess journey. I see your oak trees growing stronger every day!

And, I am grateful to the adversaries that God has put in my path along the way. You all helped me learn and grow. You all have kept the fire in my belly alive. These experiences, as hard as they have been, taught me many lessons in life.

My story is also dedicated to all who have suffered abuse, domestic violence, addiction, homelessness. We all have a story to share and your story is important to be revealed, so that we all can heal.

SPECIAL THANKS to all my "mid-wives" in the birthing process, and to those who have been instrumental in this magical and serendipitous journey.

Terrah Bennett-Smith, Leontine Lanza, Erdmann Rogge, Marlene Schifter, Alison Fuller, Lorrie Caplan, oikLiora Mendeloff, Paula Greenstein, Nola Anderson, Kohlene Hendrickson, Mimi Burns, Steve Tyler, Melissa Canaday, Ed Hyland, Frank Sawyer, Gary Ramsey, Filippo Voltaggio, Dorothy Lee Donahue, Dina Kimmel, Tim Kimmel, Zach Silverstein, David Longoria, Latisha Longoria, James (Jim) Fultz, Nicki Cardamon-Savage, Sondra Newkirk, Elle Febbo, Sheva Carr, Tom & Myrtle Keefe, Samantha Wendell, Wilda Spalding, Dean Landon, Chris Landon, Lin Evola, Steve Adorno, Gloria Hickok, Spryte Loriano, Erin Toppenberg, Erik Logan, Dani Adams, Glenn Clarke, Mitch Berman, Courtney Proffitt, Marc Bochner, Mark Day, Melody Botya, Savannah and Carly Fuller, Kelly Sullivan-Walden, Betsy Chasse, Shawn Powell, Brian Andrew, Nick Gurney, Brent Hahn, Nicole Hansen, Amy Seidman, Harpreet Mattu, John Vinestreet, Hiroshi and Kate Kato, Rene Echt, Kim Jorgensen-Adams, Camille Cellucci, Venerable Bhante Piyananda, Nancy Rivard, Fonda Whitehead, Simon Mainwaring, Szilva and Cyn Vecserdy, Lori Taubman, Cal Fussman, Yuki, Moustashi, Alberto, Bianca, Tea Defilippi, AND, the newest team to the GWEN family Xperienc-on-Demand (XOD) to offer a dream to come alive to reach millions of people through our distribution.

In loving memory of Noche and Edith Cacciatore, Harold and Pauline Davis, Kenny Conner, Anita "Nini" Cardamon "Mama 2", Mama "Dee" Clapp, Dick Caram, Stephen Shern, Dave Rodriquez, Russ Tilaro, Bill Fuller, Baxter, India Rose Jos Nakamura and to all of my dear friends who lost their battle to AIDS.

Table of Contents

Forward: Edie Fraser

Homeless to the White House is Tess Cacciatore's remarkable, powerful story of never giving up, self-discovery, self-reliance, and self-empowerment.

Tess's message is to stand up and persevere through troubles, and tragedies. We get to practice patience for the fruition of dreams, celebrations, and empowerment.

Today, Tess Cacciatore is a great producer living in Los Angeles. Reflect on her story, from her time in Africa to her journey to the White House during an experience of homelessness. Her passion never wavered, even in the face of struggle and pain.

Tess is passionate about providing a safe platform of being able to share your story, as she feels we all have a story to share. We all have made mistakes, experienced failures, and had lessons learned: Keep focused toward happiness.

Tess finds a call to action, as do millions of us today. Cacciatore says, *"The time has come. We are in a revolution and an evolution...The feminine culture and the empowerment of women is rising. We are given the choice to either take a stand, or hide in a cave."* Today with #MeToo, #TimesUp, and the social movement that Tess has started based on her story, #Reveal2Heal we can join Tess and tell our stories so we can rise up and come together for healing. We can join forces for the positives in women's empowerment, the likes of which Tess is doing with www.GlobalWomensEmpowermentNetwork.org, and what we are doing with Million Women Mentors by offering women great careers mentoring, sponsorship, internships and more.

Follow Tess's story as she begins her life tucked away in Des Moines, Iowa to embark on her journey at seventeen into the world. New York, Los Angeles, South America, Europe, Asia, and Africa. This book encompasses a life of someone who understands the beauty of the cultures of the world and to create a human family for solutions.

Tess believes that every story should be valued. Tess is clear in her "revealing to heal" messages that takes her from abuse to self-love, self-reliance, and self- empowerment. .

Currently, Tess is working with nonprofit organizations associated with various United Nations initiatives, including the annual *Commission on the Status of Women*. All of us know the stories of the world with abused women. Help them as we all work on positives.

Tess cheers us all who are taking a stand and joining actively to make a change.

Tess shows that she has *"slipped down the slipperiest of slopes and fallen down endless rabbit holes chasing carrots that have been dangled in front of me by one person or another."* But she shares a new hope for positivity. What a life she has had, filled with fearful experiences: *"guns pointed at me, walking on the edge of literal fires, flying in a plane over New York City on 9/11, living in Los Angeles during the riots."*

Tess has traveled the world for the past twenty-five years as a producer, public speaker, media leader. Tess's story reveals her darkest secrets during the height of her abusive relationships. She learned through hardship and "shedding her cocoon" to write this book. *Homeless to the White House* will have great impact on you, as it did on me!

This is a book to be read, shared, and celebrated. What a story!

Introduction

The time has come. We are in a revolution and an evolution. Markers throughout history stated that we would come to a crossroads in humanity, but we were not given the exact time, or circumstance.

This is an exciting time to be alive, however this is not for the faint of heart. The feminine is finally rising to balance the chronic masculinity that has been the way of the world for far too long. We are all faced with the choice to either take a stand and have our voices heard, or hide in a cave.

I do not believe in the fire and brimstone tales of our world coming to an end. However, I do believe we are in the midst of one version of our world coming to an end to make way for a new world. And in this new world, it is my humble opinion that we can rectify the balance between masculine and feminine to better find peace.

As I dive into the final stages of writing this book, I am preparing to travel once again to the United Nations for the Commission on the Status of Women, held each March in New York. March is Women's History month and March 8th is International Women's Day, so for me, this is a time for women to come together as one and support each other. There are too many examples, from my own experience to conversations I've had, where women have pitted against one another, instead of holding sacred our feminine powers.

The #MeToo, #TimesUp, #RevealToHeal movements are long overdue. They are platforms for all of us to speak our truth. Platforms through which we can take the time to reveal our pain, so that we can heal.

In my own life, I had to come to a place where I no longer felt like I had to defend myself for not choosing the traditional path of marriage and children. I feel it is important for women to come together and support one another, so that if a woman decides that marriage is not in her cards, or children for that matter, then there is nothing wrong with her...with us. Because there are many ways to give birth and to nurture. I have had more than a few women try to shame me into thinking that there is something wrong with me because I did not "do what God intended for our bodies to do, give birth."

To that end, we also need men to support our choices and for us to support men. We are at a crossroads witnessing the merging of both masculine and feminine aspects, which is creating a much-needed balance in the world. As women today, we are faced with new opportunities, so men are encouraged to face their emotions, express themselves, and be more aligned with their feminine side. I feel the way to obtain and sustain the balance on a global level is to hold the balance of masculine and feminine on an individual level.

There are numerous male public figures who are role models in making their mark to inspire men to be more in balance. Hugh Evans Humanitarian and CEO of Global Citizen, filmmaker Mikki Willis, actors George Clooney, Matt Damon, and Justin Baldoni (Jane the Virgin), who I actually had the pleasure of interviewing on GWEN Talks Radio to support his cause, The Wayfayer Foundation.

The United Nations is even getting into mainstream media by influencing how programming is being written and produced. Issues such as sex-trafficking and gender equality, are being pushed to the forefront of representation in television programs and feature films.

Even in Hollywood, stories of transgender and gender equality are finally being produced, and especially now, with the unveiling of the darkness that has been going on for so long in the entertainment industry these issues are being taken seriously. Men who have abused their power are now being held accountable. I cheer the celebrities and community leaders who are taking a stand, and I strive to do the same, in my own humble way.

I grew up in the Midwest, in a place that has been made famous through political elections: the Iowa Caucus in Des Moines Iowa. I was never into politics as a young person, but as life became more meaningful and I began to understand the implication of how my voice could make a difference, I have become more politically involved.

In my adult life I have lived in New York, Los Angeles, and San Francisco. I have traveled the world to places where most people only dream of going. I wake up each day with gratitude and always look at my adventures as a blessing.

This, despite the fact there has been many junctures on my road less traveled, when I have been curled up in a fetal position shaking my fists to heaven, thinking to myself, *"What in the hell am I doing?"*

I have slipped down the slipperiest of slopes and fallen down endless rabbit holes chasing carrots that have been dangled in front of me by one person or another. I keep swearing off carrots, I know that I am not a rabbit, but somehow my curiosity gets the better of me. Much to my own demise, my trust in humanity does not seem to diminish.

During the course of these carrot-chasing escapades, I have found myself in profoundly dangerous circumstances. These stories had not affected me until I sat down to write this book.

Between having guns shoved in my face, walking on the edge of literal fires, flying in a plane over New York City on 9/11 while the World Trade Center crumbled below me, and living in Los Angeles during the riots, my rabbit holes have led me far and wide. On top of this, I have lived in the confines of mental rabbit holes and even lived as a homeless person for sixteen months in 2011-2012.

I know that I have been, and continue to be, divinely protected, and my mission in life far surpasses a seemingly rocky ride. I feel it is my duty to share my story not because I feel that I am any better or worse than anyone else, but because I want to communicate that we are all on this ride together, so it is about time that we all get along.

Every time I turn on the news, I am overwhelmed by the amount of death, destruction, greed, and terrorism in the world. I know many people who have given away their television sets and are off the grid, as they do not want to be thwarted by negative news. For me, I believe it is important to be aware of what is going on and to at least try to find ways to bring social justice to the foreground. This is the time for peace-making and peace-keeping initiatives to be brought into action; I feel that this is my call to action.

I have traveled the world for the past twenty years as a producer, public speaker, media-accredited journalist for the United Nations, a humanitarian offering relief to disaster-affected areas, and a mentor to young women and men from around the world. I have dedicated my life to helping unveil worldly tribulations, and to mold these experiences into treasures that I hope will help change humanity for the better.

Homeless to the White House began while I was filming a documentary about a man who was running for President in the Democratic Republic of Congo in 2010. I traveled to the Congo by myself during a volatile national uproar to trace the steps of this man's life. He promised that when he was elected as President of the Congo, he would be committed to the women and children of Eastern Congo who, in large part due to the mining of the precious mineral Coltan, continue to be brutally raped on a daily basis. I risked my life as a pawn on his chessboard in life, and in retrospect, I wouldn't change a moment of my journey.

While filming in Congo, my safety was gravely compromised on more than one occasion. I still marvel at how closely I brushed heaven's door while in Congo, and I was reminded of this in December 2017, when fifteen United Nations Peacekeepers were slain for doing the same work that I had been doing undercover.

In effort to create the documentary on this man's life, many carrots were dangled throughout my time in Ghana, Angola, Congo, and Belgium. These proverbial carrots represent various situations throughout my life, such as record deals, soap opera contracts, publishing deals, documentary film deals, and probably the biggest carrot of all, the dangling carrot of elusive love.

Relationships have energetically manipulated my life to the core of my subconscious. I had to soul-search and claw my way back from underneath the rock-solid wall that framed the quarry of my heart. I had to find the right shovel, chisel, and hand mallet to carve away the stone to unveil a newly formed, intangible presence of self-love.

My story reveals my darkest secrets during the height of my abusive relationships. The worst of these experiences in my life were so deeply hidden that even my closest friends and family do not know the details that I am about to reveal. I had no intention of ever letting anyone in to help me. I thought I could do it alone. However, my discovery is that IF one does not fully release and heal, then the universe will continue to operate as a mirror and reflect the shadows.

I always dreamt of leaving a mark in this world, something that could transfer my pain into something good. I always had this internal fight that I was not good enough. I found that I needed to rescue myself and put on my own oxygen mask before I could ever begin helping others. I thought "they" needed me, but the fact was, I really needed myself.

After shedding my cocoon after eight long years to write this book, I feel it is important to finally surrender and give birth to my story. I get to squat in the middle of a field of sunflowers and push this book out of my creative birthing canal and then watch how it grows, rises, falls, stumbles, and dances. The consummate process of giving birth to ideas, to passions, to inventions, to beliefs. I had to go beyond my fears to know that my voice was worthy of being heard.

Through my story I want to propose a social gathering around a global campfire, to share stories that will allow for healing and change.

Homeless to the White House is where I surrendered all that I knew; emotionally, spiritually, mentally, and even physically. In 2011 I gave up my home and took a giant leap of faith into the darkest void. This story represents my personal journey of self-discovery, self-reliance, and self-empowerment. I share my journey and the birth of GWEN, as "she" is the culmination of my life purpose and my journey to healing.

It is interesting how we continue to judge ourselves so harshly. Since February 10, 2010, I have been writing this book. I have witnessed my contemporaries and friends spitting out several books during this time. My friends and family who know about this book have continued to ask me, *"When is your book coming out?"* I know they were all being supportive and that I have only myself to blame for self-judging. However, my lesson is that this book had to go through a transformation that paralleled my own transformation; and that had to come when the time was right.

If my humble story can float in the vast sea of literary greatness and can change the life of just one person, then my goal will be realized.

Thank you for taking the time to read my book. And, now my story begins. PART 1: The Rabbit Hunter. Isn't it ironic that my last name "Cacciatore" translates from Italian to English as the "Hunter."

Being that music is the important soundtrack of our lives, I have added a playlist of songs that were instrumental in my journey. I invite you to go to SoundCloud.com/HomelesstotheWhiteHouse and go to the PLAYLIST for over 50 songs that can be played along while reading my story. The songs have a buy-link to purchase the songs so that we can support the artists and the music industry. Enjoy!

PART 1: THE RABBIT HUNTER

Chapter 1

At Gunpoint

Soundcloud Playlist - Road to Redemption - Max Calo & Enrico Solazzo

Shocked solid, frozen in the back seat of a rental car, I stared down the barrel of a gun that was pointed in my direction. I was sinking in hot water and I was in way over my head. I do not think I realized how much I was in over my head until I was safely out of Kinshasa, Democratic Republic of Congo (DRC). That was the day that changed my reality forever.

"Drive!" I screamed to my translator who stared out the window in the opposite direction. He slapped the shoulder of our driver and shouted *"Kende! Kende!"* which translates to leave in Lingala, the local language of Kinshasa.

As our car lumbered down the bumpy dirt road named after the first Prime Minister, Patrice Lumumba, I looked back to see that the soldier had retreated his gun. He was on foot with no way to chase us. I exhaled.

I tumbled in the back seat of the car trying to retrieve my camera that had fallen off my lap and onto the floor of the car. I was on an undercover mission to obtain footage that I needed for a documentary that I was filming, hired by a man who was preparing to run for President of the DRC.

I had been seen by the guards as I was hanging out the car window trying to film an obscure angle of the Presidential monument. It is illegal to film in public, and even though I had been warned by my translator to be mindful of my surroundings, I was frantic to make the most of the limited time I had to get the footage that I needed so I could safely get out of this dangerous, yet beautiful, war-torn country.

I arrived in the DRC the night before. It was a long journey from Angola through Addis Ababa, Ethiopia. There was no simple way to get into Congo, and consequently, no simple way to get out.

I spent my first day in the DRC in the backseat of the car doubled over in pain from a stomach bug, trying to juggle my camera, a water bottle, and a barf bag. I wondered, *"How in the hell did I end up in hell?"*

I had been hired by this man, thinking he could become President of Congo. Eight weeks prior, on September 6th, 2010 I set out for what I thought would be a 6-day adventure to Ghana to help him launch his international campaign. I considered Ghana to be my second home based on the work that I had done they year before.

One thing led to another and I ended up being led by this "rabbit hunter" through several countries in Africa. My intentional six-day journey was extended and I did not return to Los Angeles until December 17th, 2010 - two months later.

I refer to this "rabbit hunter" as JPM. The concept of a carrot dangling in my face was an 'aha' moment for me. It occurred to me that I often got tangled in other people's' intentions and manipulations. I had to learn the hard way to follow my intuition and to not be tempted by carrots, or rabbit holes, or rabbit hunters.

Although I was hired to go to DRC on JPM's behalf, he was nowhere to be seen. He was safely nestled away in his home in Belgium, hidden from the realities that I faced alone. JPM made public accusations regarding the current President Joseph Kabila, including the allegation that Kabila captured and attempted to kill him many years before. JPM needed the support of global governments to ensure that his life would not be taken when he moved back to his homeland of Democratic Republic of Congo to run for the Presidency.

My number one intention was to draw global attention to (Blood Colton) and to bring an end to the raping of innocent women and children over the mining of these precious minerals in Eastern Congo. This was an issue I felt passionately about as I saw the inescapability of my personal responsibility in the issue. Coltan is the mineral that is extracted from nature used to create conductivity in cell phones, computers, and other electronic devices. I found myself unable to ignore the fact that the very products that run our lives are concurrently causing innocent humans to suffer on the other side of the world.

Backtracking to earlier that morning, I had entered the lobby of my hotel to find my driver and translator ready to embark on our grand adventure. I am certain that they had been hired by many tourists throughout the years, but I do not believe they had ever encountered a person who took them on a scavenger hunt like the one I did, where I had to trace through the history of JPM's life and the accused, attempted, alleged, assassination attempt and threat of JPM from President Kabilla.

While each of these locations was easily found, except for the location of his alleged assassination, every step I took to film was laden with military and danger. I am not sure that either Dido, my translator, or our driver were aware of why I was there, nor was I aware of the pending dangers that loomed on every Congolese corner.

Sitting in the back seat of the car knowing that I had put my life in danger to get this footage, I kept visualizing the faces of innocent women and children just on the other side of this country who needed my help. I felt so close, yet so far away.

Chapter 2

Politics of Love

How was it that I found myself in DRC? I had to trace back to a June "gloomy" day in 2010, when I was sitting on my bed with my laptop propped up on my crossed legs.

I was perusing Facebook when an invitation to connect popped up. This person, JPM, was looking for a documentarian to work with him on his story. He had seen my work through various sources and wondered if I was available and interested in taking the assignment. I was intrigued.

I had recently moved into a new home in Encino. The move into this house was the beginning of a slippery slope, as I had just ended an intense relationship with Maxwell from Ghana. I was heartbroken, so I welcomed the much-needed creative distraction.

JPM and I got on a Skype call. It was early evening in Brussels. During our two-hour call his wife dutifully delivered a bowl of soup for his dinner as he told me his story.

JPM was certain that the current Congolese President Joseph Kabila, had attempted to assassinate him because he was threatened and jealous of JPM.

As the story goes, several years before, JPM had gone on an extended trip to the Congo where he began a religious movement called Psalm 23. This psalm is based on the famous scripture from the Bible, reminding me of my Catholic schoolgirl days. This passage that had brought me comfort throughout the years, "The Lord is my shepherd; I shall not want. He maketh me to lie down in green pastures: he leadeth me beside the still waters. He restoreth my soul: he leadeth me in the paths of righteousness for his name's sake."

My naivety got the better of me, as JPM proceeded to share the details of his dramatic story. All of my humanitarian passions were set on fire, and my creative cells were in full flare.

An international murder attempt aligned with both political and religious implications. Now that was a great way to start a movie. My brain was already playing the opening scene and hearing the score of the music with enormous gospel voices. Please note that all of these stories, outside of historical and proven facts, were told to me by JPM. My trusting side wanted to believe, but no proof was ever given.

JPM was born and almost entirely raised in the DRC. His father was a king of one village, and his mother was a queen of another. At a young age, the king and queen came together and married. The mother never adapted to the idea of her husband having multiple wives, so when JPM was ten years old his mom left his father and married a Belgian businessman, in order to give her children a better education and life. JPM and his siblings were taken out of their African home and into a land of snowflakes and waffles.

Our conversation lasted well into the afternoon. JPM got more passionate the more he shared his story. His fast-paced, clipped accent combined with his reddened face and wide eyes spilled over onto my screen from the Skype camera. He proceeded to recount his privileged life in Brussels and his desire to go back to his homeland to help "his people" from the destruction of Kabila.

JPM began his "Psalm 23" grassroots initiative and with a groundswell of followers it became apparent to JPM that President Kabila was threatened by JPM's power and popularity.

JPM proceeded to tell me that one day he was coming out of his athletic club after playing tennis. He proceeded to a gas station across the street from the American Embassy.

JPM's car was seized by armed guards. These guards abducted him and whisked him away to prison. JPM was accused of going against the President by starting his own religious movement. After fighting to be released, JPM was put into solitary confinement. According to JPM, the President ignored his pleas to be set free. His attempts to get through to the Belgian embassy were thwarted by an unjust system within the confines of jail. JPM told his wife that he would have to resort to a hunger strike. He was in DRC on behalf of the citizens of Congo and he was going to take a stand for "his" people. JPM's wife was no stranger to the political scene as her father was a Minister within the administration of Kabila. However, even she could not use her father's political position to free her husband.

And so JPM began a hunger strike while in prison. After thirty days of no food he became too weak to carry himself. He was taken to a military hospital where the nurses tended to his health. JPM continued to refuse to eat. One night he heard loud noises in the nurses' station. He peeked out from under the blankets to see that the nurses were surrounded by armed guards. Muffled voices carried through the glass window into his hospital room. His heart began to race; he knew that they were there for him.

An older nurse came to his bedside apologizing for what was about to happen. The guards burst into his room and forced him to stand. They dressed him in scanty clothing and forced him down into the street. They blindfolded him and shoved him into the back of an empty van. His hands were tied behind his back. The van made various stops along the way and with every stop came a new prisoner. By the end of the journey there were approximately twelve other men who were then forced out of the van into an open space in the bush.

JPM's blindfold was dropped to the ground. All of the men were given shovels to break ground and dig the hole in which they were to be buried. JPM was too weak to do any digging. According to JPM, one young guard leaned in to say, *"I am a follower of your movement and I believe in you. I will not let you die. Just pretend to drop when you hear the gunshot."* When the graves were sufficiently complete, the men were lined up next to one another.

JPM shared with me that while he was walking towards the open grave a gospel song rang in his mind. It was the gospel singer, Cece Winans singing, *I Surrender All.*

Soundcloud Playlist - I Surrender All - Cece Winans

The same young guard yelled to his cohorts, *"Let's let the minister be buried on top, so that he can introduce his new friends to HIS Jesus."*

The guards' voices rang out in laughter, as a series of gunshots stung the air. JPM fell to the ground, pretending to be dead. They dragged all of the bodies on top of one another, with JPM on top. A thick plastic sheet was placed over them (this part of the story changed each time I heard the timeline) but supposedly they were all left to decompose.

JPM said that it was around 2:00 a.m. when he realized that he was the sole survivor of the ordeal and that the guards were no longer there. He slowly ripped through the thick plastic cover and climbed out of his grave, grasping for breath in the fresh night air. Having to escape the bush, he crossed onto an open road not far from the N'djili Airport. He knew he had to make it to his uncle's home before the sun rose in the sky. He estimated his journey to be sixty kilometers. He had to walk far enough off the road so as not to be seen by passing cars.

JPM arrived at his uncle's home just before daybreak. Imagine the surprise of his uncle to open the door and see his nephew standing before him. JPM had not seen himself in a mirror for many months, so the shock of weight loss, torn clothes, and the blood-stains certainly made for a curious and shocked greeting.

His uncle held him as a refuge in his attic until JPM's wife could come to the rescue. Somehow she got JPM into the bottom of a cargo jet, and he was on his way to be exiled back to Brussels.

As I hung up on the first Skype call with JPM, I had definitely taken a bite from the dangling carrot. I did not think I could go without exploring all possibilities. The carrot was well-served on a plate of promises, including the making of a film, a well-paid position, and the glory of having accomplished a humanitarian feat for the women and children of the Congo.

As the summer months lingered, the trip to Africa became eminent, and I got more involved in the historical and political scenario of Congo. As fate would have it, I met a Congolese woman who was a refugee in Los Angeles, Leontine, who to this day is a very dear sister of mine, and someone who has been a consultant and confidante on this book about the political implications of the underbelly of DRC.

My destiny felt wrapped up in her story, as well as the story of millions of other women and children who were forced into pain and suffering.

Leontine was on the personal staff to the first lady of Congo when President Mobutu held office. Even though it was the law that a President could only hold a maximum of two terms of five years each, Mobutu changed the minds of his people to the degree that the constitution was changed. President Mobutu held office for thirty-two years, and was politically supported by the European communities and America until the end of the cold war. Leontine worked for his family for seventeen years. During this time Leontine was married and raised her four children.

While in power, Mobutu formed a regime and amassed a great amount of wealth. During his reign, Mobutu established a one-party state, which caused an economic exploitation.

In 1991 Mobutu agreed to share power with leaders of the opposition, and by 1997 rebel forces led by Laurent-Desire Kabila expelled him from the country.

Mobutu then fell ill and moved to Morocco, where he died of prostate cancer in 1997. However, some people believe that he was poisoned.

When Laurent Kabila took power, the military haunted Leontine's every move. They threatened her life and the life of her family. They forced upon her the need to learn of her secrets, even though she had no secrets to share. The abuse got so intrusive and appalling that she escaped her homeland after several soldiers senselessly interrogated her, which resulted in her being raped. Her heart broken, her scars deep, she fled to the United States where today she is still an activist to help her family and countrymen.

Preparing for my trip, I sat for hours with Leontine to learn about the history of Congo. I also sat for hours with my dear friend Erdmann from San Francisco, to listen to the brilliant flow from his alien brain. I do not know anyone who has an encyclopedia inside of their mind like Erdmann. You can throw a year or date out to him and he has something to say about what happened in history, whether it be about Germany, Russia, Brazil, or the Congo. He also has the ability to speak and write in eight languages.

In his presence, I am like a schoolgirl again, in awe of how he gracefully weaves through the political and historical landscape of Congo. I only wish that I had a history teacher like Erdmann growing up, or have a microchip in my brain that would allow me to be as smart as he is one day. The details in history were awe-inspiring and his mind reeled the details of Congo.

Kinshasa was formerly known as "Leopold-ville," named after King Leopold II of Belgium. King Leopold held power from 1885 to 1908. King Leopold felt that Congo was his own personal property even though he never stepped foot into the Congo. With instructions from Leopold, his team, led by Henry Morton Stanley, pillaged both natural resources and people for decades, while King Leopold himself never so much as stepped foot into this magical, lush garden of the Congo River. While today, poverty is seen in every direction, Congo is filled with the most opulent riches of the world. The power of the Congo River alone could generate enough electricity to bring light to the entire continent of Africa. Their history is a painful one: one of slavery, stolen treasures, and the power of what one country could do if things were fair and just in the world.

Leopold paid a handsome amount of money to Stanley to pretend that he was a humanitarian, while he forced the Congolese people into slavery, while also raping the resources of the land. Rubber, copper, diamonds, coltan and the sad devastation of innocent elephants for their precious tusks of ivory were raped from the land. Men, women, children, were forced into slavery and sold like animals and brought to Belgium. Leopold forced the slaves to build a railroad that connected the

West to the East. He pretended that he was a hero for this accomplishment. The Belgium men conquered the Congolese by tricking the chiefs of the villages, by forcing them to sign contracts that gave away their entire country. None of these chiefs were able to read the language of the contract and they were tricked by small trinkets and barrels of gin, in exchange for the most precious gems of our world.

Patrice Lumumba advocated in the 1960s for a unified Congo in the 1960s. If he could manage a colonization it would be a great coo. The Belgium's imposed sanctions for five years. They demanded to be free of their predecessors. Lumumba went to the Brussels Round Table Conference and finally they were free. June 1960, they were finally granted their independence.

When I traveled to Belgium, on the last leg of the JPM journey, I ventured into the Royal Museum for Central Africa, which focuses on Congo, a former Belgium colony. There was an extraordinary exhibit that showcased the slavery of the Congolese people and the precious commodities that King Leopold had stolen. This year marked the fifty-year date of their independence, but they were still not free. I was mesmerized by this particular exhibit, as it demonstrated the horrific confines of slavery that lasted throughout the centuries. I ventured into the museum bookstore and found a music compilation called The Heritage Project. I instantly purchased the CD, found the producer who was local in Brussels and proceeded to put together a compilation of music called "Voices for Africa" to bring awareness to the conditions of the people and the plight of the human spirit that existed after all these years.

**Soundcloud Playlist - Frere Enimem - Heritage Project

Back in 1919, the protection of humanity estimated that half of the population of Congo had been killed. This would equal over five million people that were killed, which estimated to be one of the largest genocides in history.

While being driven throughout Kinshasa, I was shocked by the amount of monuments and symbolic statues that represented Leopold. This one image of a giant hand in the center of the city gave me a shudder, as I wondered if that monument represented the amount of hands that were cut off by the men who inflicted the pain to the people of the Congo. Several hours of footage and photographs are still in my archives ready to be seen by the world.

I highly recommend dipping your toes into the history of Congo to see how humanity survived under the spell of a King who thought he could do no wrong.

History was repeating itself, but with me this time, as the self-proclaimed next President thought he could do no wrong. I was told a story that was repeated so many times that even JPM believed it to be true. His story plagued my imagination and piqued my creative passions. I let myself think that if I could use my gifts as a filmmaker, I could help a nation of women and children who were victims of some of the most brutal human rights atrocities in the world today. Millions of lives continue to be taken over the years due to Coltan. Women and children are still being brutally raped on a daily basis.

Just like "blood diamond" this curse is called, "blood coltan" where this precious mineral used in the manufacturing of cell phones, digital cameras, and other electronic devices is used as a weapon to abuse the people. The largest global source of Coltan is found in the Congo, and access to it needs to be regulated so that the warlords who hold down the borders of Eastern Congo can be removed.

JPM promised that "when" he became President, he would change the laws to protect his people by changing the regulations on how Coltan is mined. Therefore, I believed that my dear Leontine, along with millions of others, would finally feel justice were I to be successful in pulling off this one feature film.

During one of our summer calls preparing for the trip, JPM shared with me that he wanted to name his political campaign Politics of Love. I almost fell out of my chair that day, as I had written a song by that same name back in 1985. I raced to the garage of my house to a stack of unpacked boxes. I scanned each one of the boxes until I chose intuitively to open one box at the bottom of the pile. I took a sharp kitchen knife and cut the box tape to open the contents inside. Sure enough, there was my large, electric blue, zippered binder that I bought while living in New York during my songwriting days, circa 1982. The binder was filled with handwritten notes and typewritten lyric sheets. We did not have computers back in the day, so the typewriter ink was slowly fading on the pages. At the bottom of the binder was the timeless treasure I was looking for, Politics of Love, which dated back to 1985. I had no idea that the lyrics I wrote in my twenties would have such a prolific impact on what I was doing almost thirty years later.

**Soundcloud Playlist - Politics of Love - Tess Cacciatore

Chapter 3

Footsteps

Have you ever set out on an adventure, thinking it was one thing and it ends up being a completely other experience?

In September of 2010, as I packed for my six day journey I felt apprehensive. I was going back to Ghana to the people I loved, but since I was going to be there for this political journey, it would be different from my experiences before.

Before leaving for Africa, I was introduced to the attorney who was leading JPM's campaign. Her name is Kim Reed. She is a smart and sharp-witted woman from Washington DC and she is still an intricate part of my life and a dear friend. I first met her when I visited DC to meet JPM's U.S election campaign office and his team.

JPM originally met Kim at a political event held in Paris when she was running the international campaign for Barack Obama in 2008. JPM asked Kim to run his campaign. Kim was sane, grounded, and exceptional. In addition to her, JMP's people were made up of a cast of characters that seemed to be good people.

There was a priest who was headquartered in DC who headed up an orphanage in Congo. He was instrumental in my entry into Congo by offering me a letter stated that I was traveling to the DRC on official business for their orphanage. This gave me a layer of protection from the military, as I was able to obtain my VISA for traveling to Congo through his office.

We waited the allotted time for JPM to come to the States for this particular meeting. However, due to some risky business that occurred in his past, he was stopped at the American border and consequently sent back to Europe.

Another person on the JPM team was a young man by the name of Cornelius Adjetey. He had become the Ghanaian Country Director for JPM's campaign, due to the fact that he was born and raised in a political family from Ghana. He and I became friends during our time together on the campaign trail, and we continue to be friends today. I consider Cornelius to be my brother.

Cornelius is the namesake of his very well-known grandfather, Sergeant Cornelius Francis Adjetey, who was an ex-serviceman and veteran of World War II. His grandfather was one of three veterans who were shot dead while they were on their way to present a petition to Sir Gerald Hallen RCeasy, a British Governor of the Gold Coast and Malta.

This tragedy was called the "Christianborg Crossroads Shooting Incident" which led to the 1948 Accra Riots. These series of events eventually led to Ghana's independence from Britain. During our time with JPM, we had many excursions. One of them being Cornelius taking all of us to the monument of his grandfather, which was erected many years before.

Cornelius takes his lineage seriously, and aspires to greatness in his own political career. It seemed like a perfect fit for a wanna-be President of Congo to mentor this young man, but no such heroic deeds were witnessed.

I cannot count how many times Cornelius and I were left holding the bag when hotel rooms, security guards, press conference details, and rentals were not paid. The worst was when JPM wanted to have a photo-op at a Ghanaian orphanage. He got out of his armed-guarded car and proceeded to bring a vendor from the side of the street into the orphanage, to share large buckets of ice cream treats to the children.

The boys and girls were thrilled to have this cold treat on such a hot and humid day. I looked around to the smiling faces and thought I had wrongly assessed JPM. Perhaps there was a heart inside of the Grinch Rabbit Hunter.

But then, he got back into his limo, escaping the heat of the day and the price of admission to pay for these treats, and rolled up his tinted, protective-glass window. He was trying to leave without paying the ice cream vendor. He had the nerve to lean over to the bodyguards and make them take money from their own pockets promising to pay them back in full. These were hardworking Ghanaian men who had families to care for and not many jobs with high-paying circumstances. This sort of thing happened many times to Cornelius and the rest of the local staff. None of them ever got paid. This should have been my first clue... and red flag.

The reason for JPM's visit to Ghana was to meet as many elected officials and former Presidents as he could. He wanted to appear in the media as a 'hero' so that when he moved back to Kinshasa to run for office, President Kabila would not kill him. In retrospect, it was like JPM was trying to repeat history and be like Patrice Lumumba. In 1856 Lumumba was invited on a study tour of Belgium for the Minister of Colonies. Upon Lumumba's return he was convicted and arrested on a charge of embezzlement from the post office. When Lumumba got out of prison he grew more active in politics and decided to go to the

All-African People's Conference in Accra, Ghana, exactly where JPM wanted to go. He was independent from other parties, went out of line to make things happen, and when he eventually became the Prime Minister to lead Congo to its independence, he would be murdered by the secessionist regime in Katanga. His death caused a scandal throughout Africa, where even his enemies proclaimed him a "national hero." In a coincidental occurrence, JPM was trying to be a national hero himself. However, he came up against one scandal after another, from owing people money, to rumors about him with younger women. He slithered through Ghana with the slickness of a snake.

I had been to Ghana several times, but never in the throws of such fanfare. We had armed guards watching our every move, 24 hours a day. I had never been surrounded by so many military weapons. Ghana is a peaceful country and not a place where that much security is needed.

During our time in Ghana, we met with the Minority and Majority Leaders, along with the former President John Kufour (Ghana President from 2001-2009). I remember filming him in his personal suite inside of his compound.

Over the years, it was challenging to film in dark rooms, with no natural light to fall on dark-skinned people who were always wearing formal dark blue or black suits. These conditions only allowed me to capture President Kafour's silhouette. He had these extremely long fingers that were like the wings of an eagle, and he spoke gracefully, using these hands to accent his words. I do not remember much of what he said, as I was transfixed by the reflection of his hands on the white-lace curtains.

My most intense and profound experience in Ghana was when we visited the slave port. I had never been there before, or since, but I can still feel the African breeze blow upon my face as clearly as I can still hear the waves that crashed gently on the jagged rocks.

I stood with my African brothers as we all silently stared over the edge of the cliff. My eyes were transfixed to the ocean waves as I envisioned hundreds of ships taking thousands of innocent men and women to a destiny that they did not deserve. I looked around at every corner of the forts, and felt the ghosts of ancestors whispering to me, urging me to continue on my mission and to share their story. I gently wept; I never understood the concept of slavery, and the fact that it still exists today.

As history came to be, from the years of 1482 to 1786, clusters of forts and castles were built along the coastline of Ghana, which back then was called the Gold Coast due to the vast amounts of gold traded with the transport of slaves. The entire coast is still filled with these ancient buildings that hold so many anguished secrets.

Before JPM left Accra, he had a flurry of radio interviews and press conferences. During one such press conference, JPM became very heated. He told the media the Kabila story, recounting how his life was threatened. During this particular retelling, it became more apparent to me than ever that his story sounded a lot like a Shakespearean play, like *Oedipus* or *King Lear*.

I am not certain if all, or even any of his story is true, but this is the story that JPM tells:

Laurent Kabila (who succeeded presidency after Mobutu) had a dear friend from either Rwanda or Tanzania. In their younger years, this friend, Mr. Kabange, was murdered in his home, leaving his children orphaned. Laurent took in one of the sons (Joseph) and raised him as one of his own children. As life went on, Laurent Kabila became President of DRC.

As in any country, when it comes to politics, there are many games behind the scenes. When Laurent was killed by his bodyguard, it was speculated that the murder was orchestrated by his "son" Joseph, so that Joseph could take over presidency. As it were, Joseph did end up succeeding Laurent as President a mere six days after his death.

If Joseph was really born in another country then JPM stated that he is ineligible to be the President of DRC. Yet, Joseph Kabilla still holds office. There is still civil unrest in the country, along with discord, corruptness, and more murder. All in the name of power.

When I was with JPM in Ghana, he held several press conference sharing this story. JPM dramatically pounded his fists on the table shouting, *"Joseph Kabange, let my people go!"*

He was trying to convince the media, his people, the Ghanians, and most of all, himself that he deserved to become President of Congo.

However, a great number of disgruntled people began to surround JPM. There was a young woman journalist who was invited to come to our compound to be on our team. I noticed many discrepancies and uncomfortable behavior between JPM and this young woman. I felt that he was abusing his power with her. I tried often to get her to feel safe with me, but she would not admit there was abusive behavior inflicted on her until JPM was long gone from Ghana. She then cried to me about her experience but did not go into grave detail. When confronting JPM about this alleged situation, he did what most men do in power, that we see every day now in the press, *"She is a liar and probably just impressed that I gave her the time of day."* Throughout our time he often called others who were in disagreement with him a liar, including me when the time came for me to stand up for myself.

When it was time to leave Ghana no one on his team had been paid, including me. You may wonder why I stayed on the project when things looked this unruly, especially considering that Kim and Cornelius had already left their positions. I suppose that I got used to the taste of poisoned carrots. And, I know that I am the only one to blame.

I do not feel like a victim, in fact, I feel victorious knowing that this experience was all for a greater cause. I truly believed that I would be paid, and that justice for the women in Congo would be served.

I was happy when JPM and his entourage left Ghana as this allowed me to see my Ghanaian family without rifles and fanfare. This was a place I considered to be my second home, to the extent that I was going to be married to a local Ghanaian (Maxwell), whose story will unfold later.

While in Ghana, I had about ten days to figure out where I would be heading next: Israel, Congo, Angola, and Belgium were all options that had been tossed around.

Finally, it was decided that I would go to Angola. My ticket had me departing on American Thanksgiving and I was desperate for an expat party that served turkey and dressing and mashed potatoes and all the treats that I missed from home. We looked at every hotel, but to no avail. I finally succumbed, and remained at the airport where I proceeded to eat an overdone chicken thigh and rice. There was an Internet connection, so I jumped online to see if I could find anyone to give me my Thanksgiving homesick fix.

Erdmann was up and getting ready to cook, as it was earlier in the day in the States. We discussed about my travels and the need to be safe in case I was sent into the Congo. I toasted my glass of wine to his cup of early morning coffee. Then, I climbed onto the plane and fell fast asleep.

My trip to Angola was broken up by a four-hour layover in Kenya. I pressed my face against the large panes of window that stretched across the Nairobi Airport. I paced from one end of the gate to the other, like a gazelle on fire, ready to jump across a river. I watched the sunrise over the peaks of Mount Kenya. I felt the spirit of the Maasai calling my name. I wanted so badly to jump out of the airport and run through the vast lands of wildlife, hugging elephants and lions along the way.

Even though I had heard many wonderful things about Angola, I never got out to see its nature and beauty. In fact, Angola ended up being one of my least favorite places to be, as I was held up for six days at a high-end hotel in the heart of Luanda. I had no idea where I was going next, or when I was going home, or most importantly, when I was going to be paid. The invoice for filming and my time on the road was ever-expanding.

Each day I moved around the lobby of the Angolan hotel to get a different perspective. I watched one diplomatic car after another shuffle in stiff-suited businessmen carrying locked briefcases, shadowed by guards with guns prominently displayed on their harness belts. I watched the diamond and gold deals dance before my eyes, even though the transactions were done with great discretion and secrecy.

The only productive filming I accomplished in Angola was an interview with the Uncle who took in JPM on that fateful night. I heard the story of JPM's escape from Uncle's perspective. I came to find out that his Uncle left his family behind for the sake of JPM, and was now exiled out of Congo, removed from his wife and children and in exile in Angola. I truly do not know all that was said or not said during our interview as he spoke only in French. I had a translator, but who knows if he translated accurately.

I did not feel safe in Angola. My passport had run out of pages, and I tried for three days to get to the American Embassy. When I finally got my passport fixed, word came that I was heading to Congo by myself. The rabbit hunter promised that his diamond deal would close any day now and that once it did, I would get paid.

The irony of the story is that the carrot I was depending on was an actual carat from a diamond deal. This is the great humor of the universe!

JPM assured me that I would get paid once I finished filming in Congo. And so my creative bug went back to the storyboard. I had to get footage from Congo so that the documentary could be finished in time for his political campaign.

How else would we be able to illustrate the drama of Psalm 23? Of the gas station, the embassy, the prison, the hospital, the capture, the torture, the escape to Uncle, and the escape back to Belgium. I was about to risk my life, but I needed this footage. Perhaps he was counting on the fact that I might not make it out of Congo alive.

Before I left Angola I gave my footage to JPM so that I could enter Congo without any evidence of knowing him. The airport was filled with the most intense energy. Perhaps it was my own secrets that caused the tingle in my stomach. I was repeatedly interrogated and almost not let out of Angola because, as it turned out, JPM never provided me with the VISA documents he promised. Without a proper VISA, one cannot legally leave a country. I was at customs without a representative and JPM was nowhere to be found. It was like he disappeared into thin air when I left the hotel, just as he had many times before, especially when I needed him for protection.

I was finally able to get on the plane. Congo is not an easy country to fly into, and as part of the entry process, it is required that one night is spent in Addis Ababa, Ethiopia

I was excited to get even a brief glimpse of Ethiopia. My overnight stay still quakes in my heart, As I woke up the next morning to the Ethiopian morning sun, this image will forever be emblazoned in my photographic mind. The morning light highlighted the brightly painted red and orange buildings. A single dog ran down the road. The shadow of a woman crossing the street appeared. A few traditional chickens scurried across the road, which forced a giggle out of me, *"Why did the chicken cross the road?... To get to the other side."*

I landed in Kinshasa in the late afternoon. The first evening I was invited to have dinner with another American who was traveling in Congo for a gold and diamond transaction. He invited me to dinner at the hotel where I was staying. I was introduced as a filmmaker to his two friends, who happened to be the sons of a man who was also running for President of Congo. They asked if I could help film their father at his 'welcome home' parade, where he was going to announce that he was running for

President. I was traveling undercover, which only heightened my vulnerability. I had to keep things low-key and not bring attention to why I was there. Needless to say, filming this parade would have been a huge conflict of interest, not to mention that it could throw me into even hotter water than I was already in. I gracefully stepped away. Even though the elder statesman, Etienne Tshisekedi, was a favored politician for the Presidency, he was known to be a bit too old to be president, as well as Joseph Kabila had no intention of leaving office.

As stated in the first part of this journey, my driver and translator met me in the lobby of my hotel the following morning and for the days I was there I traced the steps of JPM's childhood. I filmed the home where he was born, the schoolyard where he spent his elementary years, the parking lot at the gas station where he was "taken" by the military. I filmed the outside of the jail, and even snuck onto the hospital grounds where he was taken to his pending death.

Guards followed me everywhere. I hid my camera in a larger bag, sneaking footage when no one was watching. I even found the place in the bush to seemed close to the description of the location where the attempted assassination took place, and the long road that he walked on his escape to his uncles.

I had been in many precarious places in the world; surrounded by protests and riots and guns pointed at me...but never before had I felt so afraid.

Each night I fell onto a hard bed covered with mosquito netting. I slept with one-eye open, half expecting soldiers to crash down my door and take me away at any moment.

On my third day, I met up with an American guy named Thom who was in the Congo on a mission from the Catholic Church for the same local orphanage who offered me the paperwork for travel. Thom was a highlight for me, as he was from America and had the same innocence and trust as I did.

Thom was sent by the same priest that I met in Washington, who provided me with the letter of support to prove that I was there on behalf of his orphanage. Thom, Dido (the translator), myself, and the driver climbed into a car and headed to the orphanage, which was about a two-hour trek through the bush. The road was bumpy and the rainforest dense. While approaching the facility we were greeted on the road by a group of children, that in spite of their lives they were filled with smiles and twinkles in their eyes.

At the orphanage, the children were on display whenever any tourists came. They sang proper French and American songs with their adorable faces. However, as the morning went onward the twinkle in their eyes could not cover up all their sadness. This was the part of visiting orphanages that was the hardest for me, as I always wished I had a private plane to take each and every one of the children home with me. Whether it was in South Africa, Cambodia, Thailand, Ghana, Sri Lanka, El Salvador or Vietnam, every orphanage I visited reminded me that there was still work to be done in the world. There should never be a child in the world who goes to sleep hungry, thirsty, without proper medication, or an education. And most of all, no child, or person for that matter should go to sleep feeling unloved.

The highlight of the Congolese orphanage was this little four-year old girl who was going through the final stages of adoption. She was going to move to New York to be with her new mom. Between the French translator I was excited to watch her happiness that she was going to be in her new home before Christmas. I often wonder how her life turned out. The woman was a single mom who went through the ministry for international adoption. I thought this would be great for me to do as well. However, with my financial state at the time, this would not have been a conducive phase in life to raise a child.

**Soundcloud Playlist - Superstitious - Stevie Wonder

Chapter 4

China Road

I began to see the interconnectedness of the world and how something on one side of the world throughout history, could deeply affect an entire culture in another part of the world.

Thom and I marveled at the progress that was being made in DRC. The area was bustling with activity, as tractors shoveled large piles of dirt to widen the main road, which was named after Lumumba. Rumors floated that the road was going to be renamed China Road, as Kinshasa was mostly run by Chinese men in search of wealth of minerals, resources, and riches.

The town square where my hotel was located had new restaurants opening, many with Chinese owners. I found this one pizza place with Chinese workers to be quite interesting. I welcomed the new choices of restaurants, as African food can be limiting when one doesn't eat goat. Sitting in the town square, I began to look around and notice that the shopkeepers, farmers, and business owners were mostly Chinese men.

The Chinese are known for being well-planned strategists that can patiently wait for decades to implement a development. Congo is one of the wealthiest nations in our world when it comes to natural resources. Coltan minerals are necessary for manufacturing electronics, and the Chinese are brilliant at manufacturing. So it makes sense that the Chinese would come to Congo for business purposes. However, there is another reason.

In 1978, the population planning policy of China was put in place. This stemmed from an ancient tradition that dates back further than 2,000 years ago which strictly prohibited Chinese families from having more than one child. Since it is more powerful in society to have a son millions of young baby girls have either been exported into adoptions services, sex trafficked, or killed. According to the Chinese government 400 million such births were prevented. This means that an entire generation of boys grew up with no one from their culture to marry. And in my humble opinion and the second reason the Chinese came to Congo was to find wives.

Don't get me wrong... I love the thought of these beautiful African and Chinese races mixing it up to create a new generation of children, but the burden must be heavy for a cultural population to come to a potential stop. This topic could take up an entire other book, and it was a revelation to watch it happening right before my eyes. This is not a secret. This has been centuries in the making, and only since 2015 has the one child policy begun to formally be phased out. To me it seems evident that Chinese men are heading to other countries, especially Africa to find women to marry.

Thom got caught up in the story of JPM so he came along for the rest of our filming. We had a wonderful interview with Leontine's daughter and her friends on campus who were protesting the school for a better education. Another interview that I felt was important for the story of women empowerment was with Leontine's auntie, Marie Madeleine Kalala, Former Minister of Justice for Human Rights. She rattled off horrific statistics that to this day need to be fixed.

The most relevant and perhaps the riskiest place I visited was the village where JPM's father lived. I did not realize the danger I had been in until long after leaving DRC.

After JPM's mother left the King and took her children to Belgium, the father carried on with his other wives. The family grew to add fifteen more children.

It seemed that we were warmly greeted. His father had all sorts of awards, photographs, and tribal instruments laid out for display. He walked boastfully about with a long-wooden staff with a carved totem on the top. He loudly tapped the staff on the floor when he wanted command of the room, or to order his family around. Whenever I tried to change the topic to JPM, he interrupted to say that he was not yet done talking about himself. This was going to be a very long day, I thought to myself.

I set up to interview the King so that I could get his take on the progress of his son's desire to become President of DRC.

The King presented a photo album that showcased all of his children. However, none of these pictures were of JPM or his siblings. *"Out of sight...out of mind?"*

The photos were bragging rights of his accomplishments as being King and the people he knew. The one photo that was most prominently pushed in my face was a picture of the King (arm in arm) with President Joseph Kabila.

He smiled and pointed as if I was to be impressed with the fact that he was standing with the President. I looked at Thom and the translator and said, *"Does he not know that this President ordered for his son to be killed?"*

"I don't know" replied Dido. *"Should I ask?"*

I shouted, *"Yes! This is a reason why we are here. His family should know this story."*

The King wanted to know why his son had not been able to visit for him many years. It seemed that he never knew the story of the attempted assassination, so I assumed that I was going to be the one to tell him.

The King, his Queens, their children, and offspring, along with uncles, aunts, and other members of the village crowded into a small hot room. It seemed ironic to me that a white woman from Hollywood, a mere stranger to this family, was there to tell them the story of their long-lost relative.

They thought JPM got arrested several years ago for something small and that he left for Brussels for a better life. The translator told me that his family knew JPM was a successful international businessman who had the riches of diamonds and gold, but he left his family in poverty.

Still believing that JPM was a good person, I tried my best to defend him. I took in a deep breath and a long swig of Coca-Cola. I held back my tears as I recounted the arrest, the hunger strike, the coma, the guards taking him from the hospital, taking him to the forest for the execution.

I spoke slowly through my translator. I began to sob as I recounted the fact that it was by the grace of God that JPM survived a live burial surrounded by dead bodies. And, that he survived the 60 kilometer walk to his uncle's house.

I ended with a flair, as I shouted, *"It is because of this that JPM wants to run for President so that he can help his family and his country."*

I looked around to a dead-silent room. All of their faces were blank of emotion. They looked at me with wide-eyed anticipation, as tears streamed down my face. I felt as if they were watching me in disbelief. They wanted to know where the presents were that JPM was to give them. They glanced at my camera case wondering if I would open my bag to share an overflow of money and jewels.

The King swiftly got up from his chair and proceeded to walk me back over to the stack of photographs. His eyes penetrated into my soul as if to say that I should be mindful of who I share this story with, as he had been friends with the President for a very long time. I realized that I had overstayed my welcome. I took heed to the warning and knew that my angels were working overtime to get me out of there as quickly as possible. I glanced at Thom and Dido, knowing that we needed to leave. After taking a group photograph we swiftly got in our car and rambled down the dirt road.

Dido told us on the drive back to the hotel that many of the relatives pulled him aside to ask him where the gifts were and why JPM was not tending to his own blood relatives.

I did not understand the dynamic of the village nor the danger we were in until much later. How was I supposed to share the reaction of his family with JPM, knowing there was growing animosity as well as disbelief about his story and his potential run for Presidency?

JPM called on a non-traceable number, just in case I was being tapped or followed. I was able to share the experience with his family in code words. He was not surprised. He said that they looked to him to be their savior and that he had given much to them over the years.

All I can say is thank God for the cold stout ale I sipped as we sat in the town square recounting the village experience. I was getting my last glimpse of Congo and the smokey heated air, as I was headed to Belgium the day after next.

Again, I did not realize the implications of my stay in Congo until much later and to this day I have the sinking feeling that my carrot was dipped in poison and once again my angels were working overtime.

**Soundcloud Playlist - China Grove - Doobie Brothers

Chapter 5

Escape from Congo

My acquaintance from Los Angeles was getting ready to leave Kinshasa. He agreed to take my tapes of footage back to Los Angeles so that I could safely get through customs. He was traveling with a Congolese friend, so it was much easier for them to take the tapes back to Los Angeles and for me to retrieve them when I returned.

I shot all of the footage that I needed regarding Congo, and was happy to be leaving. All the footage had been captured without me being personally captured (pun intended) which was a feat and a success. I had filmed in the pouring rain, with military guns at every juncture, and with an intense stomach bug. But it was all worth it in the end.

Driving to the Kinshasa airport, the pungent fumes of fuel and smoke stung my nose. The streets seemed more alive that night, but that could be simply due to the rain letting up after many days of downpour.

A military convoy passed by our car. Soldiers carrying guns were running through the streets to alert the already congested traffic to have the cars move aside. The soldiers were banging from hood to hood so that the cars squeezed even closer to one another as if that was even possible.

There was a congested circle of huge trucks, cars and buses that were filled with an overflow of people hanging out of every window and door. People on bikes and pedestrians all twirled around us like an odd choreographed dance.

The sounds were deafening from the beeping horns, booming music, crying babies, crowing roosters, and singing voices from the local church gatherings. It was a cacophony of noise and smell, which made my experience in the Congo an unforgettable one.

While stopped at a corner waiting for the convoy to go by, I spotted a naked toddler playing in the dirt on the side of the road. He was oblivious to the craziness around him. I look anxiously around to see if his mother was near, which she was, selling her wares out of a basket that was balanced on her head. The women in Africa are mostly the breadwinners, bread-makers and backbone of the family.

I only had the clothes from my original six day journey and none of them were appropriate for a European winter in December. I bought a pair of crazy, ugly closed-toe shoes for two dollars and a pair of men's socks out the window of the car. I borrowed a puffy windbreaker that was three sizes too small from Leontine's daughter. I had to prepare for the dead of winter, as in Belgium, it was nearing Christmas time.

Ready to venture onward, I was excited to arrive at the airport. Once inside of the security area I was stopped and bullied by the military. Five tall, armed guards ran up against me knowing that I was traveling alone. They tried to bribe me for more money, of which I did not have since JPM had not paid me.

I frantically waved to Thom and Dido who were on the other side of the glass wall that divided us. I mouthed the words, *"Do not leave me yet."*

I was taken aside and my bags were dumped upside down. I wanted the officers to know that I knew local people who spoke their language, so I pointed again in the direction of Thom and Dido. They waved back.

I have gone nose-to-nose with military from other countries before, which I do not recommend. However, I had to have some sort of strategy to stand up for my rights, or else I could potentially have been taken out.

Finally, an officer stepped up with his baton pointing at my bag. I could only suffice that he was saying to get my bag packed. I quickly threw my belongings back in the suitcase, as the last officer was closely inspecting my camera. I was so grateful that I had no film with me.

I waved goodbye to Thom and Dido, whose noses were pressed against the glass waiting to pounce at any moment. I narrowly escaped. I sighed a deep prayer of gratitude when finally, I felt the wheels of the plane lift off the ground.

I had done it. I had traveled throughout Africa: Ghana, Angola, Ethiopia, and Democratic Republic of Congo. I only narrowly escaped Congo by handing my footage over to the hands of another American who could fly back to the States under the radar without suspicion.

I boarded the plane to Belgium to conclude the filming of JPM's life story. I was commissioned to dive into his most intimate tidbits of his life...his wife, his mother, his siblings, his home.

The last five days in the Congo felt like they had lasted two months. I imagined the smell of Belgium waffles, hot European coffee, and the feel of cold snow on my nose and toes. Coming out of high humidity and extreme heat, this would be a welcomed shock to the body. Except for the fact that I only had African summer dresses and open-toed sandals. Outside of the scary, ugly granny shoes that now adorned my feet.

**Soundcloud Playlist - Kibuno Mu - Ghanda Boys

Chapter 6

Basking in Belgium

Being in Belgium for three weeks gave me the opportunity to see King Leopold II from the other side. I will never agree with the King's antics in the Congo, however I cannot deny that he was a visionary when it came to building railroads and businesses for his people.

Battling the winter wonderland of Brussels was actually surprisingly marvelous. I am not a snow bunny, but the landscapes of Europe are fantastic.

I smelled the street vendors selling waffles and thought I had been transported to heaven. There is something that still lingers in my mind, with the sensory overload of being outside in the bitter winter cold, taking off my gloves that I bought at the corners stand, and biting into a crispy waffle with a dollop of Nutella dripping off the side.

Outside of the trouble that was brewing with JPM's campaign, I met a parade of wonderful people through Jean Pierre, a Belgium businessman who was part of the JPM train. Through this man I met incredible Belgium artists, musicians, activists and more. We enjoyed the bubbles of French champagne, meals with his wife and family, long walks through museums, and of course the common thread that tied us together – JMP's pending election.

I was out of money. My bills were piling up in Los Angeles. My landlord was becoming more impatient with my tardiness on rent. My car payment was overdue and my utilities were about to be shut down.

The carrot of money that was promised to me upon my arrival in Brussels had not yet been given. Nonetheless, I hit the ground running, filming press conferences and off-site meetings. The press was beginning to make waves for JPM's campaign, and there were many people in various countries who were asking for him to step out of the election.

I kept thinking of the women and children in Eastern Congo. How could I help them if he was not President? I had to stay close for my dose of carrots. I had to make this film to share his story. I stayed for two more weeks and filmed his life in Europe with his wife, his mother, his siblings, and even his high school teachers. Everything seemed to be panning out. I dove into the history of Belgium and visited the museum of King Leopold. I fell in love with the music from a CD that I bought in the museum store. It was edgy and brilliant. I made contact with the producer and became friends with him and the musicians. All the while I was writing my own song for the score of the film, Politics of Love, based on the lyric I had written years ago.

This was the appropriate time for the release of my song, combined with the other songs from these French Congolese artists. I had over twenty hours of footage from my journey, along with the music of amazing African musicians. Including a local Belgium jazz artist, Nadine Nix, who wrote and sang many African fusion songs,

Soundcloud Playlist - Asempa Lo Bodio - Nadine Nix

The day I was to leave Brussels, JPM sent his wife to take me to the airport. He was nowhere to be found. She handed me a red envelope, which in Chinese tradition, symbolizes good fortune and is supposed to ward off evil spirits. I was so excited that he had kept his word and that I was going back to Los Angeles to edit the film. His wife smiled, handed me the envelope and said, *"This is a gift from JPM, just in case you need any incidentals on your travels back home."*

I quickly ripped open the envelope to find a 100-Euro bill and no check for my work. Devastation and disbelief swallowed me whole. I shared with his wife the promise of getting paid. I saw her hands clutch the steering wheel as she choked out an apology and her disbelief that he would do such a thing. I thought as a woman that she would have my back, as she had her husband's ear. Wishful thinking got me nowhere. I held my tongue, but I wanted to lash out and tell her how awful her husband was on the road with inappropriate behavior with the young journalist, how much money was owed people from around the world, and that she was being complicit of his behavior of taking advantage of me financially, not to mention the road where I was heading back to Los Angeles where I would become homeless.

I landed in Zurich for a layover. A snowstorm hit the Swiss cities so bad that no planes could take off. The airlines had no idea how long we would be grounded. I got ahold of JPM but we had only a brief conversation. JPM said that he had no money to help me. Just like when he abandoned me at the Angola Airport, so he abandoned me again in Zurich. I tried to call another time and his wife answered. She refused to pay something to help me in Zurich as well. She hung up on me. That was the last time we ever spoke.

My angels were watching over me though, as I was able to squeeze onto the Internet and, luckily, my dear friend Erdmann was on Facebook. He spoke German and French so he was able to get me into a hotel with food. I was able to somehow jump from one miracle to another, until I landed back in Los Angeles.

JPM had no remorse of the dangerous situation that I had been in on his behalf. I went back to Los Angeles empty-handed but full-hearted, as I was still committed to bring the story of the Congolese women and children to life.

Chapter 7

A Voice from the Congo

It was December 17th, 2010. This was a strangely rainy season for a Los Angeles winter. I gave notice to my landlord to use my deposit for that last month rent, and I told them that I would be moving out on January 15th, 2011. I took the holidays and sat on my bed and taught myself how to edit film. I edited a short film called A Voice from the Congo by changing the perspective of the footage that I had, so that the story was my voice and my point of view, rather that any story that pertained to JPM's campaign. I finished the edit, recorded the song, Politics of Love, packed my bags, and gave away the rest of my belongings.

I jumped into the abyss.

I had already given up many of my belongings and threw my most valuable things into storage. And so began this new chapter in my life of not having my own home. I began this journey by living with dear friends, Dina and Tim, who were married with two kids. I helped cook for the family and helped Dina start her new business: We Rock the Spectrum Kids Gym.

I was completely distraught as I had to find a place for my cats to live. One of my best friends, Marlene, had a friend who I had known over the years. Lori was an animal maven with a menagerie of animals of her own. My dear cats, India and Yuki, settled into her guest room for the following months, which proved to be the most stressful of all. I was grateful that I was never in a dangerous situation, living on the streets, or sleeping in my car, but it was eye-opening and horrific to be without my fur babies and without my home.

I finally moved out of the Kimmel's and ventured onto many other places with two suitcases and two cats, Not many friends nor any of my business network knew what was going on with me. From the outside, it appeared as business as usual. I would show up at all networking events and conferences, still with a smile on my face, wondering where God's assignment would take me next.

Through all of this, I never left my passion for Congo. I combined efforts with my dear friend Leontine, who has become the activist voice for her countrymen and expats.

It was solely based on my friendship with Leontine that I became an underground reporter for the protests that the expats held at the CNN building in Los Angeles. These gatherings were to provide support to their fellow countrymen to not re-elect Joseph Kabila into office in 2011. He made it back into office, much to the dismay of the Congolese people, and he is still in power after the botched up election of December 2016. Needless to say, JPM was not allowed to run for president that year.

I followed Leontine into the streets and outside of the CNN building in Hollywood during the Congolese election. Back in 2011 there was a movement growing to inspire the Congolese to fight for their country and to not let Kabila take over again. It was a time when the people on the streets were still non-committal, not wanting to make waves. However, the Congolese expats from the United States and Europe knew they had to get to those who lived there and have their voices heard.

I heard from friends in Europe that my videos were going viral, but not much impact was being made inside their country. They were unsure if their Congolese friends and family were not taking action due to their fear, or disinterest.

Kabila got re-elected.

When speaking to Leontine about the current affairs in Congo, I am saddened beyond belief. Throughout history, the rebels in Rwanda, along with their President, have wanted to take over Eastern Congo. I know the political scene in Africa is much more tangled that I can ever understand or explain. I am simply looking at the situation through a humanitarian lens, and will always be in support of helping victims and giving a voice to the voiceless.

Because of what the expats in the streets in 2011 achieved, the Congolese are now standing up, unified, and ready to fight back for their country. The past Congolese election turned violent, and mass murders occurred in the name of politics.

Military from other countries were brought in, while people were being burned in the streets on a daily basis. I remember Leontine sharing with me five years ago, "The Congolese are not yet awake, or they would not let this happen. However, when they wake up, you will never see such courage and strength. There will be nothing that can stop them. They will be ready to die for their country, and that sadly, will be what happens."

More recently, Leontine told me that she thinks her countrymen are now awake and are taking a stand for themselves and their country.

Five years ago, I was appalled at the fact that five million people had been killed in Eastern Congo over blood Coltan, but now the statistics are showing that the number has grown to somewhere between eight and twelve million. Every day, that number grows. The people of Eastern Congo are now taking matters into their own hands, which is going to further the civil unrest. Civil wars, and world wars, are pending depending on who comes into power and who remains in power.

I believe that this circus is cracking wide open of what has been hiding for so long The spiritual implications are a gift and all of this had to be brought to the surface regarding racism and global doom. This is for us to see that humanity truly needs to have this shake-up so that we can move past the darkness and get closer to the light.

I had this strange idea when I was about seven years old that any President was a puppet. As I grew up I realized that there were indeed things that we will never see or hear from behind the scenes, and that the "powers that be" have a global agenda that runs deeper than any ocean. It is all tangled up in such a mess that I am not sure what comes next.

However, I know what it is like to live on the edge, I feel that God gave me the passion to tell my story so that others can tell their story to heal.

I hear the voices of the people of Africa, Cambodia, Thailand, South America, and the United States, swimming in my head after all my travels to orphanages, villages, camps, kingdoms and more. And so I take a stand to become voice for the Congo.

During my stint of being homeless I went wherever God sent me. I was thankfully never in the streets, nor sleeping in my car, but garages, couches, and guest rooms became a familiar setting. I still have the images in my mind of people sleeping in the streets under the bridge near the freeway, or in an area downtown Los Angeles called Skid Row, where thousands and thousands of people live in a tent city in a five-block radius, trying not to be forgotten. I would stare in wonder, knowing that I was two small steps away from being in their position. Being homeless is not always tied to mental illness and addiction. There is a stigma that is attached to being homeless, and the needless situation of being part of the disenfranchised, when all people need is to keep their dignity, faith, and hope.

Sometimes people end up being homeless, like me, due to circumstances that are seemingly out of our control. This could be due to financial mishaps at work, or the economy. Sometimes a person can get in an accident and they do not have enough medical coverage. In the case of children and teens they tend to get tossed around in the foster care system or they are the unfortunate ones to have abusive parents and/or caretakers. These runaways get caught in the loop which is a hard ride to get off. Life can be a ride down a slippery slide that needs to be examined deep inside the programming of our emotional life from childhood. Then there are our precious people who serve our country, who come back home after war with too many mental and physical afflictions. They are tossed aside. To me, this is criminal. Do not get me started on all the other unfair injustices that occur in our beautiful world.

I went from house-sitting positions, to living in the garage of my best friend to help her move back from Florida, to my final stint where I lived in the guest house of a friend to help sell her childhood home after the death of her father. I can write an entire other book about the attachment to objects and organization within our life, as it is a lesson on how much we consume and hang onto things in our life. I dis-assembled all the belongings from her childhood and helped put the house on the market. From a stuffed coyote in their garage to Q-tips, I saw it all.

The house was going into escrow soon, so I felt the calling to get on the road and move back to San Francisco.

Coming into this next phase, I had to take a deeper look into my life, to witness and acknowledge the self-induced patterns that created my reality. I needed to become self-aware so that I could become self-reliant and that had to be done by having self-love. How was I going to do that? I had to go dark and deep to be able to shine a light on my own shadows.

"Our shadow is our dance partner — ready to shine the light." Journal Entry: 10-10-16

**Soundcloud Playlist - Shadow Boxer - Fiona Apple

PART 2: DARK KNIGHT OF THE SOUL

Chapter 8

The Prince vs the King

In the distance, on top of a mountain, sits an ancient castle. Its intense green moss sweeps across jagged rocks that point past the waters' edge. A gentle stream bubbles softly around the bend of the moat that circles her kingdom.

This woman stands solid, near tall thick wooden doors adorned with inlaid carvings, representing the various stages of her life.

Wild birds dance and coo to call out to their mates, as she peers through the morning mist to see a horse and carriage approaching.

She is not the princess type. This Queen was never one to dress up as a princess like they do in fantasy movies, nor was she the type to believe that a Knight in shining armor would ever come to rescue her on a white horse.

However, hidden deep within her soul, she longed to have a King by her side. The backend story in the forefront of her mind.

Throughout the years, the Queen attracted a few princes-in-the-making, and the occasional pauper with a good heart. She hoped that one could grow to be her twin flame. But every time, the flame was blown out by the wind.

Could it be that her fated mate had not yet crossed her path? Could it be the love she had experienced in her life was her only chance, and that love had passed her by? Or, could it be that whenever there was a flicker of hope, a King in waiting, the Queen would run through her castle pulling back the draw bridge, closing all the oriel windows, gates and doors to protect her heart from ever being broken again?

I was not the princess type of girl who wore a princess gown to bed and refused to take it off for days. I did not even own a Princess dress. I had no desire to be a Princess...however, to be the Queen of my own castle and kingdom was my dream.

I was a tomboy by most standards. Even though I was a ballet dancer from age seven and played with Barbies, I much preferred to jump across the nearly frozen creek and chance the odds of not falling through to frozen water. I loved to make dollhouses using the strategies of architecture and design rather than actually playing with dolls. By the time I gave up dolls I only had one Barbie left. She was a Malibu Barbie with one leg missing and her hair cut off, thanks to having a rebellious older brother in the midst.

I was an odd and silent creature. While most children played by themselves talking out loud using character voices for their stuffed bears, I sat silent at the head of our dining room table in front of a bowl of ice cream. Little did anyone know that I had a table full of interesting spirit friends sharing in their own slice of my ice cream pie. They shared their stories from distant lands. If my parents or brothers walked into the room they never knew that I had a party going on at the table. They just saw me sitting alone eating ice cream and staring softly into space.

I was not a great orator of words and I was extremely shy. My mom recounted stories from my childhood where people asked me a question, or commented about my dress, or blue eyes. I would stare at them without any response. Most considered this to be rude behavior, but I had no way of forcing the words out of my mouth. If a neighbor or relative asked me if I wanted a piece of candy, or a ride to school, I avoided eye contact and walked away as fast as I could.

I needed to feel that I belonged somewhere… anywhere… and yet I felt the need to be hidden. I was deeply spiritual and depended on my faith. I refer to God through a variety of titles, God, Source, Spirit, Infinite Wisdom, Higher Self, because I respect the vast names that God has been given throughout the ages and cultures. From the early age of seven I knew there was one source that everyone referred to, despite having their own names for it. I have always seen it as, We are all one! I was raised in an Italian Catholic house, but my mother was more spiritual than religious. She was into the almanac and astrology, rather than the Bible, so I got a healthy dose of variety regarding spiritual thinking.

At a certain age, I went to church alone each week, so I had a good deal of time to reflect about consequences and theories. My two older brothers were not particularly interested in attending church in those days and my parents were not recognized by the Catholic Church as married, so they chose not to go. I was a curious soul and I was fascinated by religion. I put on my white anklet socks, starchy plaid cotton dress, and black patent leather shoes. I was the typical vision of a Catholic schoolgirl. My blonde hair was cut in a sixties style called a pageboy. My eyes were larger than my face, and when I smiled, the gap of my missing front teeth could be seen. However, I mostly looked out of place in photographs during my younger days, and I rarely smiled. I think I was still wondering what I was doing on this strange thing called planet Earth.

Until the mid-seventies, when the Pope changed the law of wearing a veil, girls were required to cover our heads in church. I carefully carried my white-laced veil to church, and gently placed it on my head before entering the sanctuary. After the obligatory genuflecting and blessing my forehead with holy water, I walked straight up to the altar and sat in the front pew.

Every week, the same family sat in that same front pew. When they saw me walking up the aisle, they quietly moved over to make room for me. The mother was round and cushy and looked like she gave good hugs. The father sat at the other end of their two children. I never uttered a word to any of them and they never spoke to me. It was like I adopted them in an unspoken dance between us all. I often wondered if they talked about the odd girl showing up in their pew each Sunday.

I wanted to be close to the action of the altar, close to the looming statue of Mother Mary. I had fond memories of Mary, as a child I remember watching an entire generation of older girl cousins getting married in the Catholic Church. I was envious of them in their beautiful white dresses, with the long-laced train of fabric that whooshed behind them as they knelt at the feet of Mother Mary statue on the altar. The bride knelt and prayed, "Hail Mary, Full of Grace" for blessings for her marriage. I remember loving this ritual and I wanted to be a pure bride when I got married so that I could give birth to one who could save the world.

During those years, Mass was given in Latin. Words flowed out of the priest's mouth like an eerily melodic doldrum chant. Trying to decipher the message of God through this ancient and strange language, I dutifully did my best to genuflect, kneel, stand, sit, pray, reflect, and confess.

I was the silent observer, the non-talker, the alien from another world. My mom often said to others, *"We don't know where she came from...an alien spaceship left her on our front porch."* Sarcasm was my mom's dear friend.

Secretly though, I prayed to God that I was an alien, so I would not have to experience death. I thought at times I heard God say, *"Do not be afraid my child, I have special plans for you."*

On my quest for truth in religion, I went to other churches to see what people were taught and what they believed. I did not understand how people considered themselves to be Christian when they listened to the priest during mass and then waddled back to their cars gossiping all the way.

In the second grade, I befriended two sisters with whom I became inseparable for many years to come. Karen and Sondra had a dear mom (Mama Dee) who married the widower who owned the house on the corner. Mama Dee was instrumental in keeping us girls occupied. She took us to swimming pools, trips to museums, and to bible camp every summer. At the various bible camps, I partook in the services of Baptist, Methodist, and Lutheran churches. From an early age I thought that churches appeared to be the pulpit from which religion made money to manifest power. I began wondering why couldn't we all be one with the same God, and with the same universal understanding that we all live on this tiny planet together.

Since I attended my neighbors' churches, I thought it only fair for my friends to experience my traditions in return. I brought the sisters to my church and proceeded to have them follow me to the altar for Holy Communion. The intimidating priest came up to me after mass to say, "You are not allowed to bring those who have not yet had the sacrament of Holy Communion in the Catholic Church." I looked up at him and innocently replied, *"Why not? Aren't they also children of God?"* The priest stoically walked away, shaking his head.

As a child I remember feeling like people were sleepwalking through life. I had deep conversations with God as I drifted off to sleep each night. I asked God questions, like *"What does it mean when the church says there is no beginning, and no end?"*

At the age of five I saw my first dead body in a casket. It was my great grandfather Graziano's funeral. The funeral home was filled with weeping Italian women. This was my entry into the world of death and the search for deeper meaning in life.

I often left my body during sleep—a phenomenon known as astral traveling— and I vividly remember sitting high in the willow tree in our backyard. I saw through the walls of the house and into my bedroom. I saw my body sleeping in the bed below. I knew from an early age that there was something much wiser and more wonderful outside the confines of our bodies. However, the thought of death still haunted me.

I saw the potential in all things. Was this an attribute, or a handicap? During the summer of fourth grade my friends and I formed a Mulberry Club. We carried empty ice cream buckets on our nature walks and picked the wild mulberries that grew on the bushes next to the creek behind our houses. We ate the tart berries which turned our lips and tongues blue. We stayed out until the sun went down. We had homes and cars that were left unlocked throughout the night. We lived in a very different era, with different expectations.

We danced through the backyard gardens of our neighbors, gathering stalks of rhubarb and crisp tart green apples off the trees. We ran home to make pies. My dad grew tomatoes in our backyard. The red, juicy orbs were divine as they were warmed on the vine. We took tires and made them into tire-swings. We hung the swings from the trees and jumped off twenty-foot cliffs, leaping wildly over the creek into a sandy patch of dirt.

Growing up with brothers and the neighborhood boys, my competitive edge was nurtured. Being around male energy was more familiar to me, so it became important to learn how to strike a balance between the feminine and the masculine in my life. I noticed from this time that girls were competitive and could be very mean. I did not understand that concept.

During one of our explorative summer days, our group of friends came upon a burned down barn. The smell of smoke still lingered in the air. The side of the barn was crispy black with soot and the light grey paint had cracked from the heat. I felt compelled to enter the barn, obviously understanding the risk that if I did not watch my step, I could fall and break something, or worse, have the barn walls collapse upon me. I took the door that was hanging from its hinge and gently pulled it aside. The door opened into the main room of the barely standing structure. The smell of fire and smoke is still vivid in my mind.

I stepped inside and I was instantly transported to a house with finished painted walls, beautiful furniture, and white-lace curtains.

I ate buckets of mulberries and sat inside the burned up barn, imagining the potential of what "could" be.

Later on, that concept of potential became an "aha" moment for me as I took that into my relationships, seeing the potential rather than reality.

I felt that I could make things better for the people in my life. I was the rescuer for my parents, my friends, my lovers, but not for myself. Inevitably, people took my kindness as a sign of weakness, which triggered the verbal and emotional abuses, which the silent abuses can be the hardest to define. These are the gateway abuses to the more deadly ones to occur.

I saw the potential in that burned-down barn but no matter how many white-lace curtains I hung in the windows I could not make the barn a fully functioning home. I tried to do the same in my relationships, to transform them into these beautiful safe havens, but the floors of the barn fell out from under me and the walls collapsed around me.

**Soundcloud playlist - A House is not a Home - Luther Vandross

When I took a deep look at myself and the people around me, I was confronted with disappointment, which was a big deal for me. I had to see that relationships served as a mirror for me to look at myself and realize that I could not make everyone happy. But that was me...the people pleaser. I was the diffuser between my parents when they engaged in loud fights and silent treatments. I did the tap-dancing to make things right. Patterns began from an early age that were deeply embedded. I did not have the proper tools to find a way out. I needed a mentor or someone who had gone through the fire and safely made it to the other side. At the time any potential role models were deep in their own fire, so they could not see their own way out, let alone guide me.

I have met people from all over the world who have shared their own tragic stories, so I feel that my story pales in comparison to those who have been brutally raped, thrown into sex trafficking, or molested by their relatives. However, each of us has a story to share. We each have our own discoveries and lessons of breaking of cycles of abuse.

My parents are no different. Each of them have their stories, as do my brothers who lived in the same house with different perspectives.

In retrospect I know my parents did their best and I know deep in my heart that they loved me. They did their best to provide a safe home, give me a good education, and teach me the value of the strong work ethic that has been an important cornerstone for my bohemian, cutting-edge, and entrepreneurial lifestyle.

My parents placed the breadcrumbs along the path to find my voice, even though I did not see the crumbs until much later in life. Self-love, self-discovery, self-reliance are the lessons that guided me to my passion and purpose. I simply needed to open up my heart, my eyes, and my mind to see them. And that… is easier said than done.

**Soundcloud Playlist - Lucy in the Sky with Diamonds - Beatles

Chapter 9

Lucy, I'm Home!

"I have an everyday religion that works for me. Love yourself first and everything else falls into line. You really have to love yourself to get anything done in this world."

~ Lucille Ball

Love yourself? What a concept! I had no idea that self-love was a necessary cornerstone to an empowered life.

Lucille Ball is one of my heroines. My mom's beauty and personality was very much like Lucy. My mom was called Lucy throughout her life. *"Lucy, I'm home"* is that cliche quote from the TV series and one that reminded me of my homelife growing up.

Lucille Ball was a powerhouse in the entertainment industry, as well as the first woman-owned studio in Hollywood. Lucy was married to Desi Arnaz and their production company was called Desilu. Lucy and Desi produced many hit shows throughout the years, but due to Desi's wandering eye, Lucy divorced him and she bought out his shares of the company.

It is a shame that most women in the entertainment industry, like Lucy, are not given proper credit of the impact women made in the industry. Lucy pioneered many methods of production that are still in existence today.

Lucy invented production techniques, such as filming before a live audience, implementing multi-cameras for shooting sitcoms, and she created the ability for several adjacent sets to exist on a soundstage. This was her innovative way to save on production costs.

Lucy was also an executive producer of her own series: *I Love Lucy, The Lucy Show,* and *Life with Lucy.* After Lucy divorced, she went on to produce other hit series, including *Mission Impossible* and *Star Trek.*

I relate to Lucy on many levels. Like me, she came from a small town. Lucy was from Jamestown, New York and I was from Des Moines, Iowa. We were both from a middle-class family, and also like me, she did not let the small town take her out of her big city dreams. She achieved most of her success later in life, which I always took as a message to never give up on my dreams.

Desilu was one of the original models of a successful independent studio. Inspired by it, I borrowed the idea and combined my parents' names, Carolynn and Lou, to create my production company CarLou Interactive Media & Publishing.

The reason of my referencing Lucille Ball, besides my intense respect of her talent, my parents were affectionately referred to as Lucy and Ricky. My dad with his dark, Italian roots mirrored the Cuban Ricky, and my mom, with her fire-redheaded beauty and wacky sense of humor mirrored, *"Apples don't fall far from the tree...doncha know!"* This was a constant reminder from my mom throughout the years.

My parents met while they were walking down the street in downtown Des Moines. My mom was on lunch break with her girlfriend when my dad walked past them. He only noticed the red-head, so he whistled to get her attention. My mom's friend knew my dad from school so she cheerfully shouted, *"Louie, what are you doing out here?"* He looked up with surprise, recognizing his school-mate and figured this was the best way to get introduced to his future wife. My mom and dad began to date, until he got drafted into the navy.

My mom moved to Los Angeles to follow her dreams of being a singer. My dad had an early discharge from the Navy due to a heart condition, so he followed my mom to California. They got married by the justice of the peace and shortly thereafter, she got pregnant with my oldest brother, Mike. They moved back to Des Moines to move in with her parents. Three years later my middle brother Rick was born.

It was not paradise between my parents. Mom had a miscarriage after my second brother and not long after this, my parents were divorced. After a couple of years of them apart Rick fell ill with the mumps. My dad went over to check on my brothers and one thing led to another and, before they knew it, I was on my way. I suppose that mumps and my brother was part of my destiny.

My parents got married for the second time after I was born, to live happily ever after, or so they thought. They would eventually marry a third time, which I will get into later. My brothers have their own views about our childhood. I am sure they were deeply affected by the roller coaster ride of our parents, but I can only speak for myself. I had the bedroom next to my parents, so I witnessed the up-close and personal fighting. I heard the emotional abuse and the constant threat of leaving one another. I believe this set up the cornerstones for my insecurity and my fear of abandonment, and self-conscious behaviors. These were subconscious actions that coincided with the relationships that I would attract later in life.

On many occasions through elementary and middle school I would step out the door. My mom yelled after me, like she was telling me to not forget my lunch box. *"Hey, you need to decide by the end of the day who you're going to live with: your father or me!"*

Each time this happened I went to school devastated. I tried to focus on schoolwork but sometimes, I just couldn't control the tears streaming down my face. It was apparent that something was wrong. One day my teacher sent me to the principal's office. The adults in the office pressed their faces into mine, drilling me, asking me what was wrong. Eventually, I broke down and confessed that my parents were getting a divorce. Somehow the gossip train ran rampant throughout the community like fire in a dry-wooded forest. Divorce was not an option in those days, especially in the Catholic Church.

By the time I got home from school my mom was waiting for me with a string of verbal lashings. She accused me of spreading private family matters in public. I figured this had something to do with those nosey neighbor ladies who loved to gossip. I am sure they helped her feel ashamed, so she took it out on me. I hid under my bed shaking until my father got home. Those church-going women in the community did not let a minute go by without sending someone up the flagpole to hang them in a cloak of judgment.

My parents had the worse case scenario of 'who cried wolf' and I suffered from their game. Their idle threats and silent treatments went on for weeks. My brothers had their own roles to play, but throughout my life, I was my mom's rescuer and negotiator. I tried to find the calm in the storm. From where I stood, sat, slept, and witnessed throughout my life, my parents were forever stoking each other's' fire of pathologies, trying to trigger each other's' fears and anxieties. I witnessed a lot passive-aggressive behaviors between husbands and wives, so I put commitment, communication, and compassion on my list of things to have when I found my mate. My oldest brother's role was to be the comedy relief and the book smart one to distract and to save. My middle brother was more of a rebellious typical middle-child with a monstrous heart of gold.

We lived in a safe midwest neighborhood where children from several families played together into the summer nights. There was a place behind our house that we referred to as "the circle" even though it was a cul-de-sac consisting of families with twins, triplets, and many other children from good Catholic families.

I grew up in a mixed Italian-Catholic family. My mom was adopted by an amazing couple who were very influential in my life, Harold and Pauline Davis. Even though these grandparents were hard-working Midwesterners, my parents mainly raised us on the traditions of being Italian.

My mom was a victim to her health issues and to the pharmaceutical industry. My parents were a dangerous cocktail of tempers mixed with hormone replacements, sleeping pills, jack-up pills, and Italian flair. Because of what I saw with my mom and other women of her generation, I am strongly suspicious of the pharmaceutical industry.

My mom lived by astrology and sun signs. She loved her dogs, her drugs, and a few choice people in her life. She often told me, *"If you can count on one hand those you truly trust, then you're doing pretty damn good."* Her other catchphrase was *"with friends like that, you don't need enemies."* That particular phrase took me decades to know what she meant, but she was trying to protect me from other kids who seemed to be out to do no good.

My mom dealt with a string of back surgeries, another miscarriage after me, and what must have been bouts of depression. I came home from school on any given sunny day, and she would be tucked away in her pitch-black bedroom, laying in her bed with the covers over her head. The drugs made her mood swings feel like we were on a fast ride through hell.

My mom had a great fear of me following in her footsteps and getting married and having children at an early age. She often threatened me by saying, *"If you ever get pregnant I will kill you."* I knew she never meant that she would literally kill me, but that phrase has rung through my mind over the years. Later in life I had an epiphany about the power of words as they relate to subconscious outcome, as I have never been pregnant.

It took me years to understand that words and energy create our programmed reality. Words burn into our thoughts, and thoughts turn into beliefs. This process can either damage or empower us for a lifetime. I feel that it is important to understand that abuse mainly comes from those who love us most; whether it is our parents, siblings, teachers, friends. Once we hit a rhythm of feeling like abuse is a natural thing, then we attract these attributes into our adult relationships, as in friendship, business and in our life partners.

This is the all-important part of my work to reveal the blueprint that was given to each of us upon birth. Whether it be what we experience in the womb, or as a newborn, or toddler to young child, our brain is a powerful engine that can turn the words we hear into a pattern of programmed beliefs. *"You're dumb, lazy, rotten, stupid, fat, horrible."* Such words can break us down and cause us to spiral into a dark tunnel leading to mental illness, addiction, self-abuse, bullying, or in the worst cases, suicide. I am eternally grateful that I did not get the depression gene. However, I have many other issues that caused me to not make the brightest decisions for myself.

I had a close bond to my mom. Most people thought I looked identical to her. Our love-hate relationship was no different from most mother-daughters. I knew she loved me more than life itself and that she did her very best, but we had a tumultuous tumble throughout our lives.

My dad was everyone's best friend. Every winter he helped my brothers' wrestling coach, and each summer he coached my brothers' little league baseball games. I suppose the reason why I feel comfortable around males is because I was surrounded by male energy on a consistent basis growing up.

During the hot summer days at the ballpark, I knew just when to interrupt my dad. I would wait until he got near the dugout on the baseball field and I would slip my fingers between the holes of the fence and bat my baby blues. He did not take his eye off the game, but he knew I was there. As he walked towards me, he would dig into his pocket for loose change, or a dollar bill. He slipped the coins into my hand and said his infamous phrase, *"Put it away before you lose it."* I ran off to get my cherry snow cone, or my favorite candy of the day.

Growing up in Iowa was wonderful. The landscape of Iowa is filled with lush farmlands, rural beauty, vast cornfields, and red barns that poke out of the scenery against the wildest blue skies. The sunsets in Iowa compare to the beautiful sunsets in Africa.

The stillness in the air has serenity, peace, calm, and the true sense of being in God's country. To give you a sense of Iowa's beauty, think of *Fields of Dreams* and *Bridges of Madison County* which were both filmed near my hometown.

I can always tell when I meet someone from the Midwest, as they seem to share the traits of friendliness and honesty. I have lived mostly in large metropolitan cities (New York, Los Angeles, San Francisco) so I take pride in telling people that I grew up in Iowa. I always hear the same reaction: 'Oh, that makes sense" OR

"I drove through Iowa once ... the people are so friendly,' AND "Wow... Iowa is really God's country!"

As a July baby, my summers growing up were filled with water skiing, roller-skating, dance camps, and birthday scavenger hunts. We grew up with drive-in movie theaters, and hot summer nights consisted of dressing in pajamas and watching a movie from the backseat of our car.

From the outside looking in, I had a great Midwestern upbringing. However, from the inside looking out, there seemed to be something missing. I always felt a bit out sorts, like the black-sheep of the family. Most of the women in my family got married early and became wonderful mothers and wives. I was the one who left for long-distance college, traveled, and kept my eyes on the prize in the entertainment industry. I had no personal role models or mentors, so I had to rely on my own tenacity to get anywhere in life. That included finding a way to leave Des Monies and start a new life.

Growing up in the sixties was pretty intense, but we had a sheltered life in Iowa. Public school offered some challenges, including a second grade teacher who tied us to chairs if we got up without permission. She would put tape across our mouths if we talked out of turn. I remember once being tied to my chair with a warning tape on the corner of my desk. I looked across the aisle at poor Tammy who had gotten the full rope and tape treatment.

She could barely breathe as tears ran down her cheeks and snot ran out of her nose across the big fat piece of tape that shut her mouth. This treatment was slightly better than the Catholic school I went to in fourth grade. The nuns were notorious of chasing us girls down and making us kneel in the hallway. They would whip out their tape measure and make sure that the hem of our skirts touched the ground while kneeling. Once we were out of their sight we would roll up the waistband and make our skirts shorter.

In sixth grade I had a nun who told me that I could not prop up my head with my hand while taking a test. She kept coming by my desk and slamming my hand down from my head. *"But why?"* I pleaded. *"Because, when you sit like that you block your brain waves."* She yelled.

I had never heard of anything more ridiculous.The last time I put my hand on my head was the last time. I saw her coming for me. Her stern face was flushed, her cheeks bright and red. The habit on her head was tilted in anger. She lifted her arm as I lifted my face. One fast, solid pop, she hit me right on the nose. My eyes instantly watered from the pain. She ran out the door and down the hallway. She was the one in trouble this time.

I always knew that I did not want to stay in Iowa. My mom told me when I was five years old that I announced that I was going to move to New York to become a dancer. I have no idea how I came up with that idea, outside of the fact that we watched the Oscars and Tony Awards each year. I dreamt that I would be in the movies, or making movies, or wherever life took me to fulfill my dreams.

When I turned six, my mom knew it was time to put me into dance class. I danced my way through grade school, middle school, high school, college, and professionally in New York and Los Angeles.

My mom witnessed the look of disappointment on the faces of the few boyfriends I had during high school. When I started talking about going away to college, my mom told me that their jaws would drop. They had their own desire to stay in Des Moines, marry a local girl, and start a family. Those ideas were just not in my plan.

My dad was the consummate provider for our family. His work ethic was strong, and he made a pure and honest living. He was a sweet and quiet man, unless he was coaching a baseball game and he felt the umpire had made a bad call. Then the across saw his Italian temper.

However, due to the lack of affection from his upbringing, he was a hard nut to crack. I knew he loved my brothers and me, but affection was not easy for him to show. My mom once shared that he was nervous about raising a daughter. Since I was not getting affection from my father, animals became the outlet for my overwhelming abundance of affection, and I would unleash my hugs and kisses on our unassuming four-legged fur family members.

I feel that a way a person is raised creates the foundation of patterns, either good or bad. I believe that we are taught from an early age about communication, work ethic, generosity, love. We are also taught racism, negativity, and judgment. Attitudes, belief systems, and traditions are passed down through the generations. Historically, one would hear racist comments directed towards the Italian and Irish immigrants while they were building the railroad, and it always confused me when racism was came from Italians towards others.

I share this story of my family, based on our upbringing, our role models, and how we learned to navigate through life experiences.

The Cacciatore Side:

At the turn of the century, there was a large migration of Italians who came through Ellis Island. My ancestors came from small villages in Sicily and Calabria, where humble beginnings and workhorse ethics were born.

There were swarms of Europeans who arrived in the States, and a great number of them began working for the Great Western Railway (GWR). I never met my great grandfather on my dad's side, as he was killed in an accident while working for the railroad.

With no rhyme or reason, immigrants traveled wherever they could start a new life. Many Italians settled in the Chicago area, and many settled in Iowa—the South side of Des Moines is considered our version of 'Little Italy.'

Our immediate clan consisted of the Cacciatore's, Graziano's and Costanzo's. All fun-loving yet extremely private people. We are not the typical loud Italian family often depicted in movies. Our family is more quiet and humble, filled with secrets behind the scenes. In our family, life lessons had to be learned on one's own, without much direction or mentorship.

I heard my older relatives speaking Italian on occasion, but not enough to learn the language. I feel sad that immigrants were not encouraged to speak their native tongue. I would have loved to learn how to speak Italian growing up.

Immigrants had to have an entrepreneurial spirit if they were going to live the American dream. Butchers, bakers, tailors, candlestick makers, and salesmen were a few categories that proved to be successful options.

My grandfather, Ignatius 'Noche' Cacciatore, began working in his teens as a salesman at a dental distribution company. He took the train that spanned so many of the Midwest cities so that he could build the relationships he needed to one day start his own business.

He eventually hired his younger brother Carl to work with him, once Carl had graduated from college. The brothers built a successful family owned business called the Iowa Dental Supply Company. The company was located in downtown Des Moines across from Mercy Hospital, where I was born. Growing up, I always thought that Billy Joel must have known my grandfather, as a lyric in his song *I'm Moving Out* states, *"He worked at Mr. Cacciatore's down on Sullivan Street, across from the medical center."*

My grandfather was strict, stoic, and not very communicative. He sat in his big cushy chair each Sunday when we came by for family dinner. I sat on their long, stiff couch that was covered in clear plastic vinyl. It was so hot in the summer months that my bare legs stuck to the plastic. I dangled my feet over the edge of the couch, avoiding eye contact. Instead, I stared at the crystal-cut candy bowl that held the Italian boxed candy I loved so much.

Each week, he asked the same short questions and each week, I gave him the same short answers. When I was dismissed I grabbed the golden box with the cameo face of a woman and tore open the wrapper. I opened the door that led to the chilly attic staircase, and sat on the stairs chewing the soft, nugget creaminess, ignoring the sound of the Bonanza theme song blaring from their television set. My brothers and cousins gathered around the television watching, The *Ed Sullivan Show* and *Bonanza*, while I sat alone in the attic staircase. Our immediate Italian family had dinner at our grandparents house most Sunday nights. My cousins consist of three brothers and two sisters. All of them, including my Aunt and Uncle are down to earth and hard-working sweet people.

I loved my grandma Edith and her sister Aunt Annie. These adorable and loving sisters were Graziano's until Edith married a Cacciatore and Annie married a Costanzo. They both had exquisite taste in clothing, decorations, and artifacts. The sisters' cooking was filled with love, especially when it came to Christmas feasts and Italian cookies.

They were the matriarchs of the family, and were strong behind the scenes. It was fun to watch my grandmother cooking Italian food for Sunday dinners. I quietly watched my Grandma and tried to stay out of her way. My Aunt Annie is still alive at ninety-five, still smart and strong. I want to be like her when I grow up.

Edith was sweet and generous. She wore her long, flowered kitchen apron that always had a folded-up tissue in the pocket. She always had a smile from ear to ear and a funny giggle. She loved to take me shopping and would always bring me gifts from her travels. It was her way of showing affection. I heard much later in life that she had had a nervous breakdown, and that through her journey she had turned to painting porcelain objects and handmade Christmas ornaments, which still adorn my tree each year. Eventually she had a stroke, and had to live the rest of her elder years in a wheelchair.

My grandfather's brother, Uncle Carl, was one of those jovial guys who everyone liked. Carl always had a twinkle in his eye when he squeezed my cheek and slipped a ten-dollar bill into my hand. He would drive up in his shiny Cadillac, wearing his white, starched shirts and perfectly donned suits and shoes. My grandfather and great uncle both had their suits and ties custom-made in Chicago by the best Italian tailors, and their wing-tipped shoes were always shiny. My father followed in their footsteps, and the Italian gene for great taste in shoes was passed down to him as much as his brother. He took out his wooden shoe box each Saturday afternoon and polished every pair of shoes in the house. He loved when I came home from college. I would line up my shoes for him to shine. My dad often said, *"You can tell a lot about a man by his shoes and his teeth."* To this day I find myself glancing at both shoes and teeth.

The family business was passed down to my father, his brother, and their cousin who all became its second-generation owners. My brothers took over in 2000 when my father's health began to decline. My brothers were the third (and last) generation to own the company, which made the Iowa Dental Supply Company a family owned business for close to ninety years.

The other side of the Italian family was also entrepreneurial. The Graziano brothers joined forces to open the Graziano Brothers Italian Market in 1912. The store still exists today and has been run by my younger cousin, Francis, the first woman to take over the store, for the past twenty-five years. Every Saturday my dad and I would visit this market to pick up the Italian lunch meat for the week. This was a highlight for me, as I cherished alone time with my daddy, even though the only sound was his whistling, or the sound of silence. The only part of the outing that I did not like was this tiny green bridge we had to cross to get to the south side of Des Moines. I was so afraid of this tiny bridge. When I visit Des Moines now, I see how small it is, but as a child the bridge seemed to be bigger than London Bridge itself.

My family, with all the turmoil and drama that seemed to haunt me, in retrospect was nothing much in the scheme of things.

They are all hard-working and sweet people, doing the very best that they can.

The entrepreneurial gene was passed onto me, as I never wanted to work for another person let alone a large corporation. I started many solo-businesses over the years, but I never had a proper mentor. I would have loved a relationship with my grandfather, one in which he would teach me about running a company, but I never expressed interest in the family business, so that opportunity was never given.

After I moved to New York and was on my own, I remember going to see my grandfather in his office. I tried to strike up a conversation and ask for his advice. I asked for a small business loan, $1,000, to begin a personal shopping business in New York. His response was, *"Little lady, I have learned a valuable lesson over the years, which is to never loan money to a friend."* A look of confusion crossed my face. I wanted to say, *"Grandpa... I am not your friend, I am your granddaughter. I want to learn, I want to succeed in business, and I need a role model, someone to take me under their wing."* However, I didn't say any of this. I was too shy to ask. I got up, thanked him for his time, and left his office.

Growing up, us kids were often sent off during the weekends to our grandparents. My oldest brother spent a most of his time with the Italian side of the family, while I spent time with the grandparents on my mom's side. My middle brother floated between the two sides and spent a great deal of time with our great-grandmother and aunties on my mom's side.

The Davis Side (My Mom):

My grandfather was a blue-collar worker who gave his life to raising my mom in a good home with a lot of love. My grandmother was a stay-home mom who ran a tight ship of humble hamburger dinners. She and my grandfather treated themselves to one single "highball" (whiskey and Squirt soda) each night as a treat. Other than that, I never saw drinking in any of the homes. I would have Squirt on ice, pretending that I was having a cocktail with them.

My mom was adopted when she was six months old and was raised in very humble beginnings. She had a lot of wonderful female energy and mysticism in her midst. My great-grandmother and the two aunties lived near one another and in their elder years, they all lived together.

My mom loved her parents so much that she barely thought of finding her biological parents. However, when I was living in New York my mom's best friend (Nini) worked at the courthouse as a clerk. She met a woman with the same last name as my mom's 'real' name. With a bit of detective digging, they found my mom's biological mom. She found out that she had two younger sisters and a brother.

This story could take up an entire other book, but I am grateful to find relatives from my mom's side, as it gives me breadcrumbs of ancestry that I did not have growing up. I became close to one of my cousins (Brenda), her husband and her kids when we were in our thirties. I often hear Brenda say, *"That mannerism you just did was so much like Grandma Bethel."*

Due to the economic differences between the two families, along with of the fact that my mom was not Italian, nor Catholic, the rub between them all was present throughout our lives.

My mom's parents were instrumental in raising me and I learned many life lessons from Grandpa Harold. He spent hours playing cards with me. One time I cheated at one of the games. I can still see the disappointment on his face, which still haunts me today. He told me that he would never play with me again if I cheated. He eventually played with me, but his reaction was a great lesson in life.

When I stayed with them, the anticipation built up during the day, waiting for Grandpa Harold to come home from work. The highlight of my day was hiding in his closet between his wool suits. The smell of mothballs permeated my nose. I heard his footsteps on the creaky, wooden floorboards. He called out my name pretending that he had no idea where I was hiding. Day after day we went through this ritual. He opened the closet door, as I sprang out of the closet to surprise him. Grandma Polly always had rose-colored cheeks and a smile on her face. She loved to sing with a bit of an operatic voice and she called my name with that same wobble in her voice.

When I turned sixteen, my grandfather was suffering from the final stages of emphysema. He was deep in a coma, sputtering 'sweet acidophilus' from his lips, as that was the famous milk commercial of the year.

I sat by his hospital bed squeezing his hand as hard as I could. I cried for him to wake up. I was not ready for him to die. He did wake up and was able to go home, but just for a short period of time. Harold P. Davis was a humble man, and his work in the factories gave him emphysema. He took the bus to and from work.

The funny and sweet story that was told, that still sticks with me is when one night he came home and told my grandmother that he had an accident on the bus. He walked strangely to the bathroom and came back out holding his stained pants, standing in his boxer shorts. My grandmother said, *"What in the world happened Harold?"* He said with a wry smile, *"Polly, I learned a very important lesson today...and that is to not put too much faith in a fart."*

My grandfather died a few months later. He is still in my heart and soul to this day. During my grandfather's transition I also experienced my first romantic heartbreak. The timing could not have been worse.

I met my first boyfriend in eighth grade. He was the first "love" of my life. We both went to different middle schools and our schools were rivals in sports. My girlfriends and I were at a basketball game sauntering around thinking that we knew it all.

I looked to the basketball court and saw a blonde guy on the opposing team running down the court. My heart skipped a beat. He was obviously one of the better players. We were both extremely shy, so it took our mutual friend Mike to introduce us. My first date with Brian was at the local roller-skating rink. This was the social gathering place of the seventies.

My girlfriends and I spent hours getting ready. We did our best hair impression of the Farrah Fawcett flip. We wore cropped paisley shirts and well-ironed extra-wide, bell-bottom blue jeans. Brian and I circled around the roller rink trying to figure out who would speak first. Brian finally asked me to skate the moonlight slow-song and we held hands for the very first time.

Those were the times of innocence. Even though we were a slightly rebellious, we were extremely wholesome. Our adventures consisted of sneaking out at midnight during slumber parties to ride our bikes to the local park to meet our boyfriends. In high school, we would have parties in the cornfield, build bonfires, and ride horses bareback. On occasion we would 'teepee' a person's front yard by throwing several rolls of toilet paper into the trees.

I remember a few times when our friend John hosted weekend parties. His mom was a pretty cool chaperone, outside of falling asleep in her oversized reclining chair. We watched the first episodes of *Saturday Night Live* with all the great comics of our time. Sometimes we would blast the music too loud until the frustrated neighbors called the police. We would all scatter like mice on a sinking ship... slipping into a dry bathtub, under a bed, or, my personal favorite, a dark walk-in closet, which gave us time to kiss and hold hands.

Brian and I dated for two years—a good length of time for being so young. He was (and still is) a wonderful person in my life. We have gone back and forth throughout the years with many synergies. His oldest daughter was born on my birthday. His son was born ten minutes before my birthday. Both of our fathers died on the same day, eight years apart.

Brian broke up with me when we were sixteen, around the time that my grandfather died. This was a double-whammy of pain and heartbreak, which still lingers with me today. My mom loved Brian so much that she had him be one of the pallbearers at her father's funeral.

I was devastated by the breakup, which happened around the time of our Sophomore homecoming dance. I accepted an invite to go to the dance with a sweet, adorable guy from my art class after I heard that Brian was going with my locker mate. I felt so bad for my date when we ended up at a party with older teens, along with Brian and his date. It was hard to see Brian hanging with this other girl who was supposed to be my friend. The seniors at the party were serving up slow-gin fizz drinks. It was bitter and sweet and did not go down well. One thing led to another and I ended up sick and spinning on the bathroom floor. I locked myself in the bathroom trying to make the spinning stop. Brian eventually talked me into opening the door; my classmates were extremely worried. Needless to say I got sick in the car on the way back home and I missed my curfew by two hours.

My father was up pacing the floor when we drove in the driveway. My punishment was to get up two hours later and go to my waitressing job at the International House of Pancakes. I did not make it through that shift as the smell of pancakes, syrup, and eggs made me sick at every turn.

It took me a long time to get over that breakup with Brian. We remained in touch over the years and even attempted to date in our adult years after he raised his children and got divorced. It was a great reunion and a solidifier of him being a lifelong friend and someone who will always have a place in my heart.

In recent years Brian explained to me why he broke up with me back in high school. He thought other boys liked me and that I would eventually break up with him. This was a revelation to me, as I had no intention of breaking up with him. We spent many hours on the phone at midnight, making plans to be together. We named our future children. We were young, but there seemed to be a solid foundation of love.

For decades I carried around the idea that I was not good enough because of him breaking up with me. The 'not good enough' theme became a dangerous thought-pattern that caused me to make terrible decisions in my life. I had no role models and no one to look to who had already forged the path where I wanted to go. I had not tackled the concept of self-love or self-awareness. I truly believe I would have handled life completely differently if I had someone to show me the way.

All through my life I have felt awkward and shy and because of this my buttons got pushed over the years. I had to learn how to rise and take my power back. I am sure there are blessings to having this sort of experience so that I could experience rejection to toughen myself for the myriad of disappointments that occurred and to see these occurrences as blessings.

Freshman year in High School, I was not chosen to be a cheerleader. I was devastated, as most of my girlfriends were chosen. However, this tragedy changed the course of my life forever.

I walked down the hallway and saw a flier hanging on the social board that read *"Mr. Fagin Wants You!"* It was an announcement for the casting of the play *Oliver*, so I decided to audition. I stood on that theatre stage with short breath, knees knocking, trying to sing, *Consider Yourself* not knowing if even a note of sound was coming out of my mouth. I got cast in that production and every show onward, so I knew I had a home. Ms. Freda Nahas was a legend at the school and she was impressionable to all of us throughout the years. She wore a cotton-candy shaped brunette wig, that swept over her left eye. She always had a dramatic flair for her liquid eyeliner that balanced out her face with her distinguished long nose.

**Soundcloud Playlist - Consider Yourself - Oliver Cast

The summer after freshman year I attended a theater workshop at Iowa State University. I remember the feeling of freedom being on a college campus at the age of thirteen. I screamed inside to spread my wings. We spent our days with master teachers in the areas of song, dance, acting, and art. The teachers offered us an opportunity of a lifetime when we were accepted into a program, one in which we could go to high school in the mornings and then travel to Ames Iowa to attend college courses in the afternoon. This would have allowed me to attend college in a parallel universe and graduate from college and high school at the same time. The Dean of Dowling High School and the other priests and nuns would not allow for this to happen, so I forged ahead in high school with a dream of my escape.

In high school I had friends who were cheerleaders, jocks, party-goers, geeks, and theatre peeps. They were all wonderful friends and luckily I don't remember any sort of bullying and there was definitely no cyberbullying as there was no social media or cell phones. I kind of drifted between all types of groups as I never really felt attached to any on particular clique and I liked it that way.

The one thing I wished growing up was having more diversity. Back in those days Des Moines was predominately white. The first black person I ever saw was my eye doctor, Dr Sanders, in third grade. I was so mesmerized by the difference between his skin and mine and by his gentle deep black eyes. He reminded me of Sidney Poitier and I wondered why I did not have skin as dark. We had a very small percentage of black kids in our high school. I do not think there were racial tensions, but of course that could be due to my sheltered existence as a white girl in Iowa. Other kids might be able to tell a different story. Our high school was a private Catholic high school, so we had scholarships to get the best athletes in the state.

I realized my full awkwardness during my senior year when I was nominated for the final twelve in the Homecoming Queen court. I was extremely uncomfortable and self-conscious. I could barely look at anyone. Needless to say, I was not voted to be one of the final six queens in the court. A dear friend Susie was crowned and there could not have been a better pick. She was the head of the cheerleading squad with a sweet smile and a feisty twinkle in her eye.

Long after graduation, during one of those crazy reunions an assortment of people came up to me to say, *"Wow... you're actually nice - I thought you were such a bitch in high school."* I mention this because there are so many misconceptions in society. But the truth is that shy girls can actually be nice and the bullies can actually be victims in their lives at home. We are all prisoners of our own minds until we are able to set ourselves free.

Due to my extensive dance background by the time I was in high school, I worked my senior year as an entertainer at the local Six Flags amusement park, Adventure Land. We performed eight shows a day during the humid, hot summers. My favorite time of day was when I could take a break. I ran as fast as I could to the water exhibit. This was my first time experiencing dolphins with their intense, keen ability and intuition. Dolphins in Iowa? I know...a strange concept. My animal rights passion did not agree with them being held captive. However, there was no way to release them into the ocean, with nothing but cornfields surrounding the park.

I slipped through the gate into the exhibit. The dolphins jumped, played, and clapped their fins at me. I felt that I belonged with them more than I did with my human co-workers. I stared deep into their eyes as they telepathically gave me the secrets to the universe. We had a beautiful exchange of love.

My senior year I was nominated by our high school to be a model on the teen board for our local department store, Yonkers. The experience of being on stage was another step in helping me to break out of my shell. I still had a long way to go. There were two of us from every high school in the surrounding area. Michelle and I represented Dowling. She was one of the pretty, perky cheerleaders, so I tried to fit in a bit more with that set of popular girls.

Later in my senior year, I was nominated to be in the Miss Iowa Pageant. I am not the pageant type, but my mom was so excited, and I did not want to disappoint her. My boyfriend at the time was supportive, and his mom helped me find sponsorships to help me obtain the proper wardrobe. I was awkward.

That pageant weekend was the longest four days of my life. There were four girls in each hotel room, so getting ready was intense and horrifying. I stepped on a hot curling iron that was laying on the floor. When I stuck my foot in the bathtub to run cold water over the burn, the faucet shifted to shower mode causing a large stream of water to melt my curled hair and made-up face. I felt like a washed-up dog when I went on stage for the evening gown competition.

I was mortified when the host of the pageant asked me, *"Tell us what you think about abortion?"* I stood there frozen, mumbling something about still being a virgin, tongue-tied beyond belief. I was hoping they would ask me about world peace. I was prepared to answer that question. I was not the eloquent type, but I received some runner-up position in the pageant. The friend I talked into doing the pageant with me was the one crowned Miss Iowa. I was so happy for her and equally happy that it was not me. Shelley was this beautiful statuesque blonde from another high school. She was one of the models on the teen board with me. Shelly was far more eloquent that I could ever imagine to be during my gawky awkward years.

I have always searched for meaning in life. One of the priests in our high school was a transplant from Hollywood. His claim to fame was being an actor in his younger years on a television series called *Alias Smith and Jones*.

He left the entertainment industry to enter the seminary and become a priest. This was an interesting transition, to leave Hollywood and end up, of all places, in Des Moines, Iowa. Father O'Connor taught a class called Non-Catholic Religions. I loved his class, and it became the extension of my personal religious studies from my childhood. We all enjoyed watching Father O'Conner and his borderline rebellious behavior. He rarely wore his clerical collar and more than a few times, came to a school dance with a female friend. I am certainly not implying anything was going on, but he was truly a rebellious out of the ordinary priest and I liked that.

I excelled in writing reports for his class, as I continued my passion of discovering the differences between spirituality and religion. Marching on from my childhood days, I continued to see the similarities of religions, and I continued to ask God why we did not all just worship him together as one. I felt like I lived on the edge of life, searching for angels and signs from God.

Iowa is a great state, however, every place has its dark clouds. I recently found out that the oldest sister of my friends had been molested by a neighbor for several years. Two doors down from us, in our quiet neighborhood, there was a 'family' man who took advantage of this young girl, and perhaps many others as well.

I pray for all victims of the world, as I have skated on the edge of darkness close enough to see the tunnel that might be the hardest to escape. One never knows where demons may hide. I am certain if these men and other perpetrators were questioned, we would find out that they had been molested as well. The patterns of abuse are cyclical, which means that we have to stop the cycles right now. I share my story with you to hopefully inspire you to know that there are safe places to share your secrets, so that healing can begin. You are not alone.

**Soundcloud Playlist - Don't Give Up - Peter Gabriel

Chapter 10
Stephen's Susie

I planned, dreamed, and studied the craft of acting, singing, and dancing all throughout my childhood. I got accepted into the only college that I applied to, Stephens College in Columbia, MO for a Bachelor of Fine Arts (BFA).

Stephens is in a great college town with three main universities: Stephens College, Columbia College, and the University of Missouri (Mizzou). Stephens is mostly an all-women's college, so a lot of our male interaction came from frat boys at Mizzou.

Stephens is the second oldest all-female school in the United States, and was founded in 1833. The drama department was established in 1937 by its chairman and teacher, Maude Adams who played the first Peter Pan. Stephens is renowned for their theatre department and for their famous alumnae, including Maude Adams, Joan Crawford, Patricia Barry, Annie Potts, and Dawn Wells, to name a few. George C. Scott came through as a visiting teacher, as did Patricia Barry and Dawn Wells during my years. We did a parody of Gilligan's Island in our "Off-the-Wall" theatre where Dawn re-enacted her character of Mary Ann. Jennifer Tilly was in the class before me.

From the time that Stephens was established to a few years before I attended, there were really strict rules for the students. Many of the girls came from wealthy Southern families, so they attended Stephens as a finishing school to get their MRS degree. I had no idea such a degree existed and come to find out well into my adult years, this is a tongue-in-cheek reference to women who want to find themselves husbands. No judgment there, this was just not on my radar screen.

Going back to early seventies, before my time of attending, girls were required to wear hats and gloves to class. Classes mostly consisted of homemaking and administrative courses, although the school had a great equestrian department as well, since many of the women came from wealthy, Southern families who grew up with horses. Back then students had to get parental permission to receive gentlemen visitors, or for that matter to even receive a letter from a member of the opposite sex.

"Stephen's Susie" is an infamous nickname for those who have attended Stephens. The name has many connotations, but I'll stick to the meaning that we are empowered women who stuck together throughout the years.

I took the fast track for my Bachelor of Fine Arts (BFA) degree by doing a three-year program, consisting of two intense summer theatre camps between the three full curriculum years. The first summer was a seven weeks summer stock on campus, and the second year consisted of a ten week summer stock at Okaboji Summer Theatre in Okaboji, Iowa.

Even though Stephen's College is considered an all women college, there is a small percentage of males who are given scholarships to advance their degree in music, theatre, and dance. Every Freshman year consisted of all female students. However, during the first summer theatre program we met our fellow male students, that were considered to be "our" guys. There were less than twenty guys at the entire college at any given time. If you divided them between the theatre, music, and dance departments the ratio was 1-in-100 of males to females.

Most of the guys were safely tucked away into the world of being gay. However, the ones who were straight were in for a once-in-a-lifetime adventure. Most men think going to an all-girls college is a great idea. However, dealing with charming, hormonal, competitive, young women ends up being an experience which the majority of men cannot handle.

My college days were filled from sunrise to sunset. Mornings began with a three-hour master dance class, then off to academia classes, mixed with music, theatre and writing. I often rehearsed a play in the afternoon and performed a different play in the evening. After midnight, if not at the local pub, there could be another rehearsal going on for an upcoming performance.

My freshman year was packed with adventures with my girlfriends off campus at the Mizzou Fraternity at the Fiji House.

On the social scene I briefly dated a football star from Mizzou. Looking back I think he must have been gay and he dated me so he could seem straight. We had fun though and he never hassled me to have sex. I was able to keep my "virtuous" status of being a virgin.

This would not be the last time that a gay man would want to date me, as my friendship gave them space to venture out of the closet and into the world. Men were dangerously afraid of coming out back in the day, so often the open-hearted straight girls fell into relationships of convenience. I got to keep my focus on my career, have a great male companion, and help them out as well. To be clear, this was never discussed like an arranged relationship, it was just what happened back then.

During my junior year of college I was asked to choreograph a Stephen Sondheim Show, *Side by Side by Sondheim*. As rehearsal began, the cast and crew were in a flutter. Rumor had it that the handsome English professor was going to be the narrator of the show. I will refer to him simply as D. I had not met D, but based off of what everyone said about him, he was the unattainable poet, writer, and professor, handsome in every way, with a heart of gold.

On this particular spring day we waited for the infamous D to show up for rehearsal. I was not particularly interested in the buzz about him, as I was preoccupied with my responsibility over the dance routines for the show.

My fashion-style of the day consisted of dance leotards underneath my brother's old hospital greens. My hair was long, blonde, over-permed and held back by a headband. Since I was always running in and out of dance classes, I typically did not wear a stitch of makeup. This bohemian style fit my college budget and my active lifestyle, but it did not leave me feeling prepared to meet any sort of handsome man at an all-women's college.

I was stretching out to get limber to dance. Positioned on the side of the stage I was able to see when the side door of the theatre opened. The sun burst into the dark theatre. My eyes adjusted to the light as this silhouette walked through the beam of light. It was like the opening sequence of an action movie. In walked an extraordinarily, handsome man. D was an exotic, American-Lebanese, with caramel skin, dark curly hair, and piercing hazel/green eyes. His physique was trim and muscular. At that moment I joined the ranks with the rest of the campus, and we collectively swooned when he walked by.

There was strong eye contact between us and something stirred inside of me, perhaps a deep karmic recognition. During rehearsals, we became friends. It was nearing the end of the school year, and I knew we would be separated for the summer. Before we departed, to ensure that I saw him again, we spoke of having an extra credit class that I wanted in English for writing. He said he would be happy to take me on for this extra credit.

I left for our summer break to a small lake town on the border of Iowa and Minnesota, Okaboji, Iowa; to attend the Okaboji Summer Theatre. It was great to be there, as it brought back wonderful childhood memories. Our family spent many family vacations on the lake growing up. My parents had best friends who had two kids, Billy and Nicki. Their kids were around the same ages as my brothers and me. We all played, water skied, and grew up together in the midst of good family fun. Nicki and I would go to the recreation room and put the same songs into the jukebox.

**Soundcloud Playlist - Signs - Five Man Electric Band

The owners of the resort had three cute boys. Nicki and I, at probably around eleven years old, experienced our first crushes on the Brown brothers. To this day Nicki is more of a sister than anything. We go way back to the day we when were both born. Her mom was my second mom and Nini was a great influence on me growing up and in my adult life.

Every day during the Okaboji summer theatre, our schedule consisted of learning every aspect of production. If we were not acting in a show, we were assigned to a RCew: costume, props, sound, lights, set/stage/art, stage management. Stephens had a well-rounded education program that has proven to be extremely valuable throughout my career.

In the flurry of it all I had to keep up with the fast-paced schedule, but I could not get D off my mind. Summer could not have ended fast enough. The first night back on campus, I went to see my friends at a frequented restaurant called, Fish & Friends. Much to my surprise, D was sitting at the bar. He turned around and flashed a smile. I walked over to give him a hug. We talked about our summer experiences, and about the school year ahead. He remembered that I needed to get an extra English credit, so he offered to give me a private class in poetry and writing composition.

D was my first introduction into serious writing. I always loved to write as a child, but I never had anyone to encourage my writing passion. Even though I won a national poetry contest about the American Flag in third grade, no one in my family made any big deal. My poem won top honors at our school and was sent to Washington, DC to represent our school for the nation.

I also won a speech contest in fifth grade. I had to get up in front of parents and teachers for an evening program at our school. I was insanely nervous. My heart was in my throat and my knees knocked underneath my dress. Looking back I realize that this set the stage of being an activist, as the content of my speech was about my passion for environment and humanity. Even though I was nervous to speak before an audience, I felt that night set me up for my future writing and public speaking career.

D was an amazing poet and I was grateful for him coming into my life to help bring my writing to the next level. He was very supportive of my writing, and he taught me about prose, creating images, and how to edit. Even today as I write this book, I feel D around me, and I hear his voice, *"Now Tree,"* Tree was a nickname given to me in college, based off my given name Theresa. "Tree," he would say, *"Always look at every word and don't be afraid to chop. Your piece will speak to you and tell you what needs to go."* He called me his muse, and he was definitely my muse as well.

For my assignment in D's class, I chose to write a thesis about F. Scott Fitzgerald's *The Great Gatsby.* I worked really during that six week course. I was assigned a ten-page paper, but my thesis ended up being forty-two pages. It had been my longest piece of work to date and I was really proud. I was expecting to get an 'A' on this paper. After all, in my other classes I was getting A+s. Imagine how I felt when I got my paper back and there was a big, fat 'B+' written across the top of the page. I cannot remember the accolades D wrote in the margins of the paper, or how he complimented my analogies of Fitzgerald's characters and storyline. None of that mattered. I did not get my A.

While we were in the teacher/student relationship everything was above board. He was the perfect teacher and gentleman. After our class was complete, D asked me to join him for a picnic at the campus lake. We sat by the waters' edge watching the equestrian students gallop by with perfect English form on their horses. We talked for hours. It was obvious there were intense emotions growing between us. D looked into my eyes and swallowed hard. He proceeded to tell me his story of being divorced with a young daughter. He shared that he was in a relationship with a person off-campus who was close to his age. I was proud enough to not let any emotion flicker across my face. Instead I told him that it was important that our friendship flourish, as that was what I cherished most.

Walking back to my dorm, a chilly air swept through us. Fall was fast approaching. He offered me his sweater and put his arm around me. I felt like a fast ball had been pitched into my stomach, and I knew I wanted him in my life, even if we were just friends. As we approached my dorm I gave him back his sweater. We parted ways with a friendly hug, and a promise to stay in touch.

Three days passed. I was studying in my dorm room when one of the girls came racing down the hall. *"Hey Tree...you got someone here to see ya."* I had no idea who it might be, so I raced through the hallway and down the stairs. I slowed down ever-so slightly at the end of the staircase, so I would not look too excited. I turned the corner to see D standing with his back to me. He was wearing one of those cliché professor jackets, made of brown and caramel colored tweed with the brown suede patches on the elbows.

This was long before cell phones, so we had to rely on the old-fashioned gentlemanly calls. I saw his face beaming as I walked down the stairs to greet him. *"Can we go on a walk?"* he asked. I replied, *"Of course."*

We walked for what seemed like forever, filling the air with small talk. He finally stopped and looked me square in the face to say, *"I could not stop thinking about you the entire summer, and that random run in at the bar that first night was planned. I went there every night for a week hoping to run into you."* He paused with a deep sigh, *"I ended my relationship so that we could be together."*

I was in happily in shock. He shared that he had done a lot of thinking and that his relationship was not going anywhere. He wanted to be with me. He shared our situation with a few of his teacher friends, concerned about any pending campus controversy. They were supportive of him. They knew the core of who he was, and that he had never before crossed any lines with a student. D was a genuine person and everyone respected him.

I too had thought about him all summer, and felt like a dream was becoming a reality. He reached his hand behind my neck and gently pulled me closer for our first kiss.

October 18, 1980, was our seventh date. He took me to the movies to see *The Rose*, starring Bette Midler. Our date was one of the most special nights of my life. I had picked the perfect time for my rose petals to blossom. It was definitely the sweetest and safest place to be, and it was well worth the wait until mature love had found me.

Besides being an amazing poet and professor, D was an amazing jazz drummer. We played together in a jazz quartet and I sang with the band. *Autumn Leaves* was our song. I know, so cliché, college girl falls for English Professor and scandals brew. However, since there was such deep respect for him there was really not any controversy or scandal.

I moved off campus and into his apartment. We wrote together, played in the band together, and made plans for our future. He taught me how to cook Lebanese and Chinese food. I got to know his lovely daughter, who was eleven at the time. Even though she and I were closer in age, I never felt that age difference between him and me. Bethel was a beautiful ballerina, and I watched her blossom into a lovely young woman.

During my senior year, to get my final grade for directing, we were required to direct a one-act play. Not one to follow the norm, I decided to get the production rights for a full-length play and produce it on my own. I had my heart set on *Mousetrap* by Agatha Christie. It is a three-act play that premiered in London's West End in 1952. The show has been running continuously ever since.

The play had a lot to offer for my senior project. My teacher however, did not support me, as he wanted me to follow the assignment and do a one-act play. I went around him and got permission from the head of the college to do my production in an abandoned building on south campus, which happened to be known for being haunted. As far as I knew, no student had done anything like this before.

I do not remember the details on how I got the rights to the performance, but I can be resourceful when I need to be. I bought the album of original sound effects from a music publisher out of New York to use for the music soundtrack. I found a local musician, Billy V, who created an amazing work of original music around the theme of *Three Blind Mice* and the sounds of London.

I cast the most talented actors, set designers, and crew of our school. I came back early from Christmas break, and we built the set on our own. Addison, the teacher, was beyond mad at me for not participating in his one-act play night. The director's bug had bitten me though, and there was no turning back. We got local press to attend, and local critics raved about the show, which only fueled the fires of fury against me. Many years later, I heard through my friend Melissa Canaday who was a year behind me, that Addison tried to sabotage my production and told everyone to boycott my show.

I cast D as the Italian Mr. Paravicini. He took to the accent like water, and did a marvelous job. This experience inspired D to become interested in playwriting. He was so passionate about writing that he applied and got accepted into the Summer Playwriting Symposium at Yale University.

D knew that I wanted to move to New York after graduation, so he was wise to know that this would be a great transition for us. Preparing for the end of school year, D and I planned spring break in New York. We hopped on a train for a three-day excursion to the city. This was my first train ride, and the journey was magical, watching the countryside go by, with the man I loved by my side.

I do not remember how we got the money to go, but we lived frugally on peanut butter and jelly sandwiches. It is surprising to report that until this point, I had never eaten a PB&J. I remember my first bite, the way the salty peanuts mixed with the sweet raspberry jam. It was romantic. It was just right.

Upon arriving at Grand Central Station, I was in awe of the thousands of people stirring throughout the cement cavern, as if magically choreographed from above. Time stood still as we held hands, wide-eyed, and full of excitement. I felt like I was home.

While in New York, I was daring. I did wild things, like sneak past the guards at NBC studios. While D waited down on the street for me, I rode up and down the elevator pretending I worked there. I must have looked extremely out of place, as one man even asked me where I was going. When I told him why I was there, he told me to follow him when he got off the elevator. I followed him down this long hallway that was adorned with photographs of the many stars that had graced the numerous television shows and movies.

We turned the corner, and he led me through a backstage door. He dipped behind a curtain and pulled it back for me to step forward. We entered onto that stage, and he said, *"Here is where Saturday Night Live is taped."* He looked for my reaction, explaining that, *"The theatre is much smaller in person."*

I was in the exact spot where so many great comedians had stood before. Silence hung in the air for what seemed like eternity. *"Ready to go?"* he asked. I followed him back to the elevator and I climbed on with a few NBC suited executives. He waved and smiled. As the elevator doors closed, I heard him say, *"Good luck out there."* I floated by the security guards and went through the revolving doors. I ran up to D laughing at what had just happened, that I had made it on the stage of *Saturday Night Live.*

That afternoon I answered an ad in the Backstage (an industry paper) and auditioned for a movie. I had no idea what the movie was, but they cast me to be on set the following day. They booked me for a four-day shoot. When I got on set, Jane Fonda and Kris Kristofferson were rehearsing their lines. The film was *Rollover*, directed by Alan J. Pakula. I was placed at the lead table, in a large ballroom scene. I was put into makeup and the wardrobe person dressed me in a beautiful gown. I had no idea that this sort of opportunity was not easy to get. I just walked off a train from the Midwest and onto the set of a feature film.

I excitedly called school to tell the head of theatrical department that I got a job. I assured him that I would only be one day late for school. I thought I would get congratulations! But instead, I was told that if I did not get back to school on time, the role that I was cast in would be given to someone else. I was in shock, as we paid for an education to teach us how to get out in the world to work, and I had a paying gig. But he strong-armed me to come back to school.

Needless to say my legs were shaking when I went to the 1st AD (Assistant Director) to tell him that I could not stay for the entire shoot, as I had to go back to school. I did not comprehend the seriousness of continuity in a shot, as they already established me next to Jane Fonda, and now I would be missing in subsequent shots. After many years of directing and producing projects, I see the damage I must have done.

In retrospect, I should have stayed and kept to my commitment. However, my dutiful-self rushed to the train to get back to school. When I got back to school and attended rehearsal, I found out that my part was double-cast, so I could have missed that first day of rehearsal after all. This was just one example that was part of a larger pattern of unsupportive teachers at this school. Even though I had incredible teachers, Earl Coleman, John Arnold, Brent Prentiss, to name a few.

During the run of this final show *Move Over Mrs. Markham*, we had a visitor from the head of ABC daytime casting. Fate and karma had my back as Mary Lynn came to the show. She approached me after the show. She said. "If you ever find yourself in New York, please look me up." Well, that was all I needed to hear.

D met my parents during graduation. They actually loved him, in spite of the fact that my dad was a bit squirmy of our age difference.

After graduation I choreographed the musical, *Kiss me Kate* at a local theatre. On closing night D and I packed the car and took off on our cross-country road trip to find our New Haven summer home. He was off to explore the playwright symposium, and I would find my way through the transition into the next chapter of my life.

We settled into a second floor apartment in a turn-of-the-century duplex. The wooden floors, arched doorways, and crown molding gave character to our new home. We adopted a sweet cat that we named Sasha the Spy Kitty, as she was a Russian-Blue with golden-speared eyes.

Our weekends and evenings were filled with culture, and we often attended picnic concerts and took long drives through the countryside. New Haven was an interesting mix of culture. The campus was surrounded by beautiful homes, but if you took a wrong turn on any particular street the area could became very sordid.

While D was busy writing with his new symposium buddies, I got involved with the actors in the Yale Summer Conservatory. They invited me to perform with them in the evenings. I was in heaven. I was not officially part of the summer program, but I took their invitation very seriously. I had a blast performing and nurturing my craft in the midst of amazing talent, as no one gets into Yale without being top of their game. They were very sweet people, but I was still a bit shy and awkward. To this day, I feel guilty over the time that they threw me a surprise birthday party for my 21st birthday. I was so overwhelmed by their kindness. When they walked up to give me a piece of the cake, I awkwardly declined. I was too shy to accept and I snuck out of the room. I am still mortified by my behavior and have looked for opportunities to properly thank them for the kindness.

I made contact with Mary Lynn, the casting director who came to our school. She invited me to come for an audition for *The Guiding Light,* so I jumped on a train to New York City. The audition process created the space to carve my way into my future plans. I was introduced to a famous photographer for my very first headshot. Michael photographed all the top models of the day, so I lucked out. I worked on my resume and I made a game plan to get an agent.

I traveled by train between New Haven and New York. I wanted to spend as much quality time with D as I could. I began feeling conflicted about my move to New York. I was in love with both D and my childhood dreams. I was very torn, yet I knew I had to make a decision.

D was wise beyond his years. He knew I needed a shot at my dream. Summer was coming to an end, so our time at Yale was closing in on us. It was beginning to sink in that he had to head back to school, and I that would be embarking on my new life in the big city.

This was my first loving and mature relationship. To this day D is one relationship that should have set the standards for other men. I could have used his wonderful qualities as a gauge to recognize when I was going down the wrong path.

However, I was embarking on a lifetime dream to move to New York, in a long-distance relationship with a true love. I knew I was in the right place and whatever was meant to be would be... and with moving to New York, I was finally able to say to my mom, *"Lucy, I'm Home."*

**Soundcloud Playlist - New York State of MInd - Jay Z and Alicia Keys

Chapter 11

City of Lights

It was August 1981. I was finally heading to New York to begin my new life. A heat wave had hit the East coast, and I was not used to the smothering humidity.

D and I packed the car, along with our Sasha cat, and headed out of Connecticut. The ride was filled with tortured silence, as reality was sinking in for both of us. The summer was coming to an end and we had to move onto our separate lives.

The terrain shifted from lush, green countryside to high-rise, cemented urban landscape. This was the first time I had entered the city in a car instead of a train, so the shift of the landscape seemed more harsh.

While driving down FDR Drive through East Harlem, I began to invent stories in my head about the millions of people who lived in the high-rise buildings.

We drove through past graffiti-graced buildings. I noticed laundry lines on the fire escapes that held tainted sheets and faded shirts, which also served as a perch for pigeons to coo. The bells from a nearby cathedral began to ring. The odor in the air turned smoky and gritty.

All of my belongings were stacked inside our car-top carrier. I had everything I needed for this bittersweet transition, but the flurry of butterflies grew inside me as we neared the East Village. I found a place to live with a college friend Bee. I loved the funky feel of the village and this place seemed like the perfect introduction to New York City life.

Bee made it clear that she was busy and would not able to help me get adjusted to the city. But I was ready to take the city by storm. Over the course of many trips up and down the five flights of stairs, D and I finally finished lugging all of my belongings from the car to this tiny apartment. My room was so small there was no place for furniture. D posed the idea of building a bunk bed. The top of the bunk bed had a single mattress and the bottom open-space was my closet. We headed to a local hardware store to get wood and supplies.

While he hammered away at my bed, I took funky-flowered fabric that I had found in a New Haven thrift store and sewed drapes to hide my clothes. The bed was clever, but not particularly comfortable. However, it was perfect for my first New York City digs.

New York was on fire in the eighties. The East village had a lot of characters roaming the streets. My building had the typical stoop in front, so I climbed over drug addicts and prostitutes to get in and out of the door. To me life in the village was like adding color to a sepia-toned photograph.

Mayor Ed Koch was in office. He was running for his second term in the 1981 election. Koch, along with the New York Police Department (NYPD), created a program called Operation Pressure Point. Over the years the East Village and Alphabet City would be "cleaned up," forcing homeless people out of the area turning away those in need of mental health aid away. But that was a horse of another color.

The day D drove away was heartbreaking. I saw his car bump down E. 11th Street. I stood in the middle of the street waving my arms frantically, wondering if he saw me in his rearview mirror.

It was a hot and humid August morning. A fire hydrant was gushing water and kids were running through the cascade of erupting water so that they could cool down from the heat. The addicts were cranky and restless on the stoop. I slipped inside and climbed up the five stories, as my legs feeling the weight of my heartbreak with every step. I ascended the wooden ladder to my loft bed, I curled up and I cried.

I had no idea what our future held. D told me that he would wait for two years to see what happened with my career. At the end of the two years, I could stay in New York, or, if I was ready to get out of the entertainment industry, I could come back to Missouri and we would marry. He did not want me to regret my decision and wake up one day hating him.

And so, I took the biggest bite out of the New York 'apple' that I could, and I chewed my way through my transition into adulthood. The Iowa cornfields were far from my sight. The lights of the city were my driving force.

My first week in New York, I deposited a check for a few hundred dollars into a local bank. I was not able to access the money for several days because it was an out-of-state check. I literally had one subway token and seventy-five cents in my pocket. I had a lead for a job at a high-end restaurant in midtown, so I took my only subway token and went to the interview. I was hired on the spot and began that night. I made enough money to take a taxi back home and buy groceries.

Through ups and downs, my luck slowly began to turn around, and several things began to fall into place. The first thing I did was orchestrate a plan to get an agent. I bought an industry handbook that listed all the agents and managers with their addresses. They taught us in school that we should email our résumé and follow up with a call. I figured that if everyone was doing that, then I should do something different. I defined a clear path of thirty-two agents that I planned to visit in person.

I stepped out in a storm, my backpack filled with head-shots and copies of my résumé. I would not let the rain deter me, so I plopped open my red umbrella and headed for the 14th Street subway station.

I ran up and down the subway stairs with my umbrella flapping in the wind. The first agent, Richard, was in midtown near Fifth Avenue. I walked up to the receptionist and handed her my résumé. She politely replied, *"The agents will not be seeing anyone new until October, but I'll pass this along."* I smiled and thanked her and headed for the elevator. I pushed the down button and looked down at my soggy boots. Lost in thought I heard a door open behind me. A voice called out my name and said, *"Hey, Theresa, come back please...It's October."*

Did I miss something? Had I been standing there for two months? I followed the receptionist back into the office. She escorted me into a back room. Richard stood up to shake my hand. He was a well-coiffed man dressed in a crisp suit and tie. His office was cluttered with scripts piled high to the ceiling. He cleared a place for me to sit. After a lengthy conversation, he reached across the desk to shake my hand and said, *"Welcome to our agency!"* And just like that, first agency out of the gate, I was signed. I went back to my apartment with a backpack full of undelivered résumé and a disgruntled roommate. She had lived in New York for two years and had not yet signed with an agent.

My days were filled with auditions and attending master dance classes with legends like Michael Bennett, Gregory & Maurice Hines, Phil Black, Frank Hatchett, to name a few. I also took an

African dance class that set my soul on fire. My acting classes were at the same caliber of talented teachers. I studied at HB Studios, Michael Howard, and even had special master classes with the late great Sandy Meisner. One night I shared a bus ride up to the upper west side with another actress from class. Alison and I became dear friends, and she is still near and dear in my life today.

After being in New York for a couple of months I registered for a soap opera acting class. I was trained for stage, so it was time to get on-camera training since I was being sent out on television auditions. I took a class with Mervyn Nelson who was a talented and well-loved man. He had many fun stories about working with legends like Marilyn Monroe, Harry Belafonte, Eric Estrada, and other actors who he helped groom for stardom.

Ethnic names, like Cacciatore, were looked down upon in the industry, especially when they referred to someone with blonde hair and blue eyes. Often I would be called by my agent after an audition with feedback from the casting director, who would say that my name did not match my image. So when my dear teacher, Mervyn called me one morning and said he had a dream that my name should be changed to Carla Cattori, I had to take notice. I resisted at first. I thought it sounded like a 1950's stripper. However, I eventually agreed, as Mervyn's success rate of getting actors working was extremely high. Unfortunately, this was the exact time when I was in an off-Broadway show and a critic was in the audience. He wanted to feature me in the United Airlines Magazine, as they were doing an article on actors in the industry. I was touted to be the up-and-coming starlet. However, the article was written about Carla Cattori, not Theresa (my given name) Cacciatore. It was my biggest marketing coo to date, and I was not even credited with my real name.

In acting class we were partnered with other actors to do scenes. A cute blonde guy, Todd, was my first scene partner. During a rehearsal he asked me if I could sing. I mentioned that I had done musicals in high school. He said, *"How would you like to audition for a record label as a duet?"* I replied, *"Where do I sign up?"* We spent the next few days rehearsing our scene for class, while also rehearsing the song <u>Spooky</u> (Dusty Springfield), as a duet for the record label audition.

**Soundcloud Playlist - Spooky - Dusty Springfield

We headed over to 57th and Broadway to meet with the head of Bobcat Records, which was a successful dance label during the eighties.

Bobby O was the dance club producer of the day. He had several hits on the charts, both in the United States and across Europe. I was very nervous. I had never been in a recording studio.

After we sang our song, Bobby motioned for Todd to step out in the hallway. I thought Todd was getting into trouble for bringing me, because in my mind I was not "good enough."

When they came back in the room Bobby asked if I would be interested in joining an all-girl group called *The Flirts*. Todd seemed happy to have made the introduction, so Bobby put me in the vocal booth and I recorded my first song, which became a hit, called *Calling All Boys*.

**Soundcloud Playlist - Calling All Boys - The Flirts

I was so nervous that I actually did more of a sing-song whisper than actual singing, but that was the sound that Bobby wanted. Bobby handed me a contract, which I immediately took to an entertainment attorney. *"Run for the hills"* the lawyer uttered sternly under his breath. *"You practically have to give them your first born."* I immediately went to the label and signed the contract. I knew what I was getting into and I wanted the experience.

Within a few short months of living in New York I had a theatrical agent, a record contract, and I was already working in the soaps as a day player. I had a test shoot with Cosmopolitan magazine, but it turned out that 5'8" was too short to model, so my commercial agent booked me in print ads for eyeglasses, Heinz ketchup, and liquor ads for the Japan market.

The Flirts did not work out too well for me, however. I participated in a photo shoot for the album cover, and the other two girls made it clear that they wanted nothing to do with me. The original *Flirts* was a brunette, a redhead, and a blonde. The redhead was the one who had left the group, so now the group had two blondes. I was out of *The Flirts*, but I rotated through a few other bands on the label. My voice is still on the original recordings, which back in the day most of the club performers were singing to tracks.

I was then matched up with another blonde and we became *Oh Romeo*, with songs on the charts, like *These Memories* and other hit songs.

We toured the hottest clubs on the East coast, including The Palladium, Limelight, Danceteria, and, my personal favorite, the infamous White Party at The Saint. My favorite Limelight memory was during the spring of 1984, when Shirley MacLaine celebrated her 50th birthday. Isaac Hayes, Liberace, Gloria Steinem, and Andy Warhol were all on hand to celebrate in style. Rubbing elbows with these giants, as a small town girl from Iowa, I was beginning to drink the Kool-aid.

We mostly played gay disco clubs, which had the best DJ's and music, with the best loyal fans. The DJ's had an influence in the artistry of music, and they became celebrities in their own right. The music that was coming out in the eighties was the precursor to EDM.

We made several thousand dollars a performance, wore fabulous costumes, and were guarded by hunky men who took us to and from the stage. I thought it ironic to have to have a bodyguard in a crowd of gorgeous gay men.

We went to Miami several times a month to play in the best clubs. The Miami music scene was hot, and it was developing a sound of its own, with heavy influence from Cuban, Haitian, and other South American artists.

We topped the charts in Europe. I often got calls from friends overseas who held up the phone to let me hear our song playing in the background. This was before cell phones, so we had to use pay phones and landlines.

My best friends were two gay guys Don (a handsome Italian actor) was Jos, Japanese guy who worked with me at Chicken & Burger World. I was the token blonde in a sea of Japanese friends, as we danced our way through the clubs each weekend. The eighties in New York was filled with parties, club scenes, and disco balls. We frequented the famous Studio 54 on many occasions and I can tell you that all rumors about the decadent times are true. While I never saw the multiple floors of debauchery, I knew there were wild things occurring behind closed doors.

My twenty-second birthday was spent having a panic attack on the fire escape at Studio 54. Someone put marijuana in my birthday cake and forgot to tell me. We ate the cake after our sushi dinner and climbed into a limo to go out dancing. While exiting the limo, I felt woozy. There was the typical line of people around the block stationed behind long, red velvet ropes. I was in a group of my Japanese friends, including our wonderful friend who was a fashion designer, Morisani. High couture and punk hair with a lot of attitude was the only way to get the crowd to part ways and let us go straight to the front of the line. We glided by the bountiful bouncers and into the disco ball dance floor. I began hallucinating that a large dragon was coming out of the dance floor. I never had a hallucination before, and did not know that pot could give me such a reaction. I grabbed Jos and made him come outside with me. We must have sat out on the fire escape for hours watching and waiting for the sky to fall. Jos sat by my side and held my hand the entire time.

During that following winter of 1982, it became difficult to stay connected with D. There were no cell phones, no facetime, no internet, and the long distance was wearing us both down.

D decided to meet me in New York after I returned from Christmas with my family in Iowa. We celebrated New Year's Eve, with tickets to one of my favorite musicals, *Camelot* starring Richard Harris, at the Winter Garden. It was exciting to see this romantic classic brought to life until we realized that Richard Harris was slurring his words and stumbling around the stage. Nothing like a drunk to bring down a Broadway Show. D and I left at intermission and decided to walk through the city. The bustle and holiday spirit was clinging to the air, but we were struggling with an intangible sadness.

**Soundcloud Playlist - If Ever I Would Leave You - Robert Goulet

The snow was gently falling as we cuddled under a blanket, riding in a horse-drawn carriage through Central Park. The city could be so magical on a cold, winter night.

Our plan was to be at a party by midnight to bring in the New Year. We arrived at the Mayflower Hotel. After going through the doorman-guarded entrance, we rode the elevator to a privately owned penthouse. Stepping into the room revealed one of the most gorgeous views of the city.

Laughter filled the room, with the loudest source coming from a corner where Robin Williams was entertaining a small group of people around a grand piano. He was the light in the room and the life of the party. D was impressed to be in the presence of a great celebrity, as we did not get many of those in the Midwest.

I slipped down the hallway to find a bathroom. One of the bedrooms was slightly illuminated by the skyline lights. I crept into the bedroom and found a bathroom that did not have a line of people waiting. When I came out of the bathroom a silhouette of a man caught my eye. He was standing in the shadows staring out the window seemingly deep in thought. I did not want to disturb him, but the twinkling city lights beyond the window were irresistible.

I walked up beside this man to take in the view. There were fireworks in the distance. We both stood in silence. I felt him turn from the window and look at me. I looked over to see the most warmest smile beaming from the face of Christopher Reeve. This was way before his *Superman* days, but he was still a super man.

We talked for a short time about the entertainment industry and life in New York. This conversation was a turning point for me. There was a great display of fireworks going off over the East

River and the man I loved was in the other room. I knew the time limit for my decision was nearing and I was not ready to give up on my career, or on this magical city that held my heart.

As if directed by the angels, Christopher looked out the window and said, *"There is something about this city that takes hold of you and does not give up that easy."* Something shifted in me so drastically that I knew what I had to do. The moment was interrupted by the sound of people counting down to midnight.

I darted down the long hallway to find D. *Ten - nine - eight -* I felt like I was swimming in a strange, swirling dream that combined Dr. Zhivago, Camelot, and Midnight in Manhattan all at once. *Seven - six - five -* I ran up and hugged D. *Four - three - two - one... Happy New Year.* We kissed at the stroke of midnight. We held onto one another like the world depended on it.

I believe he knew at that point that I was going to stay in New York. He gently caressed my face and looked into my eyes and said that he would always love me. It was one of the hardest nights in my life. I loved him very much, but I did not want to drag him along any longer.

D went back to school and became more involved with the theatre department. He eventually became an honored playwright and moved to Pennsylvania to become the head of the theatre department at Penn State. We kept in touch throughout the years, sending roses, cards, or calling each other around our October 18th anniversary every year to check in on one another. We eventually met up again in 2001. I was living in Los Angeles, but found myself in New York at the United Nations for a press conference. I asked D if he was available to meet for lunch. He took a train from Pennsylvania, and we met on the upper west side.

I had major butterflies to see him again. I was now forty, the age he was when we met. He still looked great. His young ballerina daughter was now a grown dancer on tour with *A Chorus Line*. Bethel was now living in the city, but we had not yet connected.

D and I laughed throughout lunch, reminiscing on things both serious and light. The romantic side of me wanted to be with him, but I still had much more to do in this wild world. Then on August 11, 2009, I was in Ghana, West Africa finishing up a summit for our Young Leaders. This was the night I met another important man in my life, Maxwell (whose story will be shared later in this book). I felt the kismet of this evening, but did not know the significance for many months.

October was approaching, and I figured I would share with D that I met Maxwell. I called him, but his number was not working. During the past few years I would occasionally message his daughter Bethel on Facebook While skimming Facebook one day though, I saw a post on her wall about a memorial service for her father. My world came to a screeching halt. What memorial service? What would that mean? Was D was no longer alive? I immediately wrote to Bethel and Googled his name. I found out that he died in a car crash the very day that I met Maxwell.

Bethel and I talked about getting together for many years. March 2017, I was in New York for the *Commission on the Status of Women* at the United Nations. Something told me to reach out to Bethel to see if she was around. The time felt right after all these years. She was in New York and she was available. Could it be that we would finally see each other after all these years? The last time I saw her was in 1981, when she and her best friend came to visit me with her dad. She was twelve at that time.

My head and heart were pounding as I approached the tiny pub where we were to meet. It was on the Upper West Side, near the place I last saw her dad many years before.

I arrived first and chose a small table in the corner. Bethel walked into the empty pub. I stood to greet her and we hugged and cried for what felt like forever. The memory of her father washed over both of us. We sat for hours and shared stories, chatting about a little bit of everything, and drinking wine. It was strange seeing the face of the little girl I knew as the face of this beautiful, grown up woman. I knew her father was sitting with us, with his beautiful smile and twinkling green eyes.

I told her stories that she did not know about her father and me. She always knew that I loved him more than life itself and she shared how much he loved me as well. She told me that her father shared with her that I was his muse and to this day, he definitely is a muse of mine.

I told her the Autumn Leaves story and that it was our song. Tears rolled down her cheeks. I asked *"Why the tears?"* She smiled and said, *"That was the song I chose to play at his memorial."*

Ah, those autumn leaves that drift by my window,

The summer kisses and sunburned hands I used to hold, The winter's song and days grow long,

But I miss you most of all my darling,

When those autumn leaves begin to fall.

**Soundcloud Playlist - Autumn Leaves - Eva Cassady

Chapter 12

Escape from New York

In 1983, we were revolving artists in a rotating record label. We all knew one another in the dance club scene. There was this little-known artist who performed the same club circuit. We often saw her name scribbled on the walls in the dressing rooms, and of course we heard rumors about how she worked the DJ's to get her music played. Necessity became the 'mother of her invention' and she made it big. We were all living in the East village wearing crop tops, leggings, lace gloves, with punk hair tied with funky fabric around out head.

However, it was Madonna who made it and she became the rebel of our day. She had the thickest skin of all. The ingredients for success: thick skin, connections, forging oneself onto the scene. Three strikes against me. Her marketing prowess and self-creation took her far away from all of us struggling singers in the East village.

**Soundcloud Playlist - Holiday - Madonna

I stashed away a lot of money and eventually left Bobcat Records, which I came to realize did not have room for creative growth. Not to mention that the head of the label, Bobby, did not allow us to make royalties on the songs we performed and once actually said that he *"considered artists to be the pawns on the chessboard in life."* He never wanted to be dependent on any artist, so we never performed under our real names. Even today if you look at any of the pictures of the girls groups, the ones pictured came after the original girls and they performed to our recordings. Also, the checks that we received for performing were signed from someone at a Laundromat, not our label. Seriously, a laundromat? So cliche!

I eventually got another management team, which consisted of a sweet Jewish husband and wife duo. They managed me along with a few other artists. One artist that they handled was an icon of our time, Grace Jones. I would go into the office on any given day and ask for the husband, Syd. Elaine, the wife, would say, *"Oh he's off to Fire Island to help get Grace out of trouble... Again!"* I had a feeling they experienced a lot more than they could ever say, as she was one of the most rebellious stars of the eighties.

One of my wildest gigs was playing as the group Lime, who were a duo out of Canada. They wrote many hit songs, but never performed them live. They had a male-female duo perform their songs by singing to tracks. That was the music scene of the day. Artists fronting most of the bands were singing over tracks. When I performed with Bobcat we sang to tracks, but we also sang live. There were artists who did not record the vocals and were basically lip-syncing. This was the case of Lime.

There was a gig in Honduras, which was going to bring in a lot of money. The regular duo turned it down, as they feared traveling to a war-torn country. I was asked to go on the trip, and Syd sent me and another guy from their agency. And that is how, for one night, we were Lime.

At this point, Honduras was my first trip out of the United States. This was my first brush with international drama.

It was 1983 and President Reagan was in office. The United States had been in bed with Honduras for decades, and things were heating up on the political international scene. During the early 1980s, the United States had to maintain a military presence in Central America, on account of the Sandinista government of

Nicaragua. Sharp increases in military assistance to Honduras followed the buildup of United States troops and equipment in Honduras. When we traveled there I had no idea of this statistic at the time, but Honduras had the world's highest murder rate.

We landed at the Toncontin International Airport in Tegucigalpa, Honduras. Besides serving as the civil airport for the surrounding cities and barrios, this was also a military airport. The presence of the military was evident from the second we left the airplane. Going through customs, we were heavily searched and questioned. Our local media rep was there to handle the logistics, but since neither my duet guy nor I spoke Spanish, we had no idea what was being said or negotiated.

The heat and smell of the country was intense and intriguing. The terrain of Honduras, filled with mountains and jungles, was the most exotic I had yet experienced.

One of our first stops was the local farmers market, where tropical fruit was laid out on blankets, piled high to the sky. The fruits and vegetables were colorful, with a variety of oranges, yellows, reds, and green. In disturbing juxtaposition to this rainbow of fruits was the fact that almost everyone on the street was armed, including small children who carried large rifles under their arms as they skipped down the street. I watched nurses walk through town as if they had been transported through time, dressed in traditional white nursing uniforms with white-starched caps and blue-striped trim. They looked as if they just stepped out of a 1950's magazine. They too carried rifles.

We were whisked through radio station after radio station for interviews leading up to the big Saturday night concert. Again, everything was in Spanish so I am not certain our translator said exactly what we said, but it was a fun experience.

The night of the concert we were taken to a football stadium where our concert took place. We were brought to the football locker rooms, which doubled as our dressing room. To say the locker rooms were not maintained would be an understatement: low lights, a flooded floor, broken toilet seats, and a cracked mirror hung on the wall. I put on my makeup and wardrobe as best as I could, but I felt like I needed a sanitizer shower before we went on stage.

I had never performed in such a place. The stadium was enormous, with a capacity of 34,000 people. We were taken from the dressing room to the stage in a Volkswagen convertible. Top down, propped up in the backseat, waving to the crowd. It was surreal. The music began, and the crowd was cheering.

Once I was on stage dancing, the energy of the crowd swept me away. I left the stage at one point and bounced all over the stadium grounds. I wanted to reach all people. I jumped and sang and screamed, while dancing up and down the field.

We still had a few songs left of our program. The people of Honduras were under duress and their emotions were high. During the middle of our show, a wave of people stood up, loud voices, lots of action. This did not feel like typical crowd behavior. Something was wrong. I looked to our bodyguards. They looked concerned as well, because a riot was breaking out in the stadium. My few years of Spanish class in high school allowed me to say nothing more than *"Por favor...por favor..."* which, needless to say, did nothing to calm down the impassioned crowd. I have no idea how we got out of there alive, but I remember being surrounded by a group of fans outside of the stadium. I had a brief chat with a handsome man who was holding his six-year-old son. His English was much better than my Spanish. I was distracted by our road manager who was moving us into the car to leave. In a flash of an eye, the man approached me again and said that he wanted to see me again. I thanked him politely but said that I was leaving to go back to the States the following day. I gave the adorable boy a quick hug and a kiss on his little cheek.

As I climbed into the car, the man put something in my hand. *"This is a very special piece from my family...I want you to have this."* I looked into my palm to see the most magnificent turquoise and silver amulet on a thick dark blue rope. I shook my head, *"Oh no...this is too valuable. You must keep it for yourself."* He smiled, and disappeared into the crowd. My heart melted as our car drove away. To this day, I still cherish this precious gift, and hold the energy of his family near to my heart.

Sometimes brief encounters in life can change a destiny that lasts forever.

In my twenties while most women were hunting for husbands, I was ruling Manhattan. Since D and I were not getting married, I had no desire to be married. I continued to build my career, respectfully date around, and make a few choice mistakes. I dated a soap opera star, a Wall Street executive, a bartender, and a dancer.

New York in the eighties was filled with cocaine, free love, and crime. It was truly sex, drugs, and rock & roll. I seemed to be oblivious to the crime, as I skirted the dangers by a wing and a prayer. I went out dancing after my waitressing shift with several hundred dollars tucked in my bra, wearing this stupid fur coat that my friend Celeste and I saved up for months for each of us to have our own fur coat. I did not think about the animal protest at the time as it was called the decadent eighties for a reason. I walked the streets into the early morning hours, somehow always safe from trouble.

Times Square was not the branded-commercial zone that it is today. Then, that area was considered to be the most dangerous part of the city. During the eighties over two hundred crimes were reported in the subway system on a weekly basis, which made New York the most dangerous mass-transit system in the world. I was always in Times Square with relatives visiting from out of town, seeing Broadway shows, dance classes, restaurants, auditions. Thank God, I never had any trouble there or any part of the city.

The music scene was flourishing and the economy was getting back on track from the seventies. Republicans won control of the United States Senate for the first time in twenty-eight years, which marked the 'Reagan Revolution.' I was not politically involved, but the economy shift was definitely felt in New York.

In between acting gigs and dance classes, I worked at the trendiest restaurants, so there was not much that I did not witness over the years. There were nights when Wall Street men sobbed in their margaritas while socialites put out large lines of cocaine on glass-top tables next to their plates of untouched Nouvelle cuisine. The people sniffed, snorted, and sorted out the details of their lives during the most decadent decade of our century.

I worked at a famous hot spot on the West River called Jerry's. I became life friends with the chef, Stephen. We closed down the place for private parties when celebrities were in town for their concerts. Rubbing elbows with the likes of Mick Jagger, Keith Richards, Tina Turner, and Billy Idol was a weekly occurrence.

**Soundcloud Playlist - Dancing in the Streets - Keith Richards & David Bowie

I had a flurry of mini successes, but I kept missing the mark. I played the lead in an off-Broadway show, *Comes the Wolves*. I replaced the leading actress three days before opening. I had to learn the full script of a three-act play in 72-hours. This experience made me realize the power of the brain.

I was featured in an award-winning national commercial for Honda Scooter, *Walk on the Wild Side* with Lou Reed, which gave me eligibility for the union. This song was iconic of our day, produced by David Bowie. I suppose that the Honda corporation was not privy to the story that was telling of the times. The walk on the wild side referred to a transgender girl, Holly Woodlawn, who was a runaway from Miami, who ended up in New York hanging at famous places like, Andy Warhol's Factory club. Drugs, sex, and prostitution filled the storyline for these lyrics.

**Soundcloud Playlist - Take a Walk on the Wild Side - Lou Reed

I got upgraded on the soap opera *One Life to Life* that same week, which allowed me to get into Screen Actors Guild (SAG) and AFTRA.

I worked various music videos, soap operas, continued to dance and worked on feature films such as, *Radio Days* directed by Woody Allen, which was an experience one could never forget. I worked on a project for an off-Broadway show about the life story of Francis Farmer. I put a lot of work into the character and loved the role, but the play never took off. The movie of her life story was being produced with the wonderful actress Jessica Lange.

Around the same time, I was down to the final two for a contract player on *As The World Turns*. Meg Ryan got the role. Like every other person in the entertainment industry, I had a million close calls and stories to tell. But New York is one of the toughest cities in the world, so to quote Frank Sinatra, *"If I can make it here, I'll make it anywhere."*

A challenge to my sanity was deciphering con-men from real men. I grew up in the 'field of dreams' state of Iowa, but I had to take on a 'New York State of Mind' and play my chessboard pieces with precision and strategy. Up until the fall of 2017 most of us women just had to take this sort of occurrence as part of the business. There are so many examples in the area of #MeToo for me, but the few that rise to the top still linger in my mind and twist my stomach into knots.

I had a string of con-men who found the carrots to dangle in front of me. I will refrain from sharing their names as I prefer to have this be my story. This happened decades ago, so if these men are still alive they know who they are. One of these toads actually told me that he had cancer and that he had to sleep with me before he died. He promised to get me on as a contract player on *The Guiding Light*. Needless to say, I did not sleep with him, nor did I get that coveted contract, even though I worked a lot in smaller roles on a lot of the soaps.

Christmas 1983, I worked at Bloomingdales for extra money. I worked in the housewares department demonstrating the "Clap On - Clap Off" gadget. There was a man in a suit, with a well-dressed woman who kept staring at me. The lady approached me first and told me that her friend was very high-up in the industry and he wanted to take me to dinner. Looking back of course, it all seemed suspicious. It is important to know that sometimes women actually help men capture young women, even in cases of sex trafficking. I was persuaded to go to dinner with him. He picked me up the following Friday evening. He said his last name was Cohen and that he and his brother were filmmakers. He picked me up in a limousine and we went to the top of a building to the most luxurious restaurant I have ever seen.

After we were seated the Maitre D' approached our table with a black old-fashioned phone floating on top of a red velvet pillow. He held the pillow in front the guy, *"There is a call for you."*

I felt something was strange and that he was trying to impress me. Throughout dinner he kept trying to persuade me to going away with him. I repeatedly and politely said, "No" until he finally gave in and said it was time to take me home. While in the limo he tried to undress me, kiss me, and move on top of me. My "NO!" got more vocal and emphatic. To this day I bless the limo driver as he drove straight to my apartment. I saw the limo driver's face through the rearview mirror staring at me, pleading with his eyes that I needed to escape. I got out of the car and ran into my building. They drove away.

About a year later I saw the "Coen" brothers not "Cohen" on a talk show promoting their film. Neither of those men were the guy who molested me in the limo. That totally twisted my mind, as I had no idea who that man was and who was the woman who had originally approached me?

Another story was a guy who had a stable of women around him. He was constantly trying to persuade me to sleep with him, but I held him at bay throughout the many months. I ended up co-producing and co-hosting my first talk show, *That's Show Biz.* At least he had backing from an investor and our show got cable distribution. This was an exciting time in the industry. Cable networks and MTV were just entering the scene. The common belief was that cable would never stand a chance of existing. Doesn't that sound familiar with the internet, streaming media, social media, self-driving cars, or even dating back throughout history with airplanes, electricity and technology of any kind?

The talk show format really grabbed ahold of me. I loved the interview process. I was and always have been curious about what makes people tick, so that made me excited about the talk show format.

A few interview highlights for me included Jerry Stiller and Anne Meara (Ben Stiller's parents), George Kirby, the comedian who was in prison for selling heroin to an undercover cop, and Eartha Kitt, the beautiful Catwoman, from the Batman franchise. I had a male co-host on the Catwoman episode, and in the middle of her interview, Eartha meowed and purred at my co-host and then turned to me with her fingers formed in the shape of claws and she hissed at me like a cat. Perhaps she took her role too seriously.

Our talk show's investor was a classy and distinguished businessman from China. He was a legendary success story and he was in love with a Rockette dancer from Radio City Music Hall. Harry wore the finest suits and had the shiniest shoes.

Harry owned the World Yacht that circled Manhattan for VIP cruises. I frequented many parties on that yacht, parties where the skyline of Manhattan was in constant view. My favorite times on the boat were when I partied with people like Andy Warhol. He was quirky and shy, with darting, scrutinizing eyes that surveyed the crowd as we spoke.

On one of these occasions my boyfriend at the time pointed out men in suits with binoculars pointing in our direction on a nearby roof. As we piled into limousines, "said boyfriend" jumped in a cab, *"I'll meet you there"* he shouted and waved goodbye. I had no idea why he paid for a cab when we had this limo at our disposal. But perhaps he knew more than he wanted to say.

We would always end up in the VIP section of Stringfellow's sipping Taittinger Rose Champagne that was brought to us the club owner, Peter Stringfellow. This was a very decadent time. Artists like David Bowie, Sting, and Tears for Fears would play at intimate venues around Manhattan, making it feel like they were playing just for us in their living room.

Shortly after this strange night on the yacht, I was not able to reach Harry. I called one of the girls from the show only to find out that he was actually involved in an international cocaine scandal. I was in shock. I had never seen Harry take even one sip of champagne, let alone take drugs. However, the news broke this story and he ended up being named the biggest cocaine kingpin in North America. Harry was convicted and thrown in prison for many years. I visited him a couple of times. He sent handwritten letters to me at my parents address in Des Moines. He eventually got out of prison and married his Rockette dancer. They moved to Brooklyn, had a daughter, and they have lived off the grid ever since. Or, so I think.

I had an array of eclectic jobs to keep my boat floating. I was a bridal gown model, a hair model for the Paul Mitchell hair shows, and a print model. I even pretended that I knew computers so that I could get an office job. No one at the time knew computers, as it was 1984, so it did not matter to my bosses that I self-taught while on the job.

I worked at two restaurants at once to bring in money, and my most interesting job during that time was being a hostess at a Japanese business club. This was before Karaoke was introduced in the United States. This club hosted Japanese businessmen who came to drink liquor, close deals, and sing.

Our job was to sit at their tables, talk about whatever they wanted to talk about, and make sure that their drinks were served. Each table had a bottle of scotch, a bucket of ice, and a small bowl of teriyaki rice crackers. I loved this job. Not only was I was privy to the Japanese culture because of my best friend Jos, but the men would ask me to sing, so I was able to practice my vocal chops. As a hostess we made tips whenever we were asked to sing, and we made tips whenever we were requested to sit at a table. I became the one of the popular girls, as I had a loyal ear to their drama, when it came to the upsets in business and in love.

The job was like being a Geisha Girl, without the personal or sexual implications. I held onto their secrets and simply listened. I had late shift hours, so it gave me the flexibility to audition and work during the day.

I was also hired as a corporate model at the convention centers for trade shows and exhibits. One time, I worked the International Car Show, which is where I met the charming recording engineer J. The timing could not have been more perfect. Shortly before I met J, I had been inspired to write my own songs. After leaving Bobcat Records I had to find a way to express myself.

J invited me to his recording studio and the songwriting bug bit me hard. Once that muse was tapped, the lyrics flew out of me like a rushing river. I was never safe from being hit by a new song. It could strike me in the middle of the night, while I was getting off a subway, or halfway through a bite of pizza. When the song hit and the muses started dancing for me, I would scramble for the nearest napkin, piece of paper, or anything where I could write my ideas.

J's recording studio felt like home and his business partner Steve became my first songwriting partner. Steve and I had a prolific writing relationship and an even deeper friendship. We wrote many songs together. Steve, his girlfriend, and their band were all Puerto Rican musicians who grew up in the Bronx. They had been together since early teens, so it was a privilege to be exposed to that kind of experience and also to their cultural music influences.

J was already on the charts with gold and platinum records. He had major recording artists in the studio. We were writing song after song, hoping to get that one hit. J continued to be charming and creative, while his lips were always brimming with the promise for my solo music career. Carrot dangle!

I gave up my rent-controlled apartment on the Upper East Side and he moved from his apartment in Queens. We found a place together in the East Village, in a newly developed modern building. I was ecstatic to be back in the village. Our building was considered to be in a new, hip area. The drug dealers and prostitutes had moved on, and had been replaced by influential artists and celebrities.

Joe Jackson, the British musician, lived one floor above us. Joe was extremely private and shy, but he filled the building with amazing piano music. I would often lay awake at night, listening to him through the vents of the heater.

**SoundCloud Playlist - Steppin Out - Joe Jackson

I loved living in the East village. We lived on 11th Street near the Ritz, where many iconic performers came. One day, on my way to 14th Street subway station, I saw a moving van outside the theatre. Burly guys were taking equipment off the truck. I noticed there was no name on the marquee, so I asked who was playing that night. They were not allowed to say but they put me on the guest list for that night. As it would turn out, it was Sting, who was in town trying out his new songs from his CD, *Dream of the Blue Turtle.* It was an amazing night.

**Soundcloud Playlist - Consider Me Gone - Sting

I was drawn to J's charisma and his talent of being an amazing engineer, like a rabbit would be drawn a carrot. However, I did not know the carrot was poisoned until it was too late. His dependency on drugs and abusive nature began to surface. He began showing signs of being emotionally and verbally abusive, which was even harder for me to escape than his addiction. I kept waiting for my music career to take off, but he had another agenda. And that was to keep me down as long as he could.

I tried to confide in Steve, but I did not want to jeopardize their relationship. They say that watching for signs of being in an abusive relationship can be difficult, but one of the first signs is the realization that the abuser sequesters us into their world, and their world alone. I woke up one day and suddenly noticed that all my friends were gone.

About a year into the relationship I saw signs that should have been a trigger for me: jealousy, co-dependency, argumentative behavior, needling my self-confidence.

Again, the potential scenario stood out and I thought I could fix him. On Valentine's Day, we went to a Long Island animal shelter and we adopted the cutest puppy, Baxter. Somehow this dog was the excuse to keep our relationship alive. J had become a dark force that I could not handle. I was smart enough to realize that considering his worsening relationship with drugs, that physical abuse could be next on his agenda. It was time to leave.

Throughout the years, J and I traveled to Los Angeles every year for the Audio Engineering Society (AES) convention. I learned how to navigate California and I began to yearn to move out of the snow and into the sunshine. The winter was underway and the snow-topped buildings and garbage strikes were getting on my nerves.

Things escalated with J. He stayed up for days to finish the mix of a song. The lack of sleep caused intense mood swings. I came out in the living room in the morning and he would be hovering over a mirror with a huge line of cocaine. *"Want some T?"* he would ask, looking up at me with bloodshot eyes. *"No thanks... I'm going to walk the dog and go to dance class."* I would pick up the leash and walk Baxter out the door. I had to make my plan for escape.

They say you are the average of the five people you spend the most time with. And in this case, that was true. As J spiraled downward, so did I. I found myself sleeping on the couch at night so that I could breathe. Even though this man was right next to me, I felt all alone. He was supposed to be my rock and my partner, but I knew he was not there for me, not really.

One Saturday morning, I took a walk in the village. It was springtime, and there was serenity in the air. I walked past a bookstore that had its door open. Incense burned from inside. I felt calm come over me.

I walked through the bookstore feeling like I had been guided to enter. A garden in the back of the store caught my attention. An older woman sat in a chair at a small table. She wore a red-flowered shawl around her shoulders.

The woman turned and saw me staring in her direction. She motioned for me to sit down. I sat down on the chair opposite of her, as she gracefully took out her tarot cards and began to shuffle. We sat in silence. She began to lay out the cards. She began, *"You have someone here who is happy that you came to see me."* I quickly turned to my right knowing that I would not physically see someone standing there, but I felt something. *"There is a spirit of a young child…a little girl…she stands right beside you."* She motioned to my right. She continued to say that this young girl was my spirit guide and that she was committed to stay with me throughout this lifetime. Or, if I chose to have a child then she was the one who would come through to be born.

The woman continued, as if she was translating another language. *"It seems highly unlikely that you will have a child in this lifetime, but this spirit will stay with you regardless."* The reading continued by revealing that this little girl was not happy with the man that I chose to be with at this point in life. She said that I might be heading to a bad place. She saw a gun. The lady looked up and said, *"No matter what you decide, this girl will stay by your side always to protect you."* She ended by saying that I had many years of trials ahead of me, but life would shift in my fifties and I could become well known in the world of writing, especially children's books.

I said to myself, writing children's books…in my fifties…what? That was decades away!

While all of this was going on, a tragic epidemic hit the eighties. My beloved male gay friends were taken...fast.

AIDS hit the world hard, especially in the larger metropolitan cities. One minute everyone was celebrating and partying. The next minute, a life-threatening disease swept our lives up like a tornado.

Life was nerve wracking. I was afraid to go on the subways. We did not know if this deadly virus was airborne, so no one touched the doors in public, or the poles straps on mass transit. I wore my winter gloves into summer so that I would not pick up germs. I had panic attacks on a daily basis. Heart pounding, dizzy spells, walls seemingly crumbling around me.

Even though HIV cases dated back to early 1900s, this time the gay community was struck hard. I had many close friends who were gay. They were my brothers. And to say it was devastating to see so many of my dear friends dying would be a grave understatement. My dearest friends, Michael, Russ, Jos, John, had partners die very quickly.

I think AIDS struck a chord in us all. Something about seeing the bodies of our dearest friends melt away into scabbed, scarred, skeletons affected us in a way that is difficult to describe. The saddest part was when our friends disappeared from the world and died alone in silence. It was the most helpless time of my life. Death. Everywhere. Over, and over, and over again.

The year was 1987. I went home to Iowa to visit my family for Christmas. My family knew J, but they did not approve of the relationship. My mom met him several times over the years, but they never got along. I was with my family on Christmas Eve.

They were upset that I had to fly back to New York on Christmas Day. They figured that he was manipulating me with the goal of putting a wedge between all of us. And so we plotted my escape.

The escape went like this: I returned to New York as planned and pretended to have a good Christmas Day with J. He had spiraled down to an even darker place than he was before I left. His drug addiction was getting increasingly serious. Even his friends were beginning to comment on his behavior. The insidious verbal and emotional abuse was getting worse.

Over the next few days, J climbed even deeper into his dark cave. More drugs, more dark circles under his eyes, more abuse. There was one moment when we came into our building and he was so angry that he shoved me against the wall. If he had the nerve to do this in the lobby of our building when one could potentially see him, I knew that I could not stay another minute. I became a super-sleuth for my survival. I was happy that my big brothers were coming to save me. I laid awake for days and nights plotting my escape.

J and I were planning to move to California. I wanted to be in Los Angeles in January for pilot season. I lied to him, and told him that my father was going to be in Los Angeles for a dental convention and that he would help me find a place to live and buy me a car. I began to pack everything up and told J that I would take my load out to California, while he finished producing his artist. And then, we could move in together. Another lie to build the plan.

My brothers boarded a plane a few days later, pretending they wanted a fresh break for the holiday. J was on his best behavior as there was something intimidating about two older Italian brothers suddenly staying with us in our apartment. He was outnumbered.

My brothers helped pack me up. Rick had to leave after a couple of days, as he had to return to Atlanta for work. Mike stayed behind to work as the convenient counterpart to my dastardly duo escape. I packed all my things and hired movers to come.

The morning of my escape, I knew that J would be asleep. Mike and I took our suitcases, the dog carrier, and my purse to a friend's apartment in the Lower East Side.

Once back in our apartment I hovered at the window, waiting for the moving van to arrive. But the movers were delayed, and I was beginning to think that my plot would fail. Timing was everything. I sat on the stoop outside the building. I paced the streets standing on the corner of 11th and 2nd Avenue. I called too many times to see when the truck would come and take my things away.

The sun was beginning to set in the winter sky. My heart was pounding. J was awake and working at his mixing board, drinking coffee and smoking a joint. He did not even try to mask his foul mood in front of my brother.

Finally, I saw the truck turn the corner and pull up to our building. I exhaled. Each box that was carried onto the truck represented a brick in the wall that would protect my escape from New York. My heart began to beat faster. I watched the van pull away. Now, the next phase had to be implemented.

I called out to J. *"Hey J, Mike and I are going to take Baxter for a walk...we'll go to dinner when we get back."* I attached the dog leash to Baxter's collar. Mike and I started for the front door. *"Hey T."* J replied. *"Let's try out that new Mexican place on the West side."* I closed the door, never to return.

**Soundcloud Playlist - Eye in the Sky - Alan Parsons Project

Baxter happily skipped to the elevator. My dog looked up with his big brown eyes and winked at me. He knew what was going on. Baxter was ready to go and I knew that my brother was relieved to get out of there as well. I am fortunate to have big brothers who are always there to lend a helping hand and especially my oldest brother, who has always been my rescuer in times of need.

The air was brisk. We all walked as fast as we could, trying not to look back. I kept expecting J to come running after me. We turned the corner and quickened our pace down the street, making a beeline for my friends' apartment. I held my breath the entire way. My heart was thumping in my throat.

We grabbed the luggage and flew down the flight of stairs. People were coming home from work so the winter snow was dragged across the staircase. We skipped over the snow banks, and waved down a taxi. I threw Baxter, the suitcases, and the dog kennel into the back of the cab, and we headed for the airport hotel.

When we finally settled into our room, my brother ordered filet mignon steaks to celebrate our accomplished escape. Baxter even got his own steak as a reward for being so well behaved. I was extremely nervous all night long, and I kept imagining the ways J could find us.

The next morning, we headed to the airport. I went to my gate to head to my new life in Los Angeles, while Mike and Baxter headed to Iowa. This was a temporary move for Baxter, as I needed some time to get settled and find my way.

I felt horrible about the escape, but the plan was necessary for my safety. When you are under the thumb of an abuser, you have to be smarter than your abuser. Survival depends on drawing upon every street-smart bone in your body. This is the path back to life and to healing. I am grateful to my family who stood behind me, and to my brothers in particular who took part in one of our greatest acting jobs to date.

Shortly after moving to Los Angeles, I found out that J had hired a private detective. I had a stalker now. Could I disappear into the folds of Hollywood? Could I reinvent myself, stay out of abusive relationships, and not repeat the heartbreak?

One could only hope!

Chapter 13

La La Land

I landed in Los Angeles on December 30, 1987. The sun was shining, and in the most cliché way there was not even a trace of a cloud in the sky. I was ready to begin a new year in a new city, with a new sense of an identity, and a newfound faith in who I could become. I was free from the chains of J.

I tried to fit into sunny California. Everyone had that sun-kissed glow, so my ultra-white skin and all-black wardrobe stood out. While living in New York, I was into high fashion, designer hats, expensive shoes, and wild jewelry. Los Angeles was more casual. Everyone wore a lot of white.

I was able to shed both my winter coat and outer being to become more exposed. I was invited to stay in the posh area of Brentwood. I had become friends with a lawyer who had an extra bedroom. His apartment became my safety net to land and re-launch.

During my first few weeks in Los Angeles, I bought my very first car. It was a 1978 taxicab yellow Toyota Celica, with a sunroof. I had no idea that ego and prestige was attached to one's identity through their car in Los Angeles. I found the car in the paper and bought it for $1,200, which was a great price for a dependable car. Yes, the joke was on me, as most everyone in LA depends on their identity being attached to their cars, clothes, botox, and zip codes.

Within my first week of owning the car I drove to Warner Bros. for a meeting. This guy Joe took one look at my car.

"Sorry, I cannot be seen in that car…let's take mine."

"Why not?" I asked defensively. *"Look at that color. Where in the hell did you get this shitty car?"*

I stared at him in disbelief. He looked around to make sure no one saw him getting in the car. He motioned for me to drive away. He pulled his baseball cap down over his eyes and sunk lower in his seat. I blasted the music and drove away laughing. Welcome to LA.

My first apartment was in the hip area of West Hollywood. I lived right up the street from the newly opened comedy club, Laugh Factory. Baxter was sent to live with me, and I became the apartment manager of the building.

The building had twenty-eight units. We had a diverse crowd of tenants, ranging from a casting director, to an agent, to a drunk guy who once threw his couch into the pool over his second floor balcony. One night he threw his girlfriend in there as well.

My first summer in Los Angeles, I worked on a movie that ended up being a cult classic, *Earth Girls Are Easy,* starring Jeff Goldblum, Geena Davis,Jim Carrey, Damon Wayans, and Julie Brown. *Earth Girls Are Easy* ended up being my introduction to Hollywood.

This is where I met my first Los Angeles boyfriend. MJ was a vegetarian from a famous Hollywood family, and we hit it off from the start, getting to know each other through songwriting and acting classes. This relationship lasted for almost two years, until I found out he cheated on me with a girl that he picked up from the gas station.

I dated a wonderful man who was an acupuncturist, until he asked me to marry him. I ran for the hills out of fear. What was I going to do with a nice, established career oriented, spiritual man? I had too much to lose with my thoughts that I was not good enough.

Supplementing my income became a desperate dance of juggling odd jobs while waiting for my big break. I took a telemarketing job selling ad-space at an independent local community newspaper. I hated selling ads the traditional ways, so I would make calls to establishments that catered to my experience and interest. I called restaurants and became a food reviewer. I called clothing stores and ended up becoming a friend of the owner of a small boutique. I helped him produce his fashion show. I had to think out of the box. Routine bored me. I kept my boss at the newspaper happy and I saved myself from boredom.

I became friends with a funny Italian man who worked in the next cubicle at the paper. He brought Italian food for lunch and always had this small juice glass of red wine.

Mike was an out-of-work character actor, looking to make new friends. He used to call out my name with funny accents, *"Hey Cacciatore… what "choo" doing this weekend? I want to introduce you to a friend of mine."* He took me to his friends' home, which was a Spanish Tudor mansion in Los Feliz near the Griffith Park Observatory.

We started going over and hanging out for dinner parties and we would all cook together. His friend who owned the house was intrigued by my knowledge and passion for the entertainment business. I did not know his relation to the business at first, but I found out that he was Herbert 'Bert' Leonard; a veteran in the entertainment industry. His producing credits included a myriad of famous television series in the sixties and seventies, such as *To Catch A Thief, Naked City, Route 66,* and *Rin Tin Tin.*

Even with Bert's success, he was looking to reinvent himself, to revamp his career. When he asked me to come work for his production company, he was in the process of remaking the Rin Tin Tin legacy to re-brand as *Rin Tin Tin K-9 Cop*. I enthusiastically accepted.

We created the elements that are required to build a production for a series: character bible, series treatment, scripts, and a production plan. I learned a lot and offered many of my own ideas that, to my delight, Bert absorbed into the series. They began production in Toronto, so I held down the company in his Los Angeles home. I handled many duties, including the post production elements. It was an immersive experience and all of the bedrooms in Bert's house had been turned over for business.

I loved the entire production process, until the series ended and so did my job. Bert was newly married to his third wife and his life was going in a new direction. Of all the people that I worked with over the years, I suppose Bert came closest to be my mentor. I do wish I could have had a leg up for other jobs, introductions in the industry, or even a credit on the show, but that was not in the cards with him for some reason. Perhaps the most important lesson I learned from Bert was after my time with him: to get what you want up front and in writing.

After my time working with Bert, I began with a fun job as a ghost-writer for radio show host catering to celebrity gossip. We culled our news items from the National Enquirer and other rag-mags. I am not a fan of gossip, but the job taught me how to write in another voice, as she was a very funny, sassy, and smart African American woman.

My first jump into production of global events occurred in 1990. I was brought onto a team for a triad of concerts that was to take place in three cities: Berlin (Berlin Wall) Beijing (Tiananmen

Square) and Los Angeles (main headquarters) for a simultaneous broadcast. The event was to be called the Freedom Festival. I was on the Berlin team. I was ignited by the thought of merging social impact with my production skills. After getting my passport updated, I was ready to travel to Germany. Things were going smoothly...until things did not.

I arrived at work at my usual time, 8:00 am. A large moving truck was parked in the lot. I entered the office to find the Chief Financial Officer leaning over in his chair, ready to pass out. I noticed that no one was in the office, outside of a group of burly men moving furniture, equipment, and computers out the door. *"What's going on?"* I asked. He simply shook his head and said, in his Transylvanian accent, *"It's all over!"*

I stayed at the office until the CFO turned the keys over to the landlord. The story that unfolded was completely shocking to me. It turned out that the lead executive producers had swindled over $14M, leaving no funding left for the production.

This same group of swindling producers came together almost ten years to the day. This time was for the millennium 24-hour broadcast concert that was to begin in Tonga and wrap around the world throughout the global time zones and ending in Hawaii. When I figured out these were the same cast of characters, I had no idea that they would do this again. I figured the 1990 deal was a bad fluke. However, while raising the money for this broadcast, I remember key executives replacing their old cars with brand new Mercedes, BMWs, and Jaguars. The parking lot at the production office began looking like a Beverly Hills luxury car lot. Rumors of them buying chateaus in France and mountain top condos in Hawaii swirled through the production office.

Four days before the new year, heading into Y2K, the company folded. However, this time the money at stake was $45M. Production crews from around the world were suddenly left jobless.

In spite of the madness, I did make a few lifelong friends from this situation, which is the silver lining on a very dark cloud.

Back to 1990 when MJ and I remained friends after our breakup. He tried to convince me to get back together.

One night he took me to dinner to talk things out. However, getting back together was not the conclusion, as fate would step in and change my world forever.

We sat at an outdoor restaurant on Melrose Avenue. MJ was on a trail of nervous, endless chatter. He bounced his way through a variety of topics, but I was not listening.

I was completely mesmerized by a man who was walking down the street towards the restaurant.

This man entered the patio and sat at the table next to us. The following span of time was a mixture of emotions and divine timing. A convertible pulled up to the valet, and a man and woman stepped out of their car, and then proceeded to sit at the table with him. I heard more of what they were saying at their table rather than at my own table.

I gathered that the men were meeting for the very first time, and that the couple were married. I felt there was some sort of intrigue between the handsome man and the wife. At one point, the husband turned to his wife, while looking in my direction, and I thought I heard him say, *"This woman keeps staring at us.... I think I should go talk to her."*

He got up from his table and came right towards me. I slumped in my seat, as I felt he was going to yell at me for continuing to stare at them. He stepped up to the table, *"I'm sorry to bother you, but you look familiar. Did you ever work at a place called Jerry's in New York?"* It was Stephen, the chef from Jerry's, who was now living in Los Angeles with his wife. They had just moved from New York and while unpacking Stephen came across an article from the New York Times that had a photograph of Jerry, Stephen and me.

We exchanged numbers, and proceeded to meet up at various events over the coming weeks, becoming inseparable friends.

I knew in my heart that the other guy at the table was destined to be in my life. I will refer to him as 'Handsome Hemingway' (HH), as he was extremely handsome and a fan of avant-garde art, culture and music. More often than not, a cigarette could be dangling from his lips and a shot of scotch could be found sliding down his throat. His deep voice rattled my cage, as did his piercing eyes which were covered by bushy eyebrows.

HH and I finally had our first date and after that point it seemed like we never left each other's side. I eventually moved in with him, and our life took a turn towards the amazing. HH and I were crammed into a 700 square foot studio apartment in Beverly Hills, along my little dog Baxter. We were in a creative time of our lives and we supported one another. I had my usual variety of jobs. I worked at NBC for a game show pilot. I started a catering business where I fed thirty-person crews off of a two-burner electric stove. I even started a business with my mom's old sewing machine. I sent out business postcards to set designers in the film and TV industry. This sewing business took off to the point where a driver from the studios would show up on any given morning with all the material I needed. I did the job and then the driver picked up the finished items and paid me. I sewed set decor pieces for various shows.

I continued my personal shopping business, 'Shop, Pack & Ship' that I had started in New York. I tried my hat at everything, and loved the entrepreneurial life. HH was a working actor, but he wanted to find more stability. We talked for hours about his passions, one of which was landscape architecture. I helped him name his landscaping company, which went on to be quite successful.

We had a lot of fun together. From putting up large canvases on our living room wall and splashing them with paint as an homage to Jackson Pollack, to going on random day-long road trips with no agenda. We would find ourselves in Santa Barbara, San Francisco, Joshua Tree, falling asleep reading poetry to one another.

We only quarreled over one topic, which was the direction of our relationship. I desired a house with a garden, while he preferred a loft in the outskirts of downtown. Still, things were getting serious. HH was the only man who came back to Iowa to meet my family, and I was the only one he took to Cape Cod to meet his mother and his extended family.

During my time with HH, I pursued my solo recording career. I wrote all the songs for my album and played to small but sold out clubs to test my material. I had the time of my life. I was finally out of the shadows of past partners who wanted their careers to be more important than mine. HH was always supportive of my dreams, and I was of his.

As I started my life over in Los Angeles, I never left my New York friends behind. I kept close contact with a friend, Russ, who survived the AIDS epidemic. He was diagnosed with AIDS in 1989.

Russ often called me in the middle of the night with night terrors. We talked about his fear of dying. While HH slept sweetly by my side, I whispered support to my friend who was suffering 3,000 miles away. We cried together until the sun came up on the East coast and Russ was fast asleep.

Russ was writing a journal. He told me that his journal would be in his will for me. We had a great sense of humor with one another, so he laughed when I said, *"You're too mean to die... give me your journal and I'll do something with it now."*

He sent me his journal knowing that I wanted to do something to inspire others with his story of life with AIDS. His journal pages were filled with hard to read, hand-scribbled notes that rang of fear. But one phrase stood out to me:*"Don't be numbed by the numbers."* That phrase became the hook of a song I produced to bring awareness to the AIDS crisis. The song and the project was called <u>Numbed by the Numbers</u>.

**Soundcloud Playlist - Numbed by the Numbers - Torey (Tess Cacciatore)

Shortly after the song was released, Russ moved to Los Angeles. We tried branding the song around the gay pride parade in West Hollywood. I wanted to get the song to a celebrity so that it could gain momentum. At the time I had become friends with Michael Masser, who gave me a songwriting scholarship where I was interacting by many Grammy producers, including the famous and amazing David Foster. Masser was a legendary producer of Whitney Houston, Diana Ross, Gladys Knight to name a few.

Through my connections in the music industry, I put the song in the hands of David Foster, Bette Midler, Madonna, Liz Taylor. Each of their camps wrote back with similar polite sentiments, *"This is a good song with a wonderful story, but it seems to be a bit dark."*

The previous hit song that was produced for AIDS was *That's What Friends Are For*. I was determined to get our song out there, so I began calling around to get sponsorships for the music video. The best in the industry stepped up, and we received over $250,000 worth of corporate sponsorship.

The day Russ walked onto the set of the music video, he was totally blown away by the support for the vision of the video. I was so proud to have him there and so grateful he could live to see his journal come to life. While in post production, Russ fell ill with a brain tumor and ended up in the hospital. I wanted to keep his hopes alive so I brought rough-cut edits to his hospital room at night.

Throughout the years Russ moved back and forth between New York and Los Angeles. He worked with various Broadway producers and introduced me to these agents who had me perform on the 1992 MTV special Boathouse Rocks that taped and aired from Central Park. *Numbed by the Numbers* could finally have its day. I was one of three performers: Rupal (who was just coming onto the scene), Eartha Kitt (nice revisit from our past) and me. It was great to be premiered on MTV. My mom came to visit, so it was sweet to be back in Manhattan and feel that we had some legs for the song.

Russ's health eventually pushed him to move back to his mom's house in his hometown of Jamestown, New York. Russ lasted longer than anyone I knew with AIDS. He continued to be an advocate for other victims and worked arduously in upstate New York on behalf of activism and social services.

I am not sure of his final cause of death, but his passing left me devastated. He was alone when he passed. His mother had been out on errands and found him after knocking on his door later that day to see if he wanted dinner. Dying alone had been one of his fears he shared with me during our midnight talks. However, he lasted until age 57, which was much longer than he ever expected. I am certain that his crooked smile with a solid laugh is roughing up heaven. Russ passed in 2015, so he lasted twenty-five years with this diagnosis, so he must have been doing something right.

In 1992, I had a manager representing my solo music career. My manager had three record labels interested in signing me as a solo artist. Two labels were from Europe and one from Japan. At that exact same time I was given an offer to go on a tour with a band to Singapore, Malaysia, and Australia.

I ended up choosing to go on tour with the band, because it gave me the opportunity to work with two Motown songwriters who were musicians in the band. I figured this would allow me to pursue my songwriting career, which could set me up better for a retirement plan.

As smoothly as the rehearsals for the tour was going things were getting wobbly with HH. One night while we were cooking, we got into an argument. One thing led to another and an argument ensued. HH said, *"I don't think things are working out."* I snapped back, *"Okay - when do you want me to leave."* And he said, *"Right away!"* And I took those words to heart. At that exact moment, I stopped chopping shallots, took my purse, and walked straight out the door.

We had been arguing lately, which was so unlike us. The pressure to decide if we were going to move out of the 700 foot apartment to a house with a garden, (my choice) or an industrial loft (HH's choice) was far beyond the pressure we could take.

I walked to the nearest payphone and called my friends Lorrie and Stephen. They had been with us since the beginning and loved us both, but they invited me to stay with them for as long as I needed. I continued to rehearse with the band as if no breakup had happened.

We rehearsed at Maverick Flats, which is considered to be the 'Apollo of the West Coast'. Celebrity acts like The Temptations, Marvin Gaye, Parliament Funkadelic, Earth, Wind, and Fire, the Commodores, and more hit the Maverick Flats scene back in the day. The band was predominantly black, outside of the other background singer, a blonde Swedish girl married to the music director. The lead singer, Gwen, was with a major label, and the tour was for her album.

A few days after I moved out from HH, all hell broke loose in Los Angeles.

April 29, 1992, was a beautiful spring day. I was getting ready to drive to rehearsal when breaking news came on the television announcing that the four cops accused of beating Rodney King were off the hook. Our mouths collectively dropped to the floor.

Mayor Tom Bradley got on the air and said, *"Today, the jury told the world that what we all saw with our own eyes was not a crime. My friends, I am here to tell the jury...what we saw was a crime. No, we will not tolerate the savage beating of our citizens by a few renegade cops …We must not endanger the reforms we have achieved by resorting to mindless acts. We must not push back progress by striking back blindly."*

One news report after another came on screen, flashing images of bottle rockets and smashed storefront windows. Deep pain erupted on the streets of Los Angeles, with riots breaking out in all areas of the city. Reports on the TV were showing people looting stores, carrying out large television sets and electronics from Asian owned businesses. Windows were shattered, and businesses were set on fire. Crenshaw Boulevard was on the news, and it seemed that all the buildings in the area were on fire, except for Maverick Flats. I knew that rehearsals were cancelled.

That night, while having dinner in an outdoor restaurant on Santa Monica Boulevard, we heard faint chanting. A large crowd came into view carrying candles and marching somber through the streets. The flickering lights reflected in the eyes of those carrying the candles. Deep sadness was all around. This was a peaceful protest, not a ravenous riot, but nevertheless, the people made a point. We were all in mourning. The protest went on for days and we were living in a war-torn area.

The following days and nights were filled with turmoil. We stood on the rooftop of Lorrie and Stephen's building and watched a multitude of pockets in the city on fire. Our 'City of Angels' looked like a war-torn battlefield from an old movie.

HH and I spoke during this time, but we did not get back together. I was planning to go on tour, so I sent Baxter back to Iowa to play on a farm. It was a sad day to see him go, but he was going to be much better where he could run wild and chase cats and billy goats.

During this time I was broken in many ways. Distracted and discombobulated, I did not spend the appropriate time healing from the breakup. I suppose I was not done with my dive into the dark void. I took in a deep breath, closed my eyes, and jumped off the proverbial cliff. I dove deeper into the "Dark Knight of my Soul" to the darkest place of all.

Chapter 14

Darker - Deeper - Dive

Have you ever just wondered why you keep going deeper into the rabbit hole… knowing that there was only bad things lurking around the corner?

Our band tour was derailed on account of the racial tension that affected people all over the country. Once the riots stopped and the city went back to 'normal' our tour was picked back up. Singapore and Malaysia were still on the list, but all shows in Australia and other countries were cancelled. I so wanted to go to Australia, as that was one of the highlight points of this contract. However, the show must go on.

HH was still in my heart, but I felt that door had closed. I had not been one to go back into a relationship once I was done. He moved from our tiny apartment to a duplex with a garden. In retrospect, I suppose he was doing that for me, being that he was the one who always wanted to live in a downtown industrial loft. I was already moved out of Stephen and Lorrie's home, now living in Beverly Hills with two female roommates. I was rehearsing to leave on tour soon.

One evening HH called me to come over to his new place for dinner. It was like old times, laughing, cooking, drinking wine, talking about old times. The evening ended and he walked me to my car. We stood in the street while he proceeded to tell me everything I wanted to hear when we were together. *"I feel like my right arm is cut off being without you. I want to marry you and have a child. Let's give us a chance."*

To this day I am not sure why I did not jump back into his arms. However, I warned him from the start of our relationship that I am not an ultimatum girl. I never was one of those girls who played the game of getting someone to marry me. I always posed this same story very early in any relationship. If a man I am dating wants to be with me, then they need to let me know. I am not going to pull the ultimatum card. When I feel that the relationship is done and no decision has been made, then I will leave. By then I will not be playing a game. I will be out of love.

I do not know if this was right way to go, but I never want to play games with anyone. A male friend, David, recently told me, *"This is the way men are wired. They need that ultimatum and the challenge. All these years you might have been shooting yourself in the foot."* I replied, *"I have met the right men at the wrong time and the wrong men at the right time… when the man I am to be with is here and I am ready, then we will do it right."*

That night I gave HH a hug and told him that I would always love him. I got into my car and drove away. I missed HH, but I was having the time of my life dancing four shows a night and exploring new cultures.

While on tour, my songwriting career took a productive turn. I was writing with RC, the keyboardist, who supposedly played our songs for industry giants, including Stevie Wonder and Barry Gordy. RC relayed to me that they gave great responses to my melodies and lyrics. He told me that our publishing deal was around the corner, so it seemed that my choice to take the band tour path rather than my solo career was proving to be a good one. Or was it a dangling carrot?

My relationship with RC turned into a one of a more personal nature. I fought my feelings, and was conflicted because I still had a great love for HH. I also did not think it was a good idea to be romantically involved with someone while on tour. However, there were two other couples in the band, and they seemed to be working out fine. We kept our relationship to ourselves for as long as we could, until it became obvious to the rest of the band.

We were on and off tour between the years of 1992 and 1993. Singapore and Malaysia were exotic, special, and intoxicating. The street-food booths bordered every park, every street. After our shows ended, around 2:00 a.m., we explored the kiosks in the park that were filled with Asian cuisines. We were night owls in the music business, so going to sleep earlier than 5:00 a.m. was a rare occurrence.

Every afternoon I ordered the same bowl of Singapore noodles, with a large portion of sambal paste. The earthy, spicy, flavors of the sambal paste was just enough heat to clear my nasal passages for singing, and the noodles gave me enough energy to get through four shows a night. I would also take a shot of ginseng before the show which helped carry my long hours of dancing on stage. I was working out and dancing six days a week. I felt on top of my game.

Singapore is known for being the cleanest place on earth. Chewing gum was even illegal. On our passports, it was noted that drugs were 'punishable by death' and we witnessed a young Australian tourist jailed and almost hung for bringing in a small amount of marijuana. Singapore is an island with extraordinary modern architecture mixed with ancient temples. It piqued my passion for photography, architecture, and spirituality.

As the tour went on, I began to see a controlling side in RC that was reminiscent of J in New York. The behavior began with RC not wanting me to explore the things that captivated me. There

156

were times when someone from the audience approached us after a performance and offered to take us out on field trips to see the beauty of their country. RC would always decline the offer on both of our behalves, often jealous of the person offering. RC forced us to sit in a closed hotel room every day, doing nothing. Little did he know, I snuck out of the hotel to go on my own adventures.

Once I ventured out of the hotel slipping through the crowded streets, following the scent of incense into the local temples. I entered the temple with reverence. There was something comforting about the murmuring chant of the Buddhist monks. The tone of their voices crept into my bones and vibrated. The flickering candles offered a glow to all of the faces in the room, as they knelt and bowed and chanted. I was at peace. This feeling was reminiscent of my childhood with the chanting priests in Latin, the scent of incense and burning candles on the altar.

I knelt on the floor mat and closed my eyes. Visions twirled in my mind, parts of my life flashing before my eyes. The sound of chanting led me down a deep meditative path and my spirit floated out of my body.

I was coming out of meditation. I saw my spirit climb back into my body in the Singapore temple. And somehow, that day was the day that I knew my faith, my quest, and my never-ending search could not be stopped by some jealous man.

I quietly slipped on my sandals and ran out of the temple through the refreshing, afternoon rain. RC was still napping so he had no idea that I had left the room. My heart was beginning to drift. I wanted my relationship to work out with him, but I think it was more about the songwriting than the relationship.

My faith was pulling me in one direction, but my soul was leading me further into the darkness.

I began noticing RC out of the corner of my eye watching me on stage during our shows. It was not one of those proud looks, but more of a suspicious and menacing look. He watched me from behind his keyboard with eagle eyes and would later accuse me of flirting with someone in the audience because I smiled during the performance.

But for some reason, I stayed with him. And the longer I stayed with him, the further down he would bring me, like swirling sewage down a drain. I felt at times like one of those seagulls caught in an oil spill. I could not move. I was under his dark spell.

In between our tour dates we went back in Los Angeles and returned to the recording studio to finish the songs that were supposedly given to Motown publishers. I set up my publishing company with BMI and I was on my way...or so I thought.

RC began to show signs of having a great dependency on drugs. I knew the signs. I did survive the eighties in New York, after all. There were endless nights of his paranoia. I stayed awake with him as he fought his demons. After long hours in the recording studio, he would drive to the other side of town on an 'errand.' It took me a bit of time to realize that his trips past Western Boulevard where to meet with his drug dealer. I look back to those days and wince with embarrassment and with gratitude, that at any time we could have been robbed, or killed, or busted.

RC took these dark trips without warning. I was a passenger in his self-destructive spiral into hell. At that time I considered myself to be the 'Fix It' girl. I thought I had the strength and fortitude to make things right. I am responsible for these actions, as I refuse in this current state to view myself as a victim. I had to now pay attention to what I did not pay attention to, during those times.

The cycles of RC went a little like this: paranoia led to possessiveness, which led to extreme jealousy, which became extreme explosiveness. He would go into one of these states where his eyes would go wild and then suddenly empty, a reflection of his dark soul. He seemed to leave his body during these times as he continued to rant verbal, emotional, spiritual, financial abuse upon me. He would guilt me into giving him money for drugs. He would overpower me. He forced me onto my bed with my arms pinned down. He would stare into my eyes trying to pour darkness over me. I had to look away and force him off of me on any given night. Physical abuse was right around the corner. Does any of this sound familiar to you?

Let me take a right turn here and describe my theory of the "frog in the pot" syndrome that might help you recognize the signs of being in an abusive relationship.

The Frog in the Pot

With this story I have to put a disclaimer that I in no way mean any harm to animals or frogs, this is just a symbolic story to make a point.

So, imagine a pot on a stove with water filled halfway up to the top. A frog jumps in and begins to swim around. Said frog is feeling comfortable in his surroundings, languishing in the tepid water. A low flame is now put under the pot. The frog relaxes even more getting used to the warm water. The flame goes higher, the water goes hotter, the frog relaxes more, until the water has come to a slow boil. End of frog.

The other side of the story is that there is a pot on a stove with water at a high-boil. The frog jumps in and jumps immediately out of the water, as this is too painful to be in the boiling water. Frog is saved.

The point of the symbology is that there are very few people that are abusive who will show you that side of themselves from the start. Most of the time they are charismatic, fun-loving, supportive, sexy people. They do not wear a sign above their head stating *"Hey, I'm abusive."*

The signs to watch out for are ones that begin to slowly put you down behind the scenes, ever-so-slightly cracking the veneer of your confidence. Then they begin to put a wedge between you and your best friends and family, stating this-or-that is wrong with them. Then you finally find yourself sequestered inside of a verbally and/or emotionally abusive relationship. The danger is that these types of relationships are the most hardest relationships to uncover and to realize there is not much one can do when they are in low self esteem and not fully confident with self-love. The spiral goes down and down until the abuse can do deeper into sexual, spiritual, financial, and physical abuse.

When our tour resumed I was relieved. The distraction of performing was my best reprieve. We performed under the watchful eyes of the country police of Singapore, so that was my safety net of RC not being able to do drugs. He was a prisoner of his addiction and I was a prisoner of RC; but at least on the road, the darker demon was put to rest.

Soundcloud Playlist - What's Love Got to do With It. - Tina Turner

Ironically, one of the songs in our set was the famous Tina Turner's song, *"What's Love Got To Do With It."* This was a rinse and repeat of Ike and Tina Turner, without their fame and glory. We were off the radar and I was under a microscope. "What does love got to do with it? Who needs a heart when a heart can be broken?"

The deeper my relationship got with RC, the closer he would say that we were close to our publishing deal. Cycles of abuse and that dangling carrot held me in place. When I tried to leave, he got me excited about my songwriting career. I had given up my solo career to make this happen. This was my shot.

But still, I was so worn out. I had no idea if he was shooting up drugs. I did not see any needles, but his moods were intense and our fights got worse. I was truly scared. I remember meeting my best friend Alison in the park. She tried to get information out of me, tried to support me, but I was in deep denial. I had two roommates who had an idea of what was going on, but I was not cracking...even under pressure. I was too ashamed and I felt I was to blame. Blame and Shame... two powerful prisoners that might feel familiar to you?

One summer night RC and I were walking down the street. We were back home in Los Angeles. We did not live together, but spent a lot of time together.

I was in a great mood, feeling that our publishing deal was close. But RC's mood swung dark, and he turned and swiftly clocked me in the head. My neck snapped back in pain and I was in shock. I had never been hit before, so I had no idea what occurred. I saw stars floating above my head. I knew that I was deep trouble. At that point anything would set him off. After the abuse, then came the stage where he begged for forgiveness. This is the typical cycle that we all fall for... that never-ending cycle of the forgiveness and the showering of love and affection. *"I'll never do that again baby... I promise."* Sound familiar?

About a month later we were coming out from the recording studio. RC was in his giddy and charismatic mood, so I knew he was already on drugs. It was about 3 a.m. I wanted to go home. We pulled up in front of my house. We sat in the car for a moment when his mood swung dark again. RC was completely obsessed with this guy in our band. They had a long history and a bit of betrayal between them, so their rivalry had not died.

He kept accusing me of having an affair with this person. *"Once I get the truth from you, then we can move forward and get our publishing deal settled,"* he kept saying.

He saw me contemplating something and he assumed it was due to guilt. I was actually thinking more along the lines of *"this relationship is getting out of hand and no publishing deal is worth it."*

But it was too late. RC came out of the car from the drivers side and he opened the door on the passenger side. His mood then swung sweet. He knelt down and held my hands and kissed my cheek. He said, *"We need to put this behind us, so that we can have a clean start."*

I stuttered and looked away. My hands were tangled on my lap. My breath was shallow and my heart was racing. I knew this could be the time I put this relationship behind me. I could break up with him and be done with this horrid experience.

I looked into his eyes with fear, wanting to say something. Without giving me a chance to utter another word I felt the force of his fist upon my face, my head, my back, my arms. He screamed, *"I knew it...you were with him. You're a slut, you bitch, you're a whore."* He hit me over and over and over and over again. I felt parts of my head swell while blood was pouring down my face. I was falling into unconsciousness. RC threw my legs back in the car and slammed the door. He ran around the car, jumped into the driver's seat and sped away. The 3 a.m. silence was deafening in the streets. The screeching of his wheels must have awakened the dead.

I had no idea where we were going. Things were turning black. Was he taking me to the hospital? Taking himself to the police? I saw the street lights look fuzzy and twirling. I was nauseous. I think I might have thrown up.

RC drove like a bat out of hell. He took me over to the mid-Wilshire district and turned down a dark street. He got me out of the car and walked me up a sidewalk. He opened the door to a dark and dingy apartment. I was still in shock and I had no way of figuring out what to do for myself. By then, it was nearly 4 a.m.

I saw a lump of a body lying on a sofa with a television set that blared Christian TV. The person slightly stirred and looked up from under her blanket. RC said, *"Ma, it's just me...go back to sleep."*

I heard him talk about his mother before, but I had never met her. I curled up in a chair in the corner of the other room and cried. I had no idea what to do. I was still bleeding. More than anything I was afraid, embarrassed, and in shock. My eyes were puffy and black, and my head was pounding. The lump was getting bigger.

RC said he would be right back and that he would get me an ice pack. I heard him slip out the front door. I had a feeling he needed an excuse to get out and get drugs so that he could deal with this horrific reality. I was afraid to move, afraid to leave, and most of all, afraid to call any of my friends.

For three days I sat in silence, feeling the lumps and bumps go down. He watched me through coke-filled eyes with sorrow and disbelief that he could have done this to me. I think he was shocked that I did not call the police. In hindsight I am shocked as well, as that is what I should have done.

I eventually called my roommates to say I would be home in a couple of days. The black eyes were still there, so I lied to protect my shame and embarrassment. I told them that we got into a car accident and that I was healing and would be fine.

I knew this relationship had to end and that I had to gracefully escape. I had to get through the healing, so that I could return to civilization and find a way out. Rinse and repeat of New York, but this time I was not living with him, so leaving would be easier.

I finally went back home. No words were needed to break up with RC. I called the manager of the band and asked to get out of my contract. We never spoke of any details, but I think he knew more than he would ever let on. This also meant that I was leaving the tour, the supposed publishing deal, and my career.

I had no idea where I was going but I knew I had to leave. I threw a packing and going away party. My mom came out to help me pack. My friends told her things behind the scenes, so I felt the look of disappointment more than anything. There was no time for nurturing, for healing, and certainly not for conversation. Bury the shame and move on. One morning my friends and my mom came together for this so-called intervention. But, it was already too late as I already knew in my heart that I was planning to leave and I knew the wrong steps that I had taken. However, it was nice to know that they cared.

HH came to the party to say goodbye. I shared part of the story with him. And I told my friends that I was done with Los Angeles for good. Never to return. I looked at HH wondering if I had made the worst mistake of my life. He wanted to get married and I walked away. I know now that this was part of our destiny and perhaps I needed to go through all of this so that I could do the work that I am doing now.

I went to visit my brother and sister-in-law in Atlanta. I was thinking this might be a good transitional place and I could get into the industry in Atlanta and be with my nieces as they grew up. However, Atlanta was a bit overwhelming to me and there were too many Peachtree Streets to ever find my way around. I headed back to Iowa, only to find that my roots had been uprooted. I returned during the Great Flood of 1993. I landed at the Des Moines Airport carrying extra bottles of water in my suitcase, but as it turned out, all of Iowa was under water. Symbolic for sure, as I was flooded with emotions and memories. The raindrops were representative of the tears I was not able to cry.

Life during the flood was what I imagine the pioneer days were like. There was no electricity, no potable drinking water. We went to the military camps to get large containers of water and we wore bathings suits outside to take showers in the rain. We caught the rainwater in large buckets and heated the water on the stove to use for cooking and for baths for the children. My brother had two young children at the time. This is how we got my young niece and nephew ready for school.

I stayed between my parents' house and my brother's basement. I had been there for a few days when my mom said, *"Don't think you can stay here without getting a job."* Those words stung. I realized I would have to move through this tragedy with no counseling, no help, and on my own. I stuffed my emotions deep inside my boots and since these boots were made for walking… I did just that.

I went from one job interview to another, from local TV stations, to production companies. Each person I interviewed with looked at me from behind their cushy desks and said, *"Why do you want to be in the Iowa market, with a resume like this from New York and LA?"* I felt their judgment and I did not have an answer. I was way out of place by Iowa standards. They looked at me, as if to say, *"What's wrong with you?"*

As the floods were clearing up, I was curled in a fetal position in the basement of my brother's house. I prayed to God to reveal where I was supposed to go. The autumn leaves were soon going to fall and I promised myself to get out of Iowa before snow came.

My underground haven of a brick wall was a huge turning point in my life. Whenever anyone asks me *"What made you go down this path and begin a nonprofit"* I can always see myself huddled up on the bed, staring at the brick wall, and praying really hard to God. I was waiting for a sign to trickle down through the bricks and give me an answer. I felt like St John in his cave waiting on the angel of mercy to deliver my mission and my book of revelation.

I thought about moving back to New York, or to Chicago, or even Vancouver, but all I could see in each of these cities was a big blanket of white snow.

I still had voice mail set up in Los Angeles. This was my last connection to my old life, outside of a few choice friends that I kept in contact with from time to time.

On the day I called to cancel my voicemail there was one message left for me to hear. I was tempted not to listen, terrified that it might be RC trying to find me. However, curiosity got the better of me. The message was from a guy by the name of Mark, whom I met during the rebuild of South Central after the riots. I had participated in the community build before leaving Los Angeles. Mark was calling to inform me that he was part of a coalition of nonprofit groups and he wanted to include me. Mark and his team were creating a compilation of music to raise funds for this coalition. He left a voice message, *"Since I remember you saying that you were in the music business, I thought you might want to come on board to help us!"*

I loved the idea that I could bring my talents as a producer to this group, but I hoped it did not require for me to move back to Los Angeles.

Mark and I began talking in August of 1993. Due to the limitations of technology during those days, we had to use a fax machine to send documents back and forth. The plans for the music CD quickly fell into place, and I finally had a home for my song, *Numbed by the Numbers*.

It became evident that I would have to go back to California, so I learned the meaning of the cliché saying, *'Never say never!'*

The plan was for me to be tucked safely away in the South Bay for no more than six months. I told Mark a bit of my story and let him know that I was not too keen on getting close to the Hollywood area.

We created an entire plan around the World Trust and named the CD project *World Jam 1*. We ended up with 47 artists from around the world on a 4 CD box set of interactive music. Mark and I switched roles, as he started Worldwide Records as the music label and I founded World Trust Foundation as the nonprofit. I met a guy from San Diego who had the ability to turn the CD's into interactive experiences and allowed for the user to listen to music on their computer and watch videos at the same time. It was a concept that was ahead of its times, so it was a hard sell.

After some time, Mark and I gracefully dissolved our partnership, each following the individual roads that we needed to take. I made some really great lifelong friends during this time (Mark D, Marc B, Paula G) and eventually I felt safe enough to come out of hiding. I had already ventured up into Hollywood several times exploring the music scene to find artists.

I moved to San Fernando Valley with a new songwriting partner. He and his wife rented the top floor of their house to me, while Jones and I continued to work on music. Jones was a talented songwriter and helped me get a few of my demos done. The songs that I have written in my life are in an archive waiting for the right time to be released. My continued story of why it was taking so long to get my message or mission out to the world was becoming a broken record. I had to realize what was holding me back.

In 1994, I was taken into the technology world kicking and screaming. My friend Amy saw the potential in my writing and producing and she was building a team of people to work on some projects. Once I discovered the power of technology, I never looked back. When the world was waking up to emails, personal computers, and the internet, I saw the potential for more. I actually had an agent who sent me from client to client and city to city to work on major corporate brands as they built their online identity before anyone knew there should be an online identity to develop.

From 1994 through 2000 I worked in the philanthropic and technology arenas, learning the best ways by which to connect the world. However, as a woman in tech, I was automatically part of a small group of women in the vast sea of men. I saw small start-up companies make millions and I witnessed people's lives change forever. I remember the Mark Cuban's of the world, as we all attended the same networking groups. While I saw others making huge successes in technology, I was watching from the sidelines like a wallflower waiting for someone to ask me to dance.

My universe was filled with numerous ideas that could have – should have - made millions for the budding empire in my mind. I am sure that you as well have had numerous entrepreneurial ideas throughout your life.

For example, 1994, I was on the board of a company called Rose Croix. We almost got funded, until the potential investor told us that they did not think anyone would ever buy anything from an online auction site. September 1995 EBay was born.

In 1995, I completed a business plan for an online network called, World Trust Network (WTN). During those days they called it an IPTV, containing streaming programming. I put that on hold in 1997, as whenever I pitched the idea of streaming media, or virtual classroom content I was stared at with skeptic eyes.

In 1996, I was working for a database technology company. The CEO (Sia) was a bright and generous Persian man, who I adored, as well as everyone else at the company. I was the producer/ project manager of all of their clients for about two years. At one point I pitched an idea to Sia, based on the fact that he had the best database programmers in the business.

Being that my previous career was being an actor, I created a company that offered a much-needed service that catered to actors, that could also make a lot of money.

I wrote a business plan that included a site where actors could put up their reels, pics, and bios into a database website, so that managers, agents, and casting directors could review for casting. I did not have the funding and Sia did not have the resources, so I let the idea go. By 1998, Jeff Bezos bought a similar company for $55M which ended up being Internet Movie DataBase, otherwise known as IMDB. And then, these sort of examples did not stop.

In 1999, I created a kids product called Kitty Soup. I had the President of a major toy company who loved the idea. He was drawing up the contract, as he told my friend Marlene (who introduced me) that Kitty Soup would make the "toy of the millennium." Then, two days before the contract was to be signed, he called to tell me that his office was flooded and they were putting everything on hold. I was devastated, as everything pointed to this being my way to finally making something grand.

In January of 2000, I went to the dumpster and threw out all of my client folders and jumped off the precipice to begin an independent life of traveling the world and being of service. Out of disappointment came the ideal that one should never give up on a dream, vision, passion, or purpose. I needed to find my purpose and that had to be attached to my passion.

As the clock struck midnight on New Year's' Eve to bring in the new millennium, we found out that Y2K was not going to bring the world to a halt. This particular year would be another important crossroad in my life, because it was the year I discovered my love for humanitarian work. I began working with the United Nations and things were beginning to look a little brighter.

In 2000, I also ended yet another relationship with another damaged man, when I realized that I could not save him. This man had a compelling and devastating story, that from the age of eleven until his thirties he had been sexually abused by an older male neighbor.

I was beginning to learn the concept of forgiveness, as I remember telling him that would be a great way to heal. *"Forgive us our trespasses as we forgive those who trespass against us."* These words I had been saying for years in prayer had finally came to the surface. Now, I just had to put these words into practice.

Underneath the cycles of abuse there are patterns that are set from our childhood. I had to dive deeper to see what patterns that were set, so that I could begin to identify the problem and to also see why I kept getting so close to the destination of success, but kept missing the mark. Perhaps my perception had to change a bit as well.

I had to look deeper to see what programming (or messages) that I received from my parents, grandparents, siblings, friends, and ancestors.

What was my reflection in the mirror? What was my lesson? Who were these people in my life? Did they put me down... or empower me to greatness?

I realized I had been the rescuer, which was set from early on, as I was born to bring my parents back together. I always felt that I was here to rescue my mother.

After going on a path through a dark journey there should be light. But for me the light was too dim and I could not yet see the entire picture. I was waiting for that blast of bright light through the dark for this pattern to end. However, sometimes we need to take the first step. Step-by-step the light shines a bit brighter. I stumble on a pebble. I begin again. I fall on my face. I begin again.

What brought me to this place? How do I get out? Too many questions! So today, I focus on forgiveness! I look to the patterns of my childhood to see where I need to go next.

I say, *"Let my tears wipe away my fears and the years of abusive approach, so that this young girl's heart can be returned to love and be returned to innocence."*

**Soundcloud Playlist - Return to Innocence - Enigma

Chapter 15

I Left My Heart in San Francisco

One of my favorite cities in the world is San Francisco. The first time I visited this hilly, magical city was when I thirteen, in the summer of 1973.

This was the transitional summer before I entered high school. I had my bell-bottom jeans fiercely ironed with an intense seam down the front of my pants. My hair had the perfect Farrah Fawcett flip. I was madly in love with a boy whom I met earlier in the year. I did not think I could survive for an entire month away from him and my friends.

This was my first plane ride and my first trip away from the Midwest. We came to San Francisco and to Northern California to visit my mom's relatives. I marveled at how the orange groves filled the air with an abundant citrus aroma. I loved the sight of the farms that contained these bright, orange orbs that popped out of the bushy green trees. This was much different from where I grew up with miles of corn fields as far as the eye could see.

In every direction that I looked, San Francisco revealed another picture-perfect postcard scene. The bridges, the curvy streets, the sounds of the cable cars, I even floated on the fog from one place to another.

I found out many decades later from my brother that this trip with my mom was more of a trial separation for my parents. My mom was trying to see if she and I were going to move to California. My oldest brother was off to college and my middle brother was going to be a senior in high school, so perhaps she thought it was time to finally pull the plug on their marriage. However, we returned after a month, but not after having the time of my life with my dear Uncle Kenny and Auntie Ruth. The only time in my life when I was thinking of another career other than entertainment. My aunt had her own travel agency and the stories they shared of all the places they lived piqued my imagination. I was so intrigued with the thought of travel and living overseas, as they did, that I wanted to be part of the travel industry.

Fast-forward to my adult life, I always wanted to live in San Francisco. The internet gaming industry was gaining speed. Somehow I met a young Russian man, Yury, who worked for a Russian online game company. The game brought people together from around the world into this online community, where there was social impact at the end of the game. Yury asked me if I wanted to work with him to head up the United States main office. I said, "*Yes!*"

The year was 2003. Yury was living in Santa Cruz at the time. The CEO, Dimitri, gave us full reign to decide where the corporate office was going to be, so we began looking around Northern California, where Yury felt most comfortable. Santa Cruz was lovely, but not a great place for this wild, city girl. *"Let's try San Francisco."* I pleaded.

Yury and I jumped in a car and drove to the city. We went through many listings in the paper. However, when this one particular listing grabbed my attention, I knew this was the house.

We got an appointment with the owner. He opened the door to this Victorian mansion in Potrero Hill and the house had every single element on my wish list for manifesting a home.

When I was getting ready to decide about San Francisco, I had asked my friend, Kohlene who lives in Switzerland, if she still had anyone in the city who could help me. She introduced me to her best friend Nola. They grew up together and Nola knew the city very well and she could point me in the right direction.

I called Nola up a few days before heading up to the city, and proclaimed, *"I want to have hardwood floors, high ceilings, a walk-in closest, large kitchen, entertaining areas, a view of the city, and ample parking."* I felt the silence on the other end of the phone, as I am sure that Nola thought I was a bat-shit crazy.

And here I was, walking through this stunning 4,000 square foot Victorian mansion with spectacular views of the city.

The CEO of the company agreed to have Yury and I live in this house, as the headquarters for the first sixth months to get us acclimated to the city. Then the house would be used for out-of-town dignitaries and guests.

The owner of the house, Nick, was a sweet man who lived out of town with his family. He was excited to rent the house to someone who loved it as much as he did. I went back to Los Angeles, packed my car, threw the rest in storage, took my two cats (India and Coco at the time) and headed up Interstate 5 to my next home and new job. I was living it right! But *"don't believe me when I say I've got it down."*

**Soundcloud Playlist - Why Georgia - John Mayer

Within the first forty-eight hours of arriving in San Francisco, I noticed Yury acting out of balance. I tried to hold down the fort during those first few weeks of launching the US office, but it became evident that something was curiously wrong. Yury revealed that he had undiagnosed bipolar disorder. So, I did what I usually do, I jumped into the fire and did the work for both of us. I did not want to spoil our chances by bringing attention to Yury's instability to the CEO, who was headquartered in Russia. It seemed plausible from a distance that our launch was on schedule and all things were aligned.

Since I moved from Los Angeles in record time, there were loose ends that I needed to complete. I was part of the production team for Earth Day LA, so I had to virtually do my part to produce the event from afar. My best friend Alison, in Los Angeles, was also pregnant with her second child. I threw her a baby shower, while also planning my parents' 50th wedding anniversary back in Des Moines. I knew I could multitask and manage a lot of things, but I had to take this to a whole new level.

When I flew home to prepare for my parents anniversary party, I had no idea the importance of this occasion, but all would be revealed in God's time.

Their anniversary was extraordinarily special, as the endless train of relatives and friends came through the house to celebrate their fifty years of togetherness. My father held court from the corner of the couch, smiling and laughing, even while the tubes strung out of his nose connecting him to his tank of oxygen. My mom was thrilled that they made it to their golden milestone. I felt complete, as I was able to plan their dream party. There was joy that filled the house. After all of the years we witnessed their turbulence, when in the end they really loved one another.

I decorated the table with silk flower petals and filled the table full of wonderful food to eat. Everyone had a lovely time celebrating what I called "third time's a charm" because they had three marriages. There was the first marriage which was young love and my brothers were born, the second marriage happened after my brother Rick got the mumps and I was on my way, and the third marriage was a formality in the Catholic

Church the year before, when I was their maid-of-honor. Voila! Third time's a charm!

I made it through all my events between Los Angeles and Des Moines and decided to take a much-needed break to see my friends in Boulder.

While I was in Boulder the CEO flew into San Francisco from Russia for a surprise visit. He saw Yury's condition and in a flash of an eye, he closed down our office. We were not even five weeks in the flow. He was not fond of the idea of an American woman running his US company.

I was in the dark of his visit and his decision, until I listened to my voicemail while at a dinner party in Boulder. Laughter echoed in the background while I heard Yury's shaky voice apologizing for messing things up. A few days later Yury retreated back to his quiet ocean life in Santa Cruz and I was left wondering what to do next. I had already shut down all my work in Los Angeles and was now living in a mansion that I could not afford. In five short weeks my life had shifted once again. Solid ground was nowhere to be found.

I called the owner of the house and shared with him the misfortune of the company closing. *"Sometimes blessings can come from a curse"* Nick said. He furthered his story by sharing that he had been recently diagnosed with brain cancer and that he would be going through chemo and other treatments for the next six months. He and his wife did not want to make any rash decisions about the house, so they had me live there as a caretaker of the property. I could live there for minimal rent while he went through his treatments and then they would make a decision to rent or sell.

God works in mysterious ways, as I knew I was drawn to San Francisco for a bigger purpose and now the reason could be revealed.

My bedroom was in the front turret of the house. I would sit for hours gawking at the San Francisco skyline, which at night seemed like an electronic postcard lit up just for me. The bay was to the right of my view. I would watch the sailboats drifting peacefully on the water at sunset and wonder, *"Who are those people in those sailboats and where do they go each night?"* My creative muses loved that house and I spent a lot of time writing and manifesting future visions.

Because I was in Potrero Hill, I basked in the sunshine above the fog that settled into the base of the city each day. I held gatherings and dinner parties with the progressive thinkers of San Francisco. I finally felt like I was home. Nola and I became dear friends and her family of friends embraced me as well. Life was definitely looking up. Imagine her surprise the first time she came to the house on Potrero Hill, when she witnessed all of my wishlist had been manifested.

During my time in San Francisco, my mom came to visit over the Memorial weekend.

We reminisced about all of our adventures over the years, including New York discos, Broadway Shows, our trip to Mexico when we got lost and almost got run off the road. We had the typical mother/daughter roller coaster ride of a relationship, but I felt that my mom was most proud of my living in her dream city, San Francisco. What I did not know that this beginning for me would also be a beginning and an end of a dream. I simply had no idea how much of an end this would be.

My mom spent most of her time that weekend wandering around this huge Victorian house with a notepad and pen, in silence.

I would say, *"Ma, it's a beautiful day, let's go out and enjoy the city"* or *"My friends want us to come for dinner, let's go."* She would politely refuse and say that she was fine in the house. She just wanted to spend time with me. I watched her as she quietly mused her way from room to room throughout the mansion. Over the years, she could often get into a mode of not wanting to share me with others, but this was different. Something was drastically different.

I was also stressed out. That very weekend, my best friend was having her baby in Los Angeles. Alison was on her back, legs in the air, fighting with her doctor, who was insisting that she has a c-section. I got on the phone and fought with the doctor to let Alison have the natural childbirth that she wanted. I knew that her amazing husband, Bill, was at her side but I wanted to be there. It was frustrating to be far away, as I was planning to be in the delivery room with her. It was my chance to experience childbirth at its finest hour. Instead, I watched my mom sit in silence in a room by herself.

The last night of this strange weekend, my mom took me to dinner at one of my favorite places down the street. As the waiter slipped in and around our table, filing our wine glasses and bringing us delectable almond-crusted tilapia, my mom took out her notepad and balanced it on the table's edge.

She proceeded to flip from page to page, between bites of food and sips of wine, and told me her plan to buy the house and move in with me. Her notepad was filled with floor plans and sketches of remodeling ideas. Morbid as it was, my father's health was failing, and she only had a limited amount of time to purchase the home and decide on her next move.

My mom's plan was once my dad passed she would take vacations with my Auntie Ruth, go on shopping trips, spend quiet Sundays with a crossword puzzle, and become my business accountant. She was great at crunching numbers and she had an affinity with balancing a checkbook.

My mom left San Francisco with her notepad filled with dream house scribbles, tucked inside her bag. She was in great spirits and in great health.

By July of that summer, Nick had completed his treatments. They decided to sell their home. I had no idea where I would land, but Los Angeles was calling my name once again. My mom and I hoped that no one would come forward to buy the house, so that my mom could fulfill her dream.

Since I had no work in San Francisco, I moved back to Los Angeles, into a temporary empty house in Burbank.

I rented a 14-foot truck and hitched my car to the back of the truck. With my two cat carriers strapped in, I took Interstate 5 once again, through horrific weather. The white-knuckle drive was the least of my worries, as other large semi-trucks slide from side to side of the freeway in the windy, downpour rain. By the grace of God and angels, I sang, *"She'll be coming round the mountain when she comes."* Over and over and over again. This was the only thing I could do to keep my nerves in tack.

My friend, who lived in Burbank, had a great idea for my return to Los Angeles. She was waiting for her "ex" to buy a house across the street for her and her daughter.

The plan was to switch places once escrow closed, then I would rent her house. The purchase and escrow took longer than we expected, so I set up camp with a temporary bed and kept my belongings in storage.

That August in 2003, I took a trip to Geneva to speak at the United Nations. This was the year I received the Medal of Excellence in the category of Edu-tainment at the Festival of Excellence. It was an honor to feel recognized for my work that I had been doing since 1993 for my foundation, the World Trust Foundation.

I did not have much time to relish in the excitement of the award, as upon returning to Los Angeles I found out that my mom was to have back surgery in a few weeks and I was to travel home to take care of her.

It was sweet to hear her remind me to bring home my medal from Geneva. Over the years my mom seemed more aligned and understanding of my career as an actor or performer. Even years after leaving acting, she often forgot to correct friends who still thought I worked in soap operas. I suppose it was easier for her to describe me as an actress, as opposed to an unmarried woman who runs around the world helping people in need. With her mentioning the medal, I finally felt that my mom was beginning to understand what I was doing with my life.

My mom was in great spirits about her surgery, excited to finally be out of pain. She had a cruise planned with my aunt after the surgery and she was in process of remodeling her bedroom suite. She continued to dream of her pending move to "her" home in San Francisco as my dad's health continued to decline.

I planned to go back to Iowa for her surgery to help for two weeks. I would be back in the hot, humid summer, when the giant corn stalks were ready to be shucked. I was counting the days before I would be there to cook for my parents and help my mom heal. During the years I made my way back home often to cook for my dad. At least once a month I cooked for an entire weekend and labeled Tupperware and froze the collection of food for them to eat throughout the month.

I had not seen my father since their anniversary party. My mom warned me that he was getting more frail.

All the same, my mom continued to have a recurring nightmare that she shared with me throughout the years. In this dream she would be laying on the floor dying and my dad would not rescue her. She would say, *"I see him stepping over me while I lay dying."* I thought it was based on strange thoughts from their tumultuous marriage. I could not see her dying first, as her health was fine, while my dad's health was failing fast.

Unfortunately, I saw yet another opportunity to see how our thoughts can manifest in our lives. My mom was one week away from her back surgery. I had my ticket in hand and I was ready to go.

It was late morning, August 18th 2003. I answered a call from my brother, who had a strained and strange voice on the other end of the phone. I remember the blood drained from my head and my heart felt like it had completely stopped. He said that my mom was found unconscious on her bedroom floor. My world stood still. This did not make sense to me. Was this a joke? A nightmare? Would I wake up to find that it was all going to be fine? They had taken her to the hospital to find out what happened, but it was not looking good.

She is the only one who knows those final steps, but putting the pieces together it seemed that her worst nightmare became her reality. I assume that she woke up in the middle of a hot August night, for a trip to the bathroom. Returning to her bed she fell to the floor following an explosion in her head. My father had his own room at the other end of the house, so as a convalescent, he was trapped in his hospital bed.

I am sure he must have heard her fall, as it had to have created a loud thud. My mom's worst nightmare was coming true, as my dad was trapped inside of his own broken body. He could not come to save her. My mom lied unconscious, drifting above her body and perhaps above my father's bed, begging for help. Or, was it that she finally felt free outside of her body? That she saw the light and had no remorse of leaving me … leaving us … leaving him.

**Soundcloud Playlist - She Talks to Angels - Black Crowes

It was not until my father's nurse arrived hours later that she was found. I am sure my dad laid in bed during that time and wondered what happened to my mom. Her ritual was to wake up every morning to *Good Morning America*, unlock the front door for the nurse, visit my dad, and bring him his first cup of coffee.

The nurse, named Bobby, arrived at his daily scheduled time. He was a nineteen-year-old boy, sweet, innocent, and strong-bodied. Bobby had no idea why the normally unlocked door was still locked from the night before. He called my brothers, who rushed to the house with the paramedics on their way. They found my mom laying face down in her bedroom, brain dead. They brought her to the hospital, and tried for hours to revive her and find the reason of this sudden disaster. They put her on life support and called me for the second time. I was pacing back and forth, wondering what to do.

I waited by the phone all day to get updates. I paced the rooms of the empty house, hearing the heels of my shoes echo across the floor boards, while my breath reverberated through the rafters. No news was coming my way, or at least no good news. I got a redeye flight scheduled and I somehow packed my bags. My friend Dina took me to Alison's and then Alison took me to the airport.

I sat frozen in my seat of the airplane, as the engines stirred. The silver tube took me through the air, to the final day I would have with my mother.

My brothers picked me up at the Des Moines Airport. The waiting area in the airport always held great memories for me. This time, as I walked from the airplane to the baggage area, a time-lapse vision appeared to me. I saw the faces of my parents change from my time in college, to New York, to Los Angeles, or wherever I was traveling from to see my family. They were always standing there waiting with open arms. Eventually my brothers had children, and they too would be part of the welcoming committee. Their children went from rolling in strollers, to toddling, to running to hug their *Auntie Tess.* Their voices sounded like a unison of angels.

This time, I entered the waiting area where my brothers waited. We embraced and walked to the car. We rode to the hospital in silence. I was the last to arrive. I will never forget the antiseptic smell that pierced my nose as I entered the hospital, and the crowd of relatives that parted like the red sea as I descended down the center of the hallway to her room. The looks and the whispers were just about to drive me over the edge, but somehow I held it together. My moms body was there, tangled between the tubes, while the machines that held her to this earth, quietly murmured. I felt her spirit alive in the room. My brothers and nurses left me alone, so that she and I could have our time together.

As I was packing to come home, I had heard my mom's voice say to me *"Don't forget to bring your medal."* Perhaps since I had not gotten the Academy Award that she wanted me to have, a medal from the United Nations would do for the time being.

I pulled the heavy medal out of my purse. This large round gold medal had a peace dove molded on the top. It was cold and heavy in my hands. I slipped the medal into her hands, as her fingers entangled inside of mine. I held her hands with the medal between us and begged her to give me a sign that she was in the room with me. I waited and waited. Finally her finger slightly twitched in my hand. I knew she was there. I felt her love and her spirit soar in the room. A doctor walked in and looked at our entangled hands trying to discern what the gold flashy object was that caught his eye. Without saying a word, I slipped the medal back into my purse. I honored her request to bring the medal home, and she gave me the final sign that she was there. I felt her pride.

The hospital room door opened and my dad was brought into the room in a wheelchair. His sunken face and spirit wore strongly on his presence. My brother rolled his wheelchair as close as he could next to my mom. He sat helpless. His hand reached to out to hold her hand. Tears welled up in his eyes. I heard him say under his breath *"This was supposed to be me."* Perhaps he knew her hidden fears of him not being there, or he had the fear that he would not have her by his side when he left this earth. Perhaps she would be his champion on the other side, when he finally left his body.

Four short hours later, we all gathered by her side. Her best friends and relatives crammed into this tiny hospital room. Our family decided it was time to take her off life support. The end of life process took over an hour. We all watched her vital signs as they began to slowly shut down, one by one. It was surprising even to the doctors how strong her heart was. It was the last organ to go. I stood at her feet and fed loving energy into the pads of her soles, to her soul, as she departed her body. One of the most beautiful things I have ever witnessed in my life was her closing breath. Her arms, in unison, raised up slowly and gently folded across her body, crossing her heart. It was her final dance. Her final statement that her heart was now safe in heaven. August 19th 2003 my mom began her heavenly dance. Her song to me was Lee Ann Womack, *I Hope You Dance*. My brothers and I somehow got ourselves together and planned the service, along with a video that depicted her lovely life, as this time I got to say to her spirit, *"Mama, I love you. I hope you dance."*

**Soundcloud Playlist - I Hope You Dance - Lee Ann Womack

Chapter 16

What a Wonderful World

My father parted this world while peacefully sleeping just three months later, almost to the day of my mom's passing.

I was awakened from a deep sleep with a strong jolt to my bed. I thought at first it was a typical Los Angeles earthquake, but somehow I knew that my father had passed. I felt him in the room with me, to share so many secrets. My abilities to communicate and see to the other side are limited, so I could only talk to him in the silence of my mind. There were two times I started to drift back to sleep and each of those times he gave another thump to my bed, as if to say, *"You're not going to go to sleep on me now."*

I laid awake for the next three hours, trying hard to break the veil and see his face, hear his voice, or smell his cologne. I wanted to hear how he finally felt free. I knew he struggled so much with dying. He held on for such a long time. I often wondered if my mom chose to go before him, so that she could offer her strength for him to take his journey. I saw the crack of sunlight come through my window. The phone rang and it was my brother to tell me the news of my fathers passing. I picked up the phone, *"I know already."* I said. *"You already know what?"* he asked. *"That dad has passed. He's been here with me for the past few hours."* There was a brief, yet deafening silence on the other end of the phone. Finally my brother said, *"Okay then. So what sort of arrangements do we need to make to have you come home?"*

To me there is still an insurmountable amount of sadness that will never go away when it comes to the passing of my father. I felt that I could never be hurt by another man because the pain could not compare to the pain of losing my daddy. I had my other favorite man, my grandfather, die when I was at the tender age of sixteen. I experienced heartbreak from my first love, along with a myriad of other heartbreaks along the way, but nothing could top this cherry on the hell-sundae of life. This was my daddy and my champion and he was finally going to be put to rest.

I thought about the times when my dad and I had our alone times. I remember my mom needing time to do chores, so he would drive me around at night to give my mom some space. My father was not much of a talker, but he loved to whistle. It was this tuneless whistle that reminded me of our silent drives and time alone. I had long gotten over the fact that he had trouble communicating, as he was a man of few words.

I remembered while in college, I had to force him to open up and say that he loved me. Once that door opened there was a flood of love that kept coming. We had a special bond that no one could ever know. He believed in me, even though he had no idea what I was doing in life. I know he hoped that I would marry a nice man and stay in Des Moines. I know deep in his heart that all he ever wanted was for me to find a man who would love, respect, and protect me, but that had not occurred yet. On this night of his passing the one sound that comforted me was the memory of his whistle. I heard it from the other side and the sound made me smile.

Soundcloud Playlist - What a Wonderful World - Louie Armstrong

I headed back to Des Moines for a repeat performance of another funeral. I found myself standing in a long security line at the Los Angeles airport. Even though the airport was filled with thousands of people, I felt very alone. I was directed to a hallway that I had never been down before, in spite of traveling that same exact route many times over multiple years. Stepping onto the moving walkway, I looked around. There was not one other person in that hallway with me. Strange, since this was one of the busiest airports in the world. Where were all the other passengers?

Feeling lonelier than ever, I wondered how I was going to get through the next few days. My mom had died only three months earlier. Now, dad's loss on top of hers was more than I could bear. Maybe it was due to the unusual quiet in a normally buzzing airport, but I never before noticed the sound of instrumental music. The music quickly caught my attention. That song was so familiar! I said out loud, *"What is that song? Why did it sound so familiar?"* Of course! It was the muzak version of Eric Clapton's song, *Tears in Heaven*. The music penetrated my heart and took my breath away. Listening with all my senses, I knew it was a sign from my dad. I stopped feeling alone. I knew that I would sing *Tears in Heaven* at my father's funeral.

I have always enjoyed being on a plane and relished the exhilarating feeling of taking off and being lifted from the ground. But this time, my nose crushed against the cold window of the plane, my heart sank. Reflecting on the ups and downs of my parents' turbulent relationship, I recalled how their arguments would leave a deafening hole of silence between them for days on end. How could they go that long without speaking to one another? The question confused and tormented me throughout my childhood. The truth was, it still troubled me.

I knew that I did not want to recreate their relationship, and I knew that when I found my mate, we would have great communication and fear would not dictate the silent treatment. I took this dark time as an opportunity for me to imagine the man

I could spend my life with. I would take the love of my parents and manifest the one who could be in my life forever.

Lost in thought, I nearly jumped out of my seat when the plane hit the ground. The lurch from the plane forced me back to reality. I exited the plane, gathered my bags, and walked the familiar plank through the Des Moines Airport. There again the greeting area was filled with the ghosts of my past. However, this time I saw my parents standing there, as if I was just coming back from college. My brothers and I repeated, step by step, what we had done for our mother's funeral, only this time for our dad.

At the church once again, the three of us gathered behind the casket and proceeded up the aisle. It was much like a wedding march, with both of my brothers flanked on either side of me, but instead them wearing festive suits and me in a wedding gown, we were all dressed in black, walking behind our father's casket. The intense smell of incense, which normally calmed my nerves, circled my head and tickled my nose. I saw the crowd in the pews gingerly watching us as the casket was being rolled through the church. Strangely on display for the eyes that shed the tears for the loss of this man...my father.

I slipped into the pew reserved for the family and went into deep prayer. It was time for me to get up and sing. I walked toward the piano barely able to feel my legs beneath me. My cousins, Francis and Jim, were there to conduct the music for the funeral. Their smiles gave me strength, as I approached the piano. I stood before the congregation, before the altar, and sang to my father's casket.

"Will you know my name if I see you in Heaven?

Will it be the same when I see you in heaven?

I'll carry on....I must be strong." Eric Clapton 1992

**Soundcloud Playlist - Tears in Heaven - Eric Clapton

I thought I would sing at my mother's funeral because she loved to sing. But her death came as such a shock that it took everything I could muster to just walk down the aisle behind her casket. As I sang for my father, I realized that this song was the homage to them both.

It is hard to explain, but I felt surrounded by their presence. Somehow, I was finally able to appreciate that in spite of their tribulations, that my mother and father actually adored one another. Their relationship was strange, but now I knew their love for each other, like their love for me, was very real.

When I finished singing, I was taken aback by the unexpected feeling of freedom that suddenly swept over me. They say that there is a moment when both parents are gone in which one feels like an orphan, no matter what age. That moment had come for me. I was no longer a child torn between fulfilling their dreams and following my own true calling. I had this strange sense of independence, a sense of freedom. I had no one else to lean on, yet at the same time, all of their expectations were released from my body. I knew that I was free to make my own decisions, my own mistakes.

Independence has a great feeling, but it comes with a price. I truly believe that my mom left her heart in San Francisco when she departed that day, and that she still carries that notepad with sketches of her dream home under her arm. I feel that she has since recreated that home in heaven, wine cellar, reading room, new kitchen and all.

I had a dream shortly after she died in which I was sitting on the floor in a bedroom, packing a suitcase for her. She was pacing in front of this large window lined with lace curtains that were billowing in the quiet breeze. She stared and stared into the distance while we sat in silence. As I packed her bags, she said, "The plane is arriving...you can come with me you know." I smiled and said, "That's okay ma...I'm not ready to go yet. This journey is yours to take, but I will see you again one day." I looked up and she was gone.

My mom left her heart in San Francisco, but San Francisco is where I found mine. San Francisco was where I learned how to find the balance between home and heart. I remind myself, as I seek my next turn on the road in life, that wherever I am, life is blessed.

I realized that I had a choice on how I saw things happening to me... whether I continued to stay in the role of being a victim, or that any particular situation in life could actually be considered a blessing after all.

Life is all in the perception, offering us a time to reflect, to reprieve, and to grieve.

Soundcloud Playlist - I Grieve - Peter Gabriel

PART 3: THE BIRTH OF GWEN: THE IMMACULATE PERCEPTION

All of us have an unlimited opportunity to give birth at any given time, without giving birth to an actual child. There is the birth of an idea, a project, a company, or my personal favorite pun, the birth of reason. Obviously, the immaculate perception is spun off of the immaculate conception, also part of the birthing process. I realized that my giving birth to an actual child in this lifetime was not going to happen. However, the birth of GWEN is the culmination of my life work and the birth of a hopeful movement to inspire all of our stories to be revealed for the purpose of healing. I realized that in the crossroads of my life that I had been giving birth to the creative source since I was a little girl.

2004 marked the first year of my being without my parents. It was a time of rebirth and of cleansing from the dark winter's night. To me, life is a never-ending cycle of beginnings. At any time, on any given day, we can stand up and declare...I am starting over! And this is the beauty of life.

Birth can be translated into a myriad of circumstantial examples. Some cultures believe that birth occurs on the actual day of conception. Others define it as the moment our spirit takes flight and makes the decision to be born into a particular family, and that we are tied karmically to other souls until we learn the lessons they are meant to teach us.

Still others define birth as the day we are physically birthed into this world. I have belief in many potential truths, except for those that stipulate that death is the end, and that there is no connection to the spirit world. This does not compute to me. This is where my faith comes into the picture. Faith is the utmost glue that holds my fabric of life together.

Life gives us the opportunity to dive deep and to see those around us as either mirrors or lessons. We can shift the perspective to bring the negative or the positive into our lives. The great part of being human is that at any given moment we can choose to experience a rebirth and advance our soul to the next level of being. However, transformation and the desire to be of service in this world comes with a price. This is not easy to commit ourselves to being of service, when everywhere we turn we are being lured into many aspects of the material world, or the ego world, as we are made of matter and all have egos that need to be tended to.

When I lost both of my parents in a three-month span, I was devastated. My warrior-side had to come out and I had to soldier onward, burying my pain. I seem to do that burying thing quite readily: bury it down, batten down the hatches, carry on!

As I mentioned, after my parents' death there came a strange and unexpected feeling of being free. I cannot explain this and in no way am I demeaning the love that I have for my parents, but becoming an 'orphan' at any age has its own rites of passage. I think the feeling of becoming free was part of my growth and my independence.

There is something that happens between parents and children, where spoken and unspoken expectations and fears can turn into stress and judgment. Even though I will always miss my parents, I do have the feeling of freedom from judgment. However, I am now able to look back on the lessons that I learned being their child and this will be a part of my life forever.

I was free to explore my untouched dreams. I was free to capture my beautiful wishes that had not yet come true.

Chapter 17
Bella Wishes

New Years' Day 2004: it had only been six weeks since my father's death, and less than four months since my mother's death.

I was fighting the demons of frustration and grief, and trying to figure a resolution that was unlike any resolution I had made in years past.

I searched my soul to find something that I had always wanted to do: learn Italian, take piano, go back to dance class. All of them seemed appropriate and definitely on my passion list, but I knew that I could only handle one, so dance it was. Speaking Italian and learning to play piano would have to wait.

I was looking for a form of dance that I had not yet experienced, as I already knew modern, contemporary, jazz, hip hop, and African. I saw an ad in a local newspaper about a belly dance class at the Burbank recreation center. Well, that was certainly different from ballet, and I felt in tune with the culture and the music. I signed up for the class and bought the dance veils and hip scarves to accompany my long skirts and crop tops. I had the best time shimmying and shaking parts of my body that had not been awakened for years.

After one of my dance classes I fell into bed with sweet exhaustion. I always had this fondness for my 'middle of the night musings' typically around 4:00 a.m. The cycle of downloading creative ideas was always welcomed. I always felt the presence of angels and muses dancing around my room, singing, *"Get up... get up... there is so much to do in the world."*

One morning, early March 2004, I was awakened with the words, *"Bella Wishes makes three wishes as she swings her hips to and fro... Bella Wishes then she swishes, Bella is always on the go!"* This was spinning in my head

Out of my sleepy fog, I said out loud, *"What? Who is Bella? What are her Wishes?"*

Bella Wishes was coming into play. I grabbed a pad and pen, which I always keep handy by my bedside and scribbled the words of Bella Wishes down. Bella appeared to me as a pink, belly dancing hippopotamus with a jingle hip scarf and a pink veil. I cracked up at my vision of her.

I had recently met an amazing illustrator, Dave Rodriguez, who had been doing work on other animation projects of mine that had been rolling around in my docket of intellectual properties. Dave and I met at a networking event and from the very start of our friendship he was the ground to my muses.

I called him up the next morning and said *"Hey, we have to begin right away on this other story, I have a great feeling about it...we are giving birth to Bella Wishes - a belly dancing hippopotamus."* I screamed into the phone. He replied, *"Okay Cuzzie, whatever you say!"*

I knew he was rolling his eyes on the other end of the phone, as he often did with my cast of crazy characters. No matter what characters came to me, he was right there drawing them all the way.

Bella Wishes was on the fast track to manifestation. I had a bit of money from an inheritance from my parents, and I felt the investment into this intellectual property was much safer than the stock market, so I took a chance.

By end of March, the book was illustrated. Dave had done each page in black outline. He wanted me to color the pages, so I bought a large pallet of colored markers and pencils. Every evening I curled up on my couch and colored each page. I loved this process and found it very healing and reminiscent of my favorite childhood memories.

By the third week of March, my muses woke me again in the middle of the night, but this time with a melody in my head. I grabbed my recorder, which I also kept readily available on my nightstand. And the song *Boogie with Bella* was recorded, again in one fell swoop.

I called my friend Miguelli, an amazing songwriter, who helped compose the song and record the audio tracks for the book.

By end of July, *Bella Wishes* was coming off the press, and by September I was with Baker & Taylor for book distribution for my publishing company, CarLou Interactive Media & Publishing. CarLou was the hybrid of my parents' names, Carolynn and Lou in honor of their lives and their support in my career. The name also bore a resemblance to Lucille Ball's Desilu Productions.

Bella became a fast hit. I toured the country for book signings, school assemblies, and belly dancing events. Along the way, I saw a positive reaction to belly dancing. In addition to being fun, it was a great way to address the issues of body image, body shaming, self-confidence, and self-esteem. I partnered with my belly dance teacher, Anahata to bring the culture of belly dancing to my story. She had toured with a major dance company, performed at private events, and did concerts with artists, like Sting.

Anahata and I conducted auditions for young girls to win a belly dance academy scholarship and to secure a position in the belly dance DVD, *Pink Lotus: Belly Dance for Girls of All Ages*.

Over ninety girls came from all over California to audition, including some who traveled from Las Vegas to be part of the project. We chose twelve dancers and embarked on an eight-week dance camp. Every Saturday morning these girls and their mothers arrived at the dance studio and spent their entire day dancing. We took them through empowerment workshops, which is when I realized there was an important piece of conversation missing from empowerment efforts for young girls. This piece was the relationship to themselves, each other, and between themselves and their mothers.

We chose girls with different shapes and sizes, from different places and cultures. It was an incredible environment, and one that gave my best friends daughter, Savannah, time to grieve through the unexpected death of her father.

Savannah was confused, devastated, and out of her body. We saw a progress during her time in rehearsals. I always knew that dance has an unexplainable healing impact. Each girl had a story to share. This was healing for the mothers and was consequently healing for me, as I was missing my own mom.

The Pink Lotus Dance Troupe danced at many events and community fairs, while the production of the *Pink Lotus: Belly Dance for Girls of All Ages* DVD was underway. I knew The Pink Lotus Dance Troupe was becoming a hit when I sat in the audience at the Topanga Canyon fair.

Our girls were on the stage dancing, and I was behind a group of young girls, who would each point to the one dancer that they most resonated with and say, *"Hey, my girl is the one in blue,"* — *"Yeah, mine is the one in Pink."*

I wanted the *Pink Lotus: Belly Dance for Girls of All Ages* DVD to represent various cultures, ages, and sizes of girls, to highlight their individual beauty. The Bella Wishes book was being sold in various countries: France, Spain, Canada, Mexico, and Germany, amongst others. I even shipped books overseas to schools and orphanages, and personally gave one to Archbishop Desmond Tutu and his wife, for their orphanage and school. We were all attending a World Peace Conference in Bali, 2004.

I envisioned the Bella Wishes brand going worldwide, with an animation series called *The Bella & Bo Show*. I even designed a dance clothing line for the girls to wear. While I was in Bali for the peace conference, I hired seamstresses to sew belly dance hips scarves and veils to match the outfits. I had it all going on: DVD, clothing line, accessories, story book, compilation of music, and even a Bella Wishes plush doll.

I eventually got an offer for international distribution for the DVD, but turned it down upon hearing rumors that this particular company never paid royalties. In retrospect this might not have been the right decision, but it was a decision that taught me so much. I learned that the choice in this situation is between major distribution under a bigger umbrella with no royalties or independent distribution without making any profit. In hindsight, who is to know what was the best path to take.

**Soundcloud Playlist - Boogie with Bella - Bella Wishes - Tess Cacciatore

The Bella Wishes book was turning a profit, and Bella's name was becoming known. I pitched the *Bella & Bo Show* to major production companies, all of which loved Bella, but things dragged on and the carrots dangled in front of me had to be eaten.

Through Bella, I saw firsthand the benefit of a brand and how the concept of empowerment could be given through an animated character. I saw these young girls in workshops and book signings who related to this cute hippopotamus. I saw day after day the love for Bella, through fan notes and letters from parents and teachers. I still get emails from people who say, *"Where is Bella? Isn't she due to come back out yet?"* There is something about the spirit of Bella, that she is timeless and beautiful.

From 2004 to 2008, I peddled, pitched and continued to create songs, stories, and series episodes to build the brand. My illustrator, Dave, was with me all the way, bringing to life all of the characters I created, and one by one, they all danced their way into the pitch decks. I had reached the bottom of the barrel as far as my personal funding went, but figured it was worth every penny. At that juncture I was faced with the choice of investing in my own branded content, or the stock market, and I went with my company. The following year, the stock market crashed hard, and my decision paid off. I still had something to show for my money and figure that Bella Wishes would someday have her day in the sun.

Dave was the most prolific illustrator that I had ever met. He could sit down with only a small piece of paper and pen. In no time he would draw, Charlie Brown, Mickey Mouse, Ninja Turtles, to name a few of the characters he was hired to work on over the years. But as talented as he was, and for as many of the major studios as he worked for, he never had luck holding down a job. We both needed Bella to take off.

But fate had another idea. I was devastated when I received a call from him in February of 2014. *"Hey Cuzzy,"* he said, his voice dusted with sarcasm *"you'd better come see me sometime soon… the docs are giving me eight months to live…pancreatic cancer"* The juxtaposition between the lighthearted tone of his voice and the gravity of what he was telling me made his words feel simultaneously surreal and like a bad joke. Dave always had a wicked sense of humor. Towards the end, when we realized that Dave was not going to get well, I did whatever I could to make his final days better. I helped get him moved into his stepmom's house and I visited him on a daily basis. I saw this larger than life, large-bodied man wither away to almost nothing. Less than those eight short months that the doctors gave him, Dave slipped away. The date was September 25, 2014.

I took a vial of Dave's ashes to Central Park in New York City. Dave had grown up in the Bronx, so I knew he would like part of him to end up in New York. I walked through the park with my dear songwriting partner Steve, who had known Dave for over a year over the phone. Dave had been working on Steve's characters for his animated music project.

Steve was by my side when we found a tree on a path near a tunnel and bridge. There was a jazz musician playing music nearby, and somehow this felt like the right spot. Steve and I sat in the grass and I took a stick to claw up the dirt, forming a hole. I ceremonially shifted the ashes from the vial into the ground, covering them with the soil.

As my tears watered the dirt, I looked up to the deep, blue sky and wondrous puffy, white clouds. My eyes began to focus on the trunk of the tree and on the life in the branches. Sitting on the ground gave me a different perspective of the tree. I noticed the trunk seemed to have the distinctive shape of a cartoon rabbit, with a nose, whiskers, ears and all. It was perfect to see a rabbit, because it reminded me of a million animation stills that Dave had drawn over the years. I took a photo as a keepsake. Later, I showed my friend Frank the photo and told him the story. Frank noticed that the rabbit tree was not the only magical element in the photo. He pointed to a person who happened to be walking through the background of the photograph. It was a young man wearing an oversized blue, plaid shirt, baggy pants, and black rimmed hat balanced on the back of his head. He looked so much like Dave. This guy even wore his hat balanced on the back of his head like Dave did. How many times did I say, *"Cuzzy, pull your hat down straight."* Spooky coincidence. And sometimes, I like to think of the image in the photo was the spirit of Dave, captured on this sunny day in New York City. Last joke was on me, as it was like he was laughing, *"See Cuz, I can wear my hat anyway I like over here on this side of life, and you can't tell me otherwise."*

Dave's cartoon characters live on within me, and I pray for the day when I can see them dance in the real world in honor of their illustrative creator and my creative partner in crime.

After Dave's passing, Bella Wishes was put on pause. I did not have additional funding, for the necessary marketing and I felt lost without Dave. It was time to jump on another road.

Chapter 18

The Road to Ghana

The year was 2008, I found myself on the road to Ghana,

I immersed myself back into the world of giving-back, and to empowering young people, I went back in time and woke up my passion for the World Trust Foundation. I felt this mission was deeply embedded in my soul and it was time to reconnect to this part of my life.

World Trust Foundation had taken a back seat for a few years, as I thought it would be better to be financially free, so that I could personally fund all of my humanitarian passions on my own, rather than always having to go back to the giving well of corporations and donors. However, best laid plans. I often have done and continue to do philanthropy work on a shoestring budget.

Running a nonprofit organization without proper financial support is challenging and creates a lot of doubt. I often find myself curled up in a fetal position crying to God: *"Why God... Why me? Why would you entrust me with such a huge vision, when I have no idea about running all of this? And seriously, the names of these organizations are so big: World Trust Foundation, Global Women's Empowerment Network. What am I supposed to do with this?"*

Even though I often shook my fist to heaven, I always found my way back to the life of giving back. Moral obligations from my childhood, the passion to help others, regardless of the global and worldly names attached to this vision. I prayed that I would grow into the largeness of this mission and that God would provide.

At this time I wanted to return my focus on the young leaders of the world and to shine a spotlight on their talents and their inspirations to make the world a better place.

The two programs that had me excited during the World Trust days, was Earth Heroes and Young Leaders.

Beginning in 2000, my life was dedicated to activism, environmentalism, renewable energy, and saving the planet.

We needed to inspire young leaders to carve the path to do the right thing. My activists friends, John Quigley, Matt Peterson, Tim Carmichael, Susan Cox, Lori Woodley, Atossa Soltani, filmmakers like Josh and Rebecca Tickell, Mikki Willis, and other organizations like Sea Shepards, Tree People and all the great work Dr. Jane Goodall has done with the inspiration that was fueled by passion. I had the extreme honor to work with Dr Goodall through the years and she is one of my major she-roes.

I am blessed to be surrounded by the movers and shakers, the creators and the instigators who go up against the system to make noise in all the right places. The names of those who inspire me and do great work is too vast to mention here.

I wanted to live up to the name of the World Trust Foundation, so I created an international contest for Young Leaders called *Your Voice - Your Choice*. We created a viral video and began using social media to inspire young people from ages 18-26 to apply for the Young Leaders contest. The end result was to have the winner travel to the United States to partake in a Young Leaders Summit to be held in Los Angeles. However, the best laid plans sometimes get shifted to another reality. This was a time when I had to surrender to what showed up and it became my fate to be on the road to Ghana. This road took me on a spin so fast that I was reeling for many years. It was my path to hope and my path to hopeful love. Have you ever been on one of those paths, not knowing which way to go?

So, young people from around the world submitted to one of the five categories, which included: social awareness, sustainability, animal preservation, water conservation, and human rights through written word, videos, and photographs to this contest.

The launch of *Your Voice - Your Choice* was a symbolic thrust of enthusiasm to get the young leaders from our country and from around the world to join forces and let their passions be known. The entries for the contest came in from all around the world. In particular, I noticed there was an enormous reaction from Ghana. At this point in time, I knew very little about Ghana. I had no idea the impact that this country would have on my life. The Ghana entries for the contest was led by a young man by the name of Samuel Martinson, who lived in Accra. I appointed him to be the Country Director of Ghana.

In response to the contest, I decided to organize a 3-day conference in Ghana, for the seventy young Ghanaian applicants to attend. I considered them all to be the leaders of the contest and wanted to award them all, instead of simply electing one individual to be crowned. The group was a wonderful mix of young men and women, who were all dedicated in a variety of fields and passions.

A very generous friend from Canada donated his airline miles and the conference in Ghana was on. Samuel helped me organize everything from the hotel conference rooms, the house that we would stay in, and the housing for the young leaders who had to travel to Accra. There were many of the young leaders who came from far away. Some of them took over ten hours by bus to get to the conference.

Samuel greeted me at the airport and I met the most amazing young people, who many are still in my life today.

We opened the first day with a meditation of an oak tree, in which I presented them with a picture of a small acorn and then with a picture of a grown oak tree. We talked about what the acorn represented, and how the smallest acorn, given the right environment and determination could grow into the most magnificent tree in the forest.

I had them visualizing that they were that oak tree, standing strong. The meditation took them deeper into the roots of the tree, into their individual roots. At a certain point I guided them into feeling their roots alongside the other trees and for them to visualize an entire forest of these amazing oak trees standing together in unity. None of them had meditated before, and it was fascinating to listen to their experiences. To this day I still get messages from the young leaders telling me about their oak trees, about how they are still growing strong.

During the three-day conference we did breakout workshops and visited a local orphanage in the Oso District. Most of the young leaders had never been to an orphanage, even thought it was in their own backyard. We were all united in our gratitude for the opportunity to give back. I brought art supplies from the United States so that the young leaders had the experience of doing art projects with the children.

Visiting orphanages has always been bittersweet for me. It is difficult not to be overwhelmed with the urge to take all the children home with me. No matter where I have volunteered, whether I was in South Africa, Ghana, Thailand, Vietnam, El

Salvador, Cambodia, or Sri Lanka, leaving is never easy, and almost without fail, I crumble the minute I leave.

Over the course of the conference, Samuel's cousin Ruba and I became good friends. Ruba worked at a local television station, so we were able to get the Young Leaders on the morning talk show to be interviewed. At the end of our three-day conference we held a ceremony in which the Young Leaders received awards, along with a gift of shoes from one of our sponsors, TOMS®Shoes.

At the end of the ceremony, I was exhausted, but Saturday night beckoned, and I was itching to venture out and explore this amazing country. Samuel and my driver took me to the local expat market to get food. The market was a breath of fresh air, and I welcomed a break from the traditional goat that is so ubiquitous in traditional Ghanaian cuisine. A man's voice came over the PA system, *"Good evening customers... we will be closing the store in five short minutes. Please proceed to the checkout line."* The announcement was in English, something I appreciated guiltily, knowing that English was only the primary language in Ghana because it was colonized by Britain in the 1700s. As we know, European nations who colonized much of Africa, India, and parts of Asia dictated what language was part of their culture and the language learned in the process of colonization. Many Ghanians speak English, alongside at least one of their many tribal languages.

Standing in the aisle of the expat market I saw Samuel out of the corner of my eye waiting patiently for me to finish shopping. My eyes were fixated on the bottle of Pinotage that I held in my hands. This particular bottle of wine was from Kanonkop Estates, situated on the lower slopes of the Simonsberg Mountain in the

Stellenbosch Region of Cape Town, South Africa. I had actually been to this winery while traveling through South Africa in 2002.

The voice came over the PA again, *"Good evening shoppers...our store is now closed. Please proceed to the checkout lane."* I slipped the bottle into my grocery basket, alongside the olives, bread, cheese, chocolate, and went to the checkout stand.

Samuel and the driver took me back to the guest house. We finally had access to the internet, which was not the case for the past few days. The evening felt too special to hole-up in my room, so I gathered my treats and my laptop and proceeded to the front porch. I hugged Samuel and the driver goodbye, as they headed off to spend the evening with their families. Rarely do I feel lonely, but I felt a pang in my stomach that I was missing something that I could not put my finger on. Perhaps it was a special man in my life who could experience this adventure with me... but I had learned to push this feeling out of my head, and replace it with calm. I was alone again and that was all right. Being alone had become a familiar feeling.

**Soundcloud Playlist - Into the Dark - Jesse Cook

As I sipped my wine, I looked up. The African sky was breathtaking. These skies are some of the most powerful paintings from God than one can ever imagine. The summer breeze was just strong enough to slightly ripple my hair. I felt like I was in a National Geographic movie.

I signed on to Facebook for the first time in days, and posted *"I am here in Ghana, drinking South African wine, with the summer African breezes blowing ... with a great evening ahead."* I laughed at myself when I pushed the post button: what was going to be so great about sitting here alone on a Saturday night? But the power of manifestation came into play in less than three minutes. A car pulled up to the compound gate. I heard the loud beep of a horn.

Most of the homes in Africa are called compounds, which are enclosed by tall cement walls and heavy iron gates. The security guard got up from his post and pulled open the gate. This mysterious car crunched its way over the cobblestones, driving close to the porch. The driver parked the car several feet away from me. I waited with anticipation to see who would come out of the car. It was definitely not the other Americans who were staying at the house with me.

The passenger door opened. A stout, smiling man stepped out of the car. He waved to me as he approached the porch. *"Hello… welcome to my home. I heard that the internet was not working, so I wanted to stop by and make sure that all was fine. I'm the owner here… I'm Nana."* He extended his hand and shook my hand with friendly vigor. He had a magnificent smile that stretched completely across his face. The person in the driver seat stepped out of the car. This one had more of a swagger to his walk. Nana motioned for his friend to approach, *"This is Maxwell. We were at a party and I persuaded my friend to drive me over here to make sure that the Americans were taken care of with the internet."*

Maxwell stepped forward and also shook my hand.

I replied to Nana, *"I'm good… the internet is on and I'm enjoying the beautiful evening in your lovely home."*

The house chef stepped out the door and greeted Nana. They spoke in (Akan) so I was not sure what was said, but it seemed they were staying for dinner. I thought I was going to be alone, but the evening was turning into a merry party of three.

Nana and Maxwell sat at my table and the chef came out with goat stew. The two men sipped and sucked the spicy soup, complete with bones, all while dipping their hands straight into the soup to grab clumps of foofoo, which is boiled ground casava that is used as a starch much like our mashed potatoes. I was happy to be diving into my plate of cheese and sipping wine.

We all laughed the way immediate kindred spirits tend to do. Nana is the typical name for those in the Ashanti monarch, which also signifies cultural status. I had to find a way to distinguish this Nana from the many other Nana's that I knew, so I gave him the nickname 'Chinese Brother' as his broad smile and lighter color of his skin differed greatly from the other Ghanaians. He liked his given nickname, so he decided that I was his 'Chinese Sister.' No disrespect to any culture, as it was in fun and from a place of love.

On the other hand, Maxwell looked completely Ghanaian. He was quieter than Nana, but he smiled a lot and seemed nice. The Ghanaian culture gave their children three names; the first was a Christian name, the middle was always the tribal names of the day of the week they were born, and the third, is their surname.

It did not take long for a mutual and instantaneous kinship to be felt between Maxwell and me. After a couple of hours of laughing, eating and drinking, Maxwell asked if I wanted to go dancing. I heard myself blurt out, without pause, "*Yes!*" I was finally going to get out and see Accra in all its nighttime glory. I quickly changed my clothes, fluffed my hair, and was ready to have some fun.

The three of us climbed into the car. The guard opened the heavy gate and waved us out onto the dusty red, dirt road. There was nothing more beautiful than the red, dirt clay that served as the roads in Ghana. The night was dark but I could still see the reflection of the red clay from the headlights.

Chinese Brother decided that he was not up for the club, so we dropped him off at a taxi stand. We waved him goodbye and waited for him to get into a cab. Maxwell turned to me to say, *"I miss you."* I laughed, *"How can you miss me when I am sitting right here?"* He answered by saying something that I had always wanted to hear; a man with conviction and clarity. Maxwell continued, *"I am missing you now as I will miss you when you are gone. When I first saw you sitting on the porch I knew you were the woman I was going to marry."*

My heart skipped a few beats. It was as corny a line as they come, and one spoken from the lips many African men to many women ... or Greek men to women ... or Italian men to women ... but it was also something I had been praying for, so part of me wanted it to be true. I was tired of the men in my life giving me mixed signals until I was ready to leave. I wanted a man who knew it was love from the start.

Who was I to turn the answer to my prayer away? I had an obligation to at least play it out for the duration of my trip. My reply to him was, *"Just to let you know, I don't have any money and I will not be having sex with you until we are committed to be married. And, I will not be doing this for you to get a green card to America."* I figured this would lose his attention with the clear lines drawn in the sand. However, he instead grabbed me and hugged me hard. *"Thank you for being you!"* If he had any concoctions in his mind that I was some wealthy or stupid girl, then he had another thing coming.

As it turned out, the rest of the night was great. We pulled into the parking lot of the nightclub, and I instantly heard the Euro-hip, African beat music thumping the ground. Maxwell knew the bouncers, the bartenders, and of course the bevy of beautiful

African women who all eyed me up and down wondering who this blonde chick was, and why she was dancing with Maxwell.

**Soundcloud Playlist - Do Me - P Square

I laid it all on the floor that night as I was long overdue for a great night out dancing. Maxwell was a perfect gentleman. He took me safely home a few hours later. The next four days sped by with great traction. Everything seemed extra special underneath the canopy of the African sky. I felt so much at home, there was a familiarity about the land that made me think I could make Ghana my second home. I discussed the opportunity of opening a Ghana office for the World Trust Foundation to serve the Young Leaders. The prospects were exciting.

My final day in Ghana was sad. Maxwell took me to the airport. It was a long and quiet ride, and the car was thick with our combined stress and sadness. We had connected so deeply in such a short period of time, it felt surreal to say goodbye so soon.

I came back home to Los Angeles with my heart on fire. All of my girlfriends were taken aback by the story of my newfound romance.

They were so happy for me as it had been over a year since I had been in a relationship, with a guy who was a two and a half year of non-commitment. My friends knew my love for Africa, and they loved the idea of an African wedding. Everyone seemed to jump on the fantasy train with me, and we all had fun dreaming up plans. But before I could start seriously considering a future, I wanted Maxwell to come to the United States to see if we could transpire into something real. We could live part time in Ghana and part time in the United States.

However, the US embassy gave Maxwell a hard time of obtaining a VISA. Every week had more challenging news. Maxwell and I spoke every other day and our bond grew. December was nearing and I felt the clock ticking to find out if this relationship was real.

Soundcloud Playlist - In Your Eyes - Peter Gabriel

I reached out to one of my girlfriends, Dina, who owned a clothing store in the neighborhood. This store was a retail therapy chit/chat place where women gathered to buy clothes, eat lunch, and gossip about their lives. She and I were saddened that another VISA had been declined, and that Maxwell was having trouble traveling to the States. Dina mentioned that she had not seen me this low since my parents had passed away. I had to agree. I felt my future was wrapped up in the answer to this crazy question.

Dina looked at me with big eyes, *"How much mileage do you need to get a ticket?"* I said, *"I have no idea. Its close to the holiday so it might be a lot. I don't have any miles."* She blurted out, *"Give me ten minutes, I might have the answer for you."* She called her husband. Tim made a few calls and found out they had enough miles for my ticket. Dina and I jumped around the store as if we were high school girls who just got asked to the prom. Dina loved helping others' dreams come true, and my dream was getting back to Ghana.

As my December trip to Ghana was coming together, Maxwell and I were in a good place. We talked daily, and he was attentive, loving, and excited. Every step of the way he was generous with affection and on occasion when I saw a provocative posting from other women on Facebook, he took the posting down and deleted her from his friends. He wanted me to feel secure, as he knew I had men in my past who cheated on me. The road to Ghana was a long and winding road. There were signs along the way, but sometimes we need to make the journey so that we can experience the flight.

**Soundcloud Playlist - Long and Winding Road - Beatles

My flight to Ghana had me arrive in Accra on Christmas Eve. I thought it appropriate to arrive on the eve of the birth of Christ, it signified a new beginning, a new life. Christmas is also extremely important to Ghanaians. They begin celebrating around the twelve of December and continue until the end of January.

It was a long, anticipated wait through customs. As I rounded the corner of the airport lobby, I saw Maxwell's beaming face through the glass wall that separated the people arriving from those waiting for their loved ones. In the car ride from the airport, I looked out the window to see a city that was on fire with dancers, drummers and music streaming from cars and houses.

**Soundcloud Playlist - No One Like You - P Square

Maxwell had spent a lot of time preparing for my arrival. He moved from a one-bedroom apartment that he shared with his thirteen-year-old son, Sal, to a three-bedroom house that could accommodate us all.

Sal was visiting Maxwell's family in Northern Ghana, so Maxwell and I had some time to settle into our new home. Before my arrival, Maxwell spent weeks painting, scrubbing, and moving his furniture into the new house. He worked long hours to get the 'palace for his Queen' ready. I had brought many things from the States to decorate the house, as I wanted to feel at home as well.

The first couple of days were fine. Nothing spectacular, just fine! There were many cultural differences that we had to navigate, including everyday conversation, but things seemed fine. We spent every night with his friends, but not the same friends I had made when I was there in August. Our home was far away from the center of Accra, so I was meeting all new people. This group of people felt different.

There were a lot of adjustments to work on before we could ever lead to marriage. There were a couple of red flags, but I remained hopeful. I had my eyes on the prize of a wonderful African wedding, and perhaps the blessing of a baby.

New Year's Eve was fast approaching. I wanted to do something special, like go to dinner and dancing. Maxwell wanted to go to church. I have no problem with going to church on any occasion, but this particular church was far from our house in a building had no air circulation with a minister that would give a sermon that would last for hours, spoken in a language that I did not understand. I saw myself passing out before they rang in midnight. We went back and forth deciding what to do until we settled on going out to dinner near our home. By the end of dinner we were starting to argue, so we were home by 11:30.

Maxwell turned the television on to the Christian channel and he blasted the volume until my last nerve was struck. He intended to listen to the sermon to bring in the New Year. The minister yelled loudly. I think Maxwell turned up the volume to add to my frustration. A trick he would end up doing often. I resigned to the fact that this was my most rotten New Year's celebration. I went to sleep. Happy New Year! Boo!

Despite the disappointing beginning to my new year, I was looking forward to the roadtrip to the village where Maxwell's parents lived to meet his son. We packed the car full of boxes containing all sorts of food, a seventy-pound bag of rice, and house supplies that we would give to his relatives as gifts. I paid for it all, as Maxwell was waiting for money to come in from his business.

The night sky was black when we got on the road at the godly hour of 3:30 a.m. As we drove, the sunrise began to stir in the sky just above the outskirts of town. I saw women come out of their homes heading to their spots on the road to sell their wares. Trained from an early age to carry heavy and awkward objects on their head, they balance large trays and baskets on top of their heads filled with whatever the family will try to sell for the day. One particular notable time, I saw a woman carrying a small refrigerator on her head. In Ghana, you can purchase just about anything from the window of your car; chicklet gum, toilet paper, kitchen towels, office supplies. Even if you want to get married, you can drive down the road and purchase everything you need for a wedding, including the wedding dress.

Our road trip to Maxwell's family alternated between bumpy, paved roads to red dirt paths with deep crevices. I was nauseous as we swerved around potholes, large trucks, honking cars, and pedestrians in the early morning rush.

The military police stopped us at every juncture with their hand held out, wanting a pay-off, each one of them stating that they needed their Christmas gift. I knew they were pulling us over because there was an 'obruni' in the car. Obruni is the Ghanaian term for white person.

When the tenth officer pulled us over and asked for a Christmas gift, I was out of sorts. I respectfully said, *"Excuse me Officer, but Christmas has already passed... why are you still asking for Christmas gifts?"* He puffed under his breath and waved us onward.

We drove deep into the rainforest. The green canopy and lush landscape were simultaneously peaceful and breathtaking. We ascended into a very remote village in the eastern region of Ghana with food and fruit stands on either side of the road. There was a cemetery alongside the road where small, round headstones were surrounded by tiny, green puffy bushes. Maxwell spent most of his childhood growing up in this village. His father was the manager of a chocolate factory, as most of the cacao in the world is farmed in these remote areas. Nestle has a headquarters in Accra.

As we drove down the village road, Maxwell reminisced about his father and the chocolate factory, I was having a flashback of my own, of a time when I was in Switzerland. The year was 2001, and I was attending the Sub-Commission for Human Rights, which happens every March, at the United Nations, in Geneva Switzerland.

I had a major 'aha' moment in which I realized that chocolate and cheese were somehow connected and that environment played a big part in the quality of both of these delicious food items. In my 'aha' moment, I came to the conclusion that cheese and chocolate should be categorized into their own food group. Taking this epiphany a step further, I set out to film a story about chocolate and cheese. Gruyere is a quaint medieval village that looks like a surreal movie set that couldn't be real. This Swiss town is the place where Gruyere cheese is made. I contacted the marketing department of Gruyere and scheduled a visit. I did the same for Cailler chocolate, which is located in

Broc, Switzerland. Both of these factories are not far from one another and they are nestled between the alps, with deep, blue skies and bright red flowers that pop out from the meadows that line the mountain roads.

The flow of the trip fell into place like magic. As a filmmaker from Hollywood, I obtained permission to film the process of cheese and chocolate in each of these townships. I took with me my friend Kim, who had been at the United Nations with our other friend Camille.

Kim and I took off to the township of Gruyere. We arrived at the cheese factory just before lunch, which turned out to be perfect timing to film the process of how they made one of my favorite cheeses. The tour guide was generous. He took us to a lovely veranda with a breathtaking view of the Swiss Alps and surprised us with a delicious lunch of salad, baguette, plenty of Gruyere cheese, and wine.

We finished with a flourish and drove about an hour down the road to the Cailler chocolate factory. While filming the chocolate factory, we captured the workers and the large vats of chocolate coming off the assembly line. At one point Kim and I had to take the obligatory photo resembling Lucy and Ethel in the famous chocolate factory scene from *I Love Lucy*.

The next morning, we visited a small dairy farm where I filmed the milking of the cows. These were all sweet, Swiss cows who were well fed, greatly loved, and not at all treated like the dairy cows found in some American dairy factories. The point of view that I had for this piece was if the environment was out of sorts, what with famine, drought, or chemicals used in farming, the milk from the cows would be out of sorts too. In my mind, milk based cheese and chocolate could be greatly affected by the milk's quality and taste. I figured this might be a fun piece to produce for a kids program, as kids want good cheese on their pizza, and great tasting chocolate. If the kids began to see the connection between the environment and their favorite foods, perhaps they would be passionate about taking care of the environment.

A loud jolt interrupted my reverie as Maxwell pulled over to assess the deep pockets on the road. We were nearing the turn-off to this family's place. The road swiftly turned into a path with rocks and dirt. This was the only way to get to his family, so we were grateful there was no rain. We turned our car down a curved path, which looked more like it should be used for walking and not for a car, and of course our car got stuck. Maxwell beeped the horn twice. Several kids ran out of the tall grass from every direction. They pushed and pulled the car over the bumps. Our car finally wobbled to the entrance of their compound.

His family was scattered throughout the area. When they heard our car approaching, they all came running. The troupe was led by Maxwell's mother, who ran up and gave him a hug. They all seemed to circle around me and stare. I am not sure if they knew who I was to Maxwell. Maxwell's son, Sal, ran up to greet us. I had spoken to him on Skype so there was a familiarity between us. He gave me a big hug. They all grabbed items out of the trunk and seemed profusely grateful to Maxwell for the gifts. The fact that the gifts were from both of us, let alone that I paid for them, seemed to have been lost in translation.

They walked us over to an open-seated area. I took my place on a tree stump where I was seated within the circle of their conversation, but not quite included. Since his family did not speak English, I had no idea what was being said. I put a smile on my face and nodded my head to and fro pretending to be a part of the party. I was supposedly introduced to them as his fiancé, but in retrospect, I could have been anyone in his life.

I looked around at the lush landscape. Even though Maxwell's family did not have modern conveniences, their life seemed peaceful. There were small shacks that made up the living quarters. One shack for sleeping, an open-air hut for bathing, and at the center of it all, a large cave-like stove that served as their outdoor kitchen.

I loved watching the children and the way they played with each other rather than with phones, computers, and modern-day gadgets. The dogs chased the chickens and the chickens turned around and chased the dogs. I laughed out loud. Maxwell and his family looked at me. I shrugged my shoulders and looked to the ground.

Maxwell was having an intense conversation with his parents. Their voices rose and fell dramatically. I had the feeling I was part of that conversation, but one could never tell. I grabbed my camera and began taking pictures so that I would not appear too curious about their conversation.

Waves of tiredness consumed me. I feel sleepy-nods coming over me, as I had only gotten two hours of sleep the night before. I drifted in and out of listening, being lulled by the cadence of their lyrical language, which seemed to consist of their native tongue laced in with the sounds of French.

Maxwell's sister had been hovering over hot coals in the outdoor kitchen area. I had only seen the backside of her since we arrived. She was focused on her mission of shoving trays into the outdoor oven. She took a long stick and moved things around the flames. After about an hour she began taking the trays out of the oven. A woody, nutty scent filled the air. She handed a few of the warm bundles to one of the children, who brought one to each of us to eat.

I held this warm, wrapped banana leaf in my hands. As I unwrapped the leaf the sweet aroma of sugar and corn filled my nose. I scooped up the sweet mess and let it melt on my tongue. We had not eaten yet, so this was the most delicious treat I had so far.

His sister was sweating from her laborious work. She was dressed in a tired sarong. She stood away from the fire and wiped the sweat from her forehead. She arranged her wrapped delights on a large tray. She was quiet, like a silent storm. She walked across our path and dipped behind a curtain in a single standing hut that served as their shower, letting her sarong fall to the ground. I heard the shower water trickle, as she sang a song from inside.

She came out a few minutes later dressed in a brightly colored traditional dress. She had a long stretch of matching fabric in her hands and without thought she craftily wrapped it around her head. This headdress, aside from being beautiful, served the purpose controlling her hair, as well as creating the leveled support on her head for the tray of sweets to be carried.

She draped a white-lace fabric over her tray to keep bugs from flying on her food. As she balanced the large tray on her head she walked through the gate and onto the dirt road. As an after-thought, she turned and waved goodbye to the family.

I noticed other women with baskets on their heads, bobbing in and out of the tall grass in the distance. Throughout my global travels I photographed many of these women from around the world with baskets on their heads and baby bundles on their backs. I would always wonder about the story of their lives, and for the first time, here it was staring me right in the face.

After an hour I was satiated. I was ready to leave. We headed down to Kumasi, which is in the Ashanti region, for the weekend. Chinese Brother owned a hotel down there, so we were able to meet up with him, and others I considered to be friends, including a prince from the Ashanti tribe. We all had a great time, and that weekend we formed the Ghana World Trust Board of Directors. I had hope once again as the charming side of Maxwell came out, and a light energy filled the air.

The weekend flew by without incident. On our way home, we dropped back to the village to pick up Sal. Driving back through the rainforest was even more amazing than I remembered. Once we were back home in Accra, we settled into a routine. The problem was that the routine only consisted of what Maxwell wanted to do. I did not see Ruba, Chinese Brother, Samuel, or any of my other friends for many days. At times Maxwell left the house for hours at a time, leaving me to watch Sal and on occasion, Sal's younger half brother, who was from another mother. I love children, so this was fine with me, but I began to feel disrespected, something that was hard to communicate to Maxwell, who referred to himself as the 'king' of his domain. Things were beginning to go south.

The Golden Chicken and Black Swan

One of the simple pleasures of my life with Maxwell was going to the 'Keep-Fit Club' every Sunday morning at 6:45 a.m. The fitness group was started by an ex-Belgium police sergeant who had retired twenty-years earlier. The sergeant was married to a local woman, and he wanted to keep in shape by providing a military boot camp for the locals. There were about a hundred members in the group, and they met on the grounds of a high school, which had miles of paved paths and rolling hills. This provided several terrains for hiking, jogging, and military-style calisthenics.

Every Sunday, I began the hike with them, but after thirty-minutes, they started on their military run. I can only imagine what I must have looked like lined up behind all of these Africans (mostly men) in a single file line running down the road, their legs in long stride, swinging their arms strongly as they sang African chants to keep them in line and in time. Then there was me towards the end of the line with my recyclable designer water bottle swinging from my hip and my iPod earplugs, listening to the music that motivated me to keep to the beat. I must have looked like this strange golden chicken in a line of beautiful swans.

When they began to jog I slowly edged myself out of the line and ran to my special spot under the trees where I could disappear and do yoga. I kicked off my tennis shoes and exhaled. Barefoot, under the shade of the trees, I dug my toes into the cool red dirt, as the heat of the day was fast approaching with the rising sun in the African sky.

The 'Keep-Fit' troupe rounded the corner. I could hear their chants in the distance. They ended their run in an area near me. The leader had them all on the ground for core work and squats. I got out of yoga mode and went to ride the rest of the torture with them. My favorite part was the end of the workout when we headed for food and a cold Star beer under the heat of the sun and the beauty of the day.

The Conch Shell

The good times I did have while in Ghana were mostly because of the Young Leaders in my life, so I created a one-day reunion conference. We gathered at a local university along with several hundred other college students. The night before the conference, I had a dream where I was standing on top of a mountain with a large conch shell in my hands. I was holding the shell up to the sky, talking through it like a megaphone. The valley below had a beautiful forest and the sky above was deep blue with large, white clouds.

The next day at the conference, a few of my young leaders stood up to make a presentation to me. Wilson, Colin, Abraham, Nana, and so many others who are still in my heart, gave me the name of 'Mama Tess' and presented me with a gift that was symbolic and prophetic.

They held this gift behind their backs while they spoke of their time at the 'Your Voice - Your Choice' conference. Wilson stepped forward and pulled out a large conch shell. The exact shell from my dream the night before. Carefully penned, with a black sharpie, they wrote the following words: *"To Mama Tess Cacciatore, for your tremendous effort to develop the African Society, May the Lord Protect You in all your endeavors as a shell protects its host. Africa will forever love you, Mum."*

Tears flowed down my cheeks as the rest of the students stood and applauded for the young men and the beautiful gift. I told them about my dream. This was the magic I craved and the fuel that kept me going in life. I loved these people, and I am still so grateful to the core group who I continue to remain in touch. All of them have now graduated from college, entered the workforce, and started their own families. Wilson received his nursing degree, and has published several books of his poetry. I am as proud of them all as any Mama Tess could be. I was inspired by them all and wanted them to have a voice. I ended each workshop with them standing in a circle, letting go of the past that held them back. The "blueprint" workshops that I still do today.

Soundcloud Playlist - Say - John Mayer

I planned a health and wellness day for the spring in which the World Trust Foundation would partner with local charities and major corporations in Ghana. It would be a way we could launch young leaders' initiatives. Between my passion for renewable energy, and my contacts around the world, I could bring great things to the farmers, hospitals, and schools in Ghana, and throughout Africa.

I planned to invite Ghana-based corporations to take part in this two-day fair, but Maxwell discouraged me, saying that it was impossible to meet any of them and that he was handling things. He would leave the house for hours on supposed meeting with these contacts. I had neither transport nor knowledge of the local area, and our house was almost an hour out of Accra. I was finally fed up of being kept at home with no way to get out, so I called the corporations myself. By the end of the first day of making calls I set up several appointments with major banks and corporations. That success did not fare well with Maxwell, as I was proving him wrong.

I set up a visit in Dodowa, which is a progressive township outside of Accra. I set meetings with doctors at the local hospital and with a coalition of farmers who had acres of land across from the hospital. I traveled with a group of young leaders who were interested in renewable energy and sustainable growth in Ghana. I wanted to create a pilot program that could be emulated in other regions.

We planned to outfit the maternity ward of the hospital with solar energy. This could help when power outages occurred, which happened often in remote areas. The doctors explained that this could prevent babies dying during childbirth, as would happen when the electricity went out in the middle of a birth. I found out that the hospital needed prenatal monitors, so I wrote my friend, Dr Mark Z, who is part of the OB-GYN department at Cedar Sinai. Dr Mark donated several prenatal machines for their hospital and Airline Ambassadors donated the services to get the machines transported to the hospital within that year.

We visited a coalition of farmers near the hospital and explored solar energy options, which would also prove a great solution for their electrical needs. These farmers were dedicated to their children having a great education, and solar panels offered electricity options during the night when the children had to do their homework, or late night farming for their crops.

These farmers had cassava, avocado, and bananas. Each family employed their multi-generational relatives to do tasks within their farms. It was fascinating to watch the elders mix with the grandchildren, all partaking in the various stages of a farming to create a successful business.

With all the advancements that were occurring for me in Ghana, I was still missing something. I wanted the World Trust Foundation in have an office in Ghana. Through the help of Chinese Brother, we identified a building that could serve as our community offices. This was motivation for me to be in Ghana on a part-time basis. However, I was not willing to move there and become a silent woman in the background, waiting to be addressed.

Every night when we went out I was stuck at a table full of people who chose to talk around me, about me, but never to me, and never in English.

Neither Maxwell, nor any of his friends realized that I sat in silence hour after hour, night after night, week after week. I begged Maxwell to include me in their conversations. He said they felt insecure speaking English to an American, or that they did not like me because I never talked to them. The mental games continued. The women took advantage of the situation and my obvious discomfort. They would rub Maxwell's head, sit on his lap, and laugh between jokes spoken in their native tongue. The quick glances, the attitude all served a purpose to wear me down. And it was working. I was feeling desperately alone.

During my silent times, while the party went on around me, I looked up to the African sky and saw the stars twinkling. I prayed for God to shed light on the situation.

Orion in the Sky

It was the winter sky, so my favorite constellation, Orion, the hunter in the sky, was easily found. In those moments, I interpreted the mythology of Orion as an ongoing search for his lost love, with him pointing his arrow to the heavens hunting for love. I realized that I too was still searching. Searching for answers to the questions that I continued to ask myself. Searching for my true love.

I shared my innermost thoughts with Orion and the other stars in the sky, as there was no one else to talk to me.

I realized that I had to see how I was responsible for finding these relationships that gave no relief. I simply wanted to lay my heart in the hands of someone who I could trust. Someone who would be there for me as I would be there for them. Someone who would have my back and love me for who I was, with all my completeness and incompleteness. To lay my heart in their hands and just be me. I realized that this was something I had to do for myself, but I had no idea how to begin. Instead, I decided to lay my heart in the hands of God and pray.

Along with the emotional and verbal abuse I took from Maxwell, I let him take advantage of me financially as well. I paid for all the services of the house, figuring that this was going to be my house as well. However, every day there seemed to be a new service provider stopping by, including the cement person for the driveway, the cleaning person, the clothes washer, dry cleaning, food, fuel for the car, and of course I cannot forget the endless visits from the plumber, which never ended successfully. We did not have a septic tank and no individual supply of water so we were out of luck when the township decided to shut off water or electricity, which happened on a daily basis.

We had to fill large garbage cans and smaller buckets with water to keep in the bathroom and kitchen. Then, we kept even smaller buckets near the shower and sink so that we were able to wash ourselves, cook food, and do dishes.

Bucket showers were not my favorite way of cleansing myself, but I chose to go with the flow. This was not a hard task for a man with a shaved head, but for a woman with shampoo, blow dryers, and makeup, it was a challenge to get ready to go anywhere. At times there was no electricity and we had very high humidity, Certainly no one can dare call me high-maintenance after that adventure, as I was always was in great spirits and I found the humor in it all. Accra is filled with wonderful hotels and restaurants but not where we lived. I did my best to take it all in and love the adventure.

Our neighborhood was culturally mixed. There were a lot of expats around us, so I felt comfort in going to the local Ghanaian churches and the pubs to watch soccer. There was a Mosque across the street from our house, so I was often awakened by the sound of the 'call to prayer' in the morning and throughout the day. I loved the sound of the voices that rang through the neighborhood.

In the months since my arrival, Maxwell began treating me more like his servant and less like his queen. He treated his son the same. When it came time to register Sal for winter session in school, Maxwell feigned to not have any money for his education. I found myself taking the last bit of money I had, which was to be used for my car payment back home, and put the money towards his schooling. I could not stand to see a child suffer. I figured that my problems would work out and at least this boy could have a better chance with an education. Although doing this put me in a financial quandary, it was worth it to see him off to school each morning.

Before going to school each day, Sal got up at 5:00 a.m. to wash his father's car in the dark of the night. He also had the task of sweeping all the floors with a whiskbroom, if you could call it that, as it barely had any whisks to the broom. I do agree that children should learn responsibility through chores, but before school, without breakfast, in the dark of the night was a bit overboard in my book.

I happily got up and made him breakfast for his bus ride to school each morning. He had never had an egg sandwich, or any proper breakfast for that matter, so in the tradition of my dad, who always made our lunches for school, and breakfast I tried to make sure Sal always had something to eat before heading out the door. I was not raised to see a child in need. This did not seem to affect Maxwell. He only seemed relieved that I stepped up to take care of his son.

I was there when Sal came home from school and I helped him with his homework. This fulfilled a part of me that was missing, the part of me that wanted to raise my own children. My relationship with his son was a pleasant surprise, and it awakened me to the excitement of a possibility of having my own child.

I noticed that Sal was having trouble at school and that he was much farther behind his studies than other kids his age. Maxwell shared that he had given his son over to his own mother while Sal was a toddler, so that Maxwell could start his business. The grandmother was worn out raising her own children, so Sal was never watched. Left to his own devices, he never went to school. He slowly began slipping behind his peers and by the time I came into his life, he had the equivalent of a 4th grade education, but the age of an 8th grader.

They have great schools and access to education in Accra, so it was not like he was held back in a village with no school or teachers. My heart ached for his son, as he and I were connected in a deep way. Sal hid in his room during the day and cried himself to sleep at night. There was no love or affection coming from his father. This behavior told me a lot about this man.

I asked Maxwell why he treated his son like "Cinder-fella." Obviously, the reference to Cinderella went over his head. As I continued to show love to Sal, he began to blossom. I felt that it was through my actions that Maxwell finally started to see his son with different eyes. One day Maxwell actually thanked me for giving him a relationship with his son. That was worth the entire price of admission. His son was a warm-hearted child, as his father revealed a cold-hearted side, that I did not think possible.

Almost on a daily basis Maxwell would disappear for many hours, always on some vague trip to town that would benefit us. I wanted to go with him, but he always had a reason as to why I needed to stay home. Maxwell had strict eyes when it came to me on Facebook, or when I spoke to any of his friends. However, he saw nothing wrong with stepping out on the porch at night to take a call from a woman, or have a waitress sit on his lap, laughing, looking at me with treacherous eyes.

When Maxwell left me alone each day, I began to walk the dirt roads down to the main street. I must have looked out of place amongst the chickens and the goats that followed me down the road. I got really good at talking to the goats. They would say, "*Baaaaaa*" and I would say "*Bahhaaahhhaaa*." I think I had better communication with the goats than with Maxwell. Due to the fact that most of the Ghanaians ate goat, and I never did, they did not like me talking to the goats. They thought that I had a special telepathic communication with the goats and I was telling them to run in the opposite direction. Perhaps they were right.

A Rose by Any Other Name

My internal voice and intuition were getting louder now. My gut was twisted and I knew there was something amiss. Finally, I got Maxwell to crack. He came clean and told me that he was actually already married. His wife was not in the country and they were estranged. Her family was from a neighboring village. They had a tribal wedding about six years prior, and the only thing they needed to dissolve their marriage was getting the priest to go to the family and ask them to return a bottle of liquor that was given during the ceremony. Seriously? Return a liquor bottle and that dissolved their marriage? If it was that easy, then why was it taking so long for Maxwell to persuade the priest to go to their village and do so? And why, did he not tell me that he was married?

Some of the pieces began to fall into place, but I still felt there were many secrets left untold. I was suspicious of a woman named Rose, who had friended me on Facebook. She lived in Switzerland, but was mutual friends with Maxwell. Finally, my suspicion rose to the surface that I was not introduced to his family as his fiancé. He finally admitted that he told his family that I was his business partner, which is why they had an argument with him, as they were wondering about when the marriage would be dissolved.

This news was devastating to me. We began to argue every day and I am not an argumentative person. I witnessed arguing too much growing up with my parents, and I promised myself to never get into a relationship with that dynamic. However, here I was, steeped in the madness of arguments that seemed to come out of nowhere and go further into nowhere fast. This is what I refer to as the blueprint of our life and that calls us into our patterns along the way. Does this sound familiar?

Maxwell and I were at a crossroads. We visited the United States Embassy twice and both times, they declined to grant him a VISA. Looking back I think my country (and a few dozen angels) were looking out for me.

I planned to stay longer in Ghana, but I felt the conclusion of my trip was nearing. I was happy to be going home. I had made great strides with corporate sponsors for World Trust, but I did not feel confident that I had someone who could be responsible enough to take over and follow up with these important contacts. With my decision to leave, I was going to let down my Young

Leaders, but I knew I needed to get my own life together before I could help these amazing youth. Following the words of the old adage, *"You have to put the oxygen mask on yourself before you put the mask on others."* This was becoming my personal mantra.

Maxwell and I decided to travel to Kumasi for one last weekend getaway. His sister took Sal so that we could have some time alone. There was a bit of peace in the air, and in my heart, and I was giving us one final chance.

During our five-hour drive heading to Kumasi, we had plenty of time for fun. However, there were more bumps in our conversation than there were bumps in the road. At one point I remember saying, *"Well, we are not officially engaged because you never really proposed to me."* He began to pull the car over to the side of the road, he replied, *"Well, I will do that now!"* I screamed, *"Noooooooo."*

I knew in my heart that I did not want him to propose. When a proposal finally would happen, I want it to be with right man. I want to have a proposal in a sacred way. Certainly, not pulled over on the side of the road just coming out of a series of arguments.

Even though I have chosen not to be married yet, that does not mean that I do not want to be married. On the contrary, I want to find that special mate. I believe in the sacrament of marriage. I have had men who wanted to marry me, but their proposals came from a place of trying to save the relationship. A male friend of mine stated that women are the ones responsible to move things along; *"men depend on women to 'poke the bear"* he said. I desired a proposal to come from my partner without such tricks or ultimatums. Is it too much to ask that they would simply know that I was the one for them? Poke the bear? Why would I want to poke a bear?

The Last Straw

The Young Leaders from Northern Ghana met us at the hotel to discuss a radio show featuring their work and dreams.

Chinese Brother arrived later that night, so I was happy to have my posse back. Back in our hotel room, Maxwell and I had a disagreement about this or that, which escalated to him plating his 'shut down' card. I wanted to talk things out, and he wanted to ignore me and so he would turn up the volume on the television set. I was feeling hurt. My voice escalated to match the volume of the television to get his attention, *"Maxwell, besides the volume disturbing the hotel guests, I can't talk to you with this noise."* I reached for the remote that was on the nightstand and I muted the volume. He stared into space without acknowledging me, watching the muted screen for a strange amount of time. My gut was aching and my heart pounding.

Then, without warning, he lurched at me and grabbed the remote. The grabbing was rough and alarming. I felt a bout of PTSD coming over me. He sat down on the bed like a defiant child and looked me dead-in-the-eye as he increased the volume to an even higher decibel. He stared at me like a bull looking at a red cape.

I do not know to this day what made me snap. It must have been all those years of pent up fears and pain that I buried in my body, in my heart, in my soul. Reciprocating the suddenness, without warning, I jumped on the bed and pinned him down with a move not unlike what I had seen my brothers use in Iowa all those years growing up in wrestling matches. I stared deep into his eyes, which were now open and paying attention. *"If you ever, ever, grab at me again like that, or abuse me again, I will kill you."*

Kill you? What the fuck?

We glared at each other for what seemed like eternity, challenging each other inside the dance of disaster. I had never spoken that word 'kill' before. Heck, I am the one who takes spiders out of my house into the garden.

He shoved me over onto the bed and walked out the door. The sound of the slamming door was deafening. I broke down in tears. What was wrong with me? Why would I ever speak to anyone like that? I would never kill anyone. It is even hard to write the word kill, let alone say it.

At that point a major epiphany flooded me. I felt like I was going to throw up. The room started spinning.

I laid on the bed, staring at the ceiling. I knew what I had to do. I knew this relationship was not for me. I had to take whatever time it took to heal from my life, from my parents, my first boyfriend when I was sixteen, to the various relationships that came into my life carrying all sorts of abuse, and baggage, and repeat, and repeat, and repeat.

My life flashed before my eyes, like flash cards on high speed. All of the sudden the scene came to a screeching halt, stopping at a screenshot of my relationship with RC. I realized that I ran away from him, just like I ran away from J in New York. I had not yet healed from any of them. Instead, I stuffed it down my boot and left those feelings inside of me to rot. More than anything, the beating I took from RC was rotting inside of me, and I knew that I needed to confront it, to let it heal.

I kept repeating the same relationships. The faces changed, the places changed, the circumstances changed...but I had not. I thought of that great quote, *"Wherever you go... there you are!"*

God was not allowing for me to step away from those lessons until I truly learned the lesson.

I walked up and down the hotel hallways looking for Maxwell so that I could apologize. It was not my nature to threaten anyone. He used my apology as a leverage to be even more distant. Chinese Brother was put in the mediation position between us. We somehow got through the night and the rest of the weekend, but the drive back to Accra was long and awkward.

Valentine's Day was approaching but I was not willing to be there during his silence and watch him flirt with other women, which he continued to do. I had a feeling that he had plans with someone else and it was better for me to simply leave.

I booked my flight back to Los Angeles. My heart was heavy. I felt that I kept missing the mark in the area of love, which is ironic, because I am such a believer in love.

As we got closer to my departure, things escalated. The day before I left we had another fight. I just wanted to get home to Los Angeles.

The last day that I was there I got a call out of the blue from another American woman who was living in Accra. Upon answering the phone, she heard something in my voice. She softly said, *"What is going on… are you okay?"*

I began to cry. I could not form any words. She said, *"What is your address? I am sending my driver now and I will get you out of there for whatever you need."*

I somehow gave her the address. Hannah and her driver arrived about an hour later. Maxwell was pouting and nothing could pull him out. I asked if he wanted to come out for the day. He said, *"No…."*

Hannah and I left. Imagine my surprise when I discovered that our house was only ten minutes from the beach. I was held hostage without a car to drive, left to take care of his children, while he went out for hours at a time. And all the while, I had no idea that I could have gotten a cab and went to the beach this entire time.

Hannah and I went to a beachside restaurant and I shared my heartbreak story with her. Everyone had high hopes for a happy ending between Maxwell and I, but it had become obvious that this would not be the case. After a bottle of wine and great food, Hannah and I watched the sunset before venturing into Accra. I discovered another side of Ghana that I never knew existed. I had been beholden to his world filled with his way, his friends, and his life.

I called Maxwell and invited him to meet up with us. He again refused.

Hannah's lifestyle in Accra was much different then mine. While my life was filled with no running water, no electricity, and definitely no love, Hannah was living at the Polo Club with amazing expats from all over the world.

When I finally got back to the house, Maxwell was in a horrible mood. I laid awake the entire night waiting for morning to come. There was a mountain of darkness between us.

The next morning could not come fast enough. I threw the last few things in my suitcase. I gave Sal a big hug and I told him that I loved him. I think we both had a feeling this might be the last time we would see one another.

My heart cracked as we drove away. Maxwell and I rode to the airport in silence. This silence differed from the sadness that occurred during our August trip to the airport. There was the same sadness and despair, but for opposite reasons. The first time we were sad for the separation. However, this time we were sad because we could not wait for the separation.

My flight back to Los Angeles was February 10, 2010. This was an end and a beginning all in one. I stared out the airplane window. I felt like there was a mountain removed from my path, making way for my heart to heal. But when something goes up, it must come down! And gravity was dragging me down. I was falling fast… into the descent. A single teardrop fell. When that tear dripped down my cheek, it opened the floodgates.

**Soundcloud Playlist - Tear - Massive Attack

Chapter 19

The Descent

As we began our descent into the Los Angeles airport, the blackness of night enveloped the plane, and the roaring engines seemed to silence. The cabin pressure, which normally sounded like a sucking vacuum, suddenly went strangely quiet. The other passengers began to stir in their seats. It was just after midnight, and the airplane felt as if it was suddenly floating in space like a feather floating to the ground. I was elated to be home, and exhausted from all the tears I had shed. Twenty-five hours of travel so far, and it was not over yet. In fact, this long-awaited journey had just begun.

After all the years of global jet-setting, I have always been perplexed and amazed at how a plane carries the weight of people and all their baggage on an enormous silver tube that glides through the atmosphere, suspended in midair. Simple science I know, but that night it suddenly became an 'aha' moment for me when I realized how we humans carry the weight of our own emotional baggage and trauma with us.

It is not until we are in mid-flight that we hit the turbulence in our heart. Then, we get to see how resilient we are and how we can hide enormous pockets of emotions, deep inside our dark caverns until something, or someone, steps onto our path to give us the gift of human transformation and healing.

In my case, the plane was landing from a long flight from Ghana. I had spent six weeks in the womb of Ghana, experiencing a rebirth in myself and hopefully planting the seed to give birth to my own baby girl.

You may wonder why it was this particular man who opened up the wounds so that I could finally strip away my secrets and see that there was still darkness hiding inside of me after all these years. I figured that ghost would rear its ugly head one day, but why had it come at this juncture in my life? Why here? Why now? Why with this man, who lived halfway around the world from me in Ghana? I concentrated on this particular relationship, as this time with him created the necessary space to alert me that I had to dig down deep to release and reveal what needed to be healed.

The turbulence of the plane jolted me back into my body, and we were nearing the landing strip at LAX. Was the turbulence an indication of days to come?

When I got to my home in Burbank, I settled in with my cats and my silence. I began to journal, with hope that I could uncover the pattern that trapped me. I immediately opened my computer and without sleep from the plane I wrote for three days straight. There was a flood of emotion inside of me, and obviously uncovering the truth was just the beginning of another journey that I was not quite ready for at the time. I realized that Maxwell was the conduit for me knowing that I had not yet healed from any of my past traumas.

In the meantime, I had other things to worry about. Being that money was only going out while I was in Ghana with no money coming in, I was on the verge of losing my car to the bank, and I was behind on all of my bills.

It was a warm spring night in March and I was in a deep sleep. I heard a banging on my living room window. A large beam of light sprayed across the interior of my house and illuminated the rooms. I lived alone, so this was deeply disturbing to me. I felt safe in Burbank, but not while this big shadow of a man loomed in my window. His voice boomed into my bones, *"Tess...Tess Cacciatore,...Are you in there? Please come to the door!"* Bang, bang, bang!

"It's 4:00 a.m. Who in the hell is out there?" I said to myself, as my heart pounded out of my chest. I picked up the phone and called 911. The police instantly responded to my cries for help.

I hovered in the corner in the living room behind the front door, as this monster continued to bang on my window with the end of his flashlight. I did not want to open the door until the police arrived.

How does he know my name? Do buglers and rapists typically call out a name and make such noise? I thought.

When the police arrived I came outside to find out that the 'horrible monster' was actually a repo man... coming for my repo car. He ended up being a nice man who only wanted to wake me up so that I could get my belongings out of the car, before he had to put it on the tow truck.

I was devastated. I bawled my eyes out and whispered hysterically, *"What am I supposed to do without my car? I didn't mean to be late on payments. I thought the bank would work with me? I was trying to help out a kid for his school. I'm not a bad person."* I paced the porch hoping that my commotion would not wake the neighbors.

The police and this guy calmed me down and said that if I called the bank they would work with me to get my car back. I was devastated and embarrassed to take my things out of my car. I called the bank the next day, and with the generous help of Marc and Courtney, I got my car back.

Sal's education had been more important to me at the time, but I realized again that I had to take care of myself before I helped others. A recurring theme I know... but my lessons had not played out yet, and so the story continues.

My house in Burbank held memories of my parents passing. I had been there for nine years, which was the longest stay in any home to date in my adult years. Perhaps it was time to move, find a less expensive place to live, find a job, and give up my humanitarian work. I was confused, as I knew humanitarian work was my purpose. Certainly God would have the answer to my prayers.

As it happened, the gal, Ann, who stayed at my home while I was in Africa also wanted to move to Los Angeles. She had settled into a rhythm at my place during the weeks I was away and she found a job that made her move possible.

On a similar path of synergy there was a scientist from Iowa who found me through my work in Ghana. Her desire was to get a product that she had created and patented at the University of Iowa, into Africa. This product was an ointment that was being used in emergency rooms for burn victims. She had the attention of NASA and other large agencies, and Africa was on her wish list. And according to her, I was the person for the job.

The scientist had discovered that her ointment had the ability to cure Buruli ulcer, which is a horrible and deadly skin disease found in sub-Saharan Africa. Since Ghana was one of the countries most affected by this skin disease and since I knew many high officials in government and health initiatives, it seemed like this could be a perfect match. Besides, this job would take me back to Ghana, which I now considered to be my second home. I began researching the disease and reaching out to my Ghana connections.

Things were looking up. I had a new job offer, which would allow me to travel internationally, and do humanitarian work. I had a housemate to share expenses of a larger home, who liked my cats.

I began downsizing and selling stuff in yard sales to create more space and make some much-needed money. I was on a financial downslide and it was a slippery slope. Anyone who has steered a large ship knows that it takes time to turn it around in the harbor. I did not get into financial stress overnight, Therefore, my financial stress would not be relieved overnight. I had a plan.

Even though I was healing and figuring things out, Maxwell was still trying to stay in my life. With the pending job offer that would take me back to Ghana, there could be a time when I would see Maxwell again. I had to recount what I knew. Maxwell was married, and even though he was trying to dissolve that marriage, he had yet to do so successfully. I also knew that he was trying to get a VISA to come to the United States to reconcile with me. Finally, I knew that he was working with a new investor for his business and that his money situation was looking up. What I did not know was the true story of his wife.

It was at this point that Rose (from Facebook) popped into the picture. From the beginning, Maxwell told me that he had dated Rose for about six months before he and I met. She moved to Switzerland, but they were still friends, which seemed reasonable.

I was on Facebook enjoying a peaceful Saturday morning. The sun was shining and newborn birds were chirping in a nest outside my window. I got a message from Rose, letting me know that she was looking for Maxwell. I did not think much of this, as she would have known about Maxwell and me, if they were still friends. I told her that I knew that Maxwell had found a new investor and that he was in China on business. I suspected that this new 'investor' was actually a new love interest, but I did not want to confront that theory. Rose and I texted back and forth only to discover the kind of devastating information that only unravels when two industrious women carve out details to find the truth.

According to Rose, Maxwell told her that I was his business partner and that there was nothing between us. At least he kept his lies straight, as I heard that is what he told his family about me.

The next words out of Rose's mouth, threw me to the floor. Rose told me that she was his wife. They had been married for six years, not dated for six months. The story of returning the liquor bottle was true, but it was Rose who was trying to track Maxwell down to dissolve their marriage. Her family lived in Ghana and her uncle was trying to find Maxwell to get the liquor bottle back from him.

Rose had been tiring of Maxwell's lies, she had fallen in love with a man in Switzerland, and wanted to be free of Maxwell. However, he avoided the divorce because he was still counting on her for financial support.

Rose worked as a waitress in Lucerne and she sent him money every week. And where did that money go? Supposedly for repairs for the house, fuel for his car, education for Sal (even though Sal was not her son either). She had been sending money for the house that she considered theirs. These were all the same bills that I was paying for all that time. Rose and I were both being played like fiddles in the same fiddle factory.

Imagine her surprise when she learned that Maxwell and I were planning to be married, to hopefully have a child. Maxwell said that he always wanted to have a baby girl, since he already had two boys. And then imagine my surprise when Rose said, *"Did you know that Maxwell already has a daughter with another woman, who doesn't want anything to do with him?"* The daughter is his oldest child. I had never heard a word about his daughter until then.

This influx of new information threw me into a deeper clarity of how cruel Maxwell had been with me regarding children. I remember how he had taunted me about not being able to get pregnant in the time that I was in Ghana. My thoughts slipped back to my twenties, when the tarot reader from the East Village told me that she saw a baby girl spirit next to me. I had dreamt about this baby girl my entire life. Her name even came to me in a dream, Lucia. I still feel the spirit of this baby girl with me, but she will have to find another miraculous way to come into my life.

A Poem to Maxwell:

Dangerous lies weave deception

all tangled ties to make conception

of a baby who turns out to be this man

What course of action has his life taken

or experiences that have him shaken

to not make a pact with true love?

Has he no idea of where his heart roams

never to be at home

within, or without himself?

Where is God's presence in his life

to cause so much strife

to take a wife, or two, or three

And then he turns around in disbelief

that he is alone ...

until another lie begins!

**Soundcloud Playlist - Liar - Three Dog Night

Our journey begins within, and it is our divine right to find the path back to our own garden. To once again dig into the soil and dive in the underbelly of the earth until the emotional nutrients are released. *Plant the Seeds... Nurture the Soul* was a workshop that I created and facilitated that spring.

I had to dig deep enough to nourish myself and plant the seeds of truth, conviction, beauty, and above all self-love.I felt it was important to stay focused on my victories, no matter how small they seemed. I had to see the pattern of my relationships.

Was Einstein right about his definition of sanity? *"Insanity is doing the same thing over and over and expecting different results."*

I had to be a bit insane for the choices I made with the men in my life.

"Wasn't I sane? I was sane! Wasn't I? - I am sane!"

Perhaps, the drastic spell could be broken by chanting *"I am sane, I am sane, I am sane!"* three times, so that a new pattern could emerge.

Chapter 20

The Chant

My experience with Maxwell in 2009 triggered past memories of one long, dark journey that in retrospect was an important crossroads in my life.

Maxwell was like the 'sliding door' effect. If I chose one road over another, would my life be completely different? Was it time for me to come to my own conclusion that past fears and pain needed to emerge and be released? Could this have happened with anyone else? Or, does life bring us our mirrors and show us our karmic partners in this dance called life?

I truly belief that Maxwell was a karmic partner who was deep, fast, and significant.

Who is to say that any other road would have turned out to be any better? There is no way to know, so I simply keep my eyes on the prize for the healing of my heart and soul.

I traveled back to Des Moines, saw my family, rented a car, and drove to Iowa City for the meeting with the scientist.

As I entered her office, I was warmly greeted by her and her staff. They took me into a small boardroom where we discussed many options and opportunities. She was very clear that we could work together, but I would have to put World Trust on the back burner. I was not sure about that idea, but I was open to hearing her out.

Her plan was to have me in Ghana for most of the year for the next five years. She offered me a solid monthly stipend and travel expenses. I could find someone in Ghana to help me run World Trust, so that we would not have to shut down completely, as the work with the Young Leaders fit into the plan for the National Health Expo and I did not want to disappoint them.

I already made inroads to get her ointment into the Ghanaian hospitals. My connections, including my Prince friend of the Ashanti region, were receptive to the idea of her ointment being distributed throughout Ghana as part of a pilot program. If we could find a way to get the Kings' endorsement, then we could offer a solution to millions of people.

That afternoon we had a conference call with people from NASA, who had constructed a hyperbaric chamber in which Burelli patients could be treated with the ointment in a contained, sterile environment. All the pieces were falling into place. I was working with my connections at the main hospital in Kumasi and Dadowa, including a wonderful man named Peter who heads up the health organization in all of Africa.

The scientist walked out of the room to attend to another matter. I was sitting at my computer on Facebook when the light blinked, indicating that a friend had come online.

"Hi" popped on the instant message window. It was Maxwell. I nervously looked around to make sure no one from the office was in the room. It was a milestone to hear from him, as I hadn't spoken to him in several weeks. I was curious of the timing as I sat in this office planning for my return to Ghana.

I noticed that his relationship status on his profile was changed and he was now 'in a relationship' which I assumed was posted in regard to me. The timing could not be more serendipitous. Perhaps fate was giving us one more chance to see if we could start again. I know, silly me.

I typed in the message box, *"Who are you in a relationship with?"* The screen was blank for what seemed like a long time. I stared at the screen like a pubescent schoolgirl, hoping for a positive response. The chat indicator light finally came on. I could see him typing his answer. He said, *"You don't know her."*

My heart stopped, my head began to spin. It was a struggle to hold it together for the rest of the meeting. I put on a fake smile and masked the pain.

I had hoped that Maxwell would have the decency to speak on the phone before we officially ended our brief, yet tumultuous relationship. I know that all signs pointed to a break up, but we had not yet voiced closure.

When I left Ghana, all of my internal systems were whispering "run, run, run," but I was still dealing with the loss of the fantasy of this relationship. I seem to be fixated by the desire to fix things, but this was no fixing matter.

The scientist and I closed down a productive day, and scheduled our second day of meetings to answer questions, sign contracts, and move forward.

I slipped the key card into my hotel room door, waiting for the blinking green light to wink at me so that I could finally disappear into my vacant, yet welcoming room. It felt like a good omen that my room number was 308, which contained two of my favorite numbers, 3 and 8.

I wheeled my suitcase into the corner of the room and exhaled from the long day. I pushed the play button on my ITunes and lit a stick of my favorite incense, Nag Champa. This daily ritual was my saving grace from the crazy outside world.

I grabbed the hotel-branded wine opener and pulled out a bottle of wine from the sack (as we call it in the Midwest). I crumpled the sack into a twisted fury and let it fall to the ground. I popped the cork out of the bottle and took a hotel glass from the counter, pouring myself a large taste of wine.

I sat on the edge of the bed, thinking back on the day. It felt wonderful to be back in the Midwest, and to have the opportunity to work with a scientist at the University of Iowa. The World Trust Foundation was founded in Iowa in 1993 and here I was seventeen years later on the brink of fulfilling my dream of the World Trust becoming a virtual classroom that would connect universities between continents. This was my dream. This was my purpose. I felt that everything was falling into place, while my heart was cracking open.

I decided to take a bubble bath to go along with my red wine, music, and the smell of incense.

I pointed my big toe into the hot water to test the temperature, finally sinking my naked body into the hot, steamy bath. I uttered the mantra, *"Victim to victorious, victim to victorious, victim to victorious"* in my head, as tears streamed down my face.

How was I to become victorious after the shattered months that I had just experienced? I knew that my vast tears were just a trickle of a long-awaited outpour. I kept these emotions buried inside for all these years. I had never dealt with the abuses from my past, and especially RC.

Was I still a victim? Is being a victim a vicious cycle that one has to overcome on a continual basis? Or, was there a magic pill that one could take to become instantly victorious?

Maxwell had still been on my mind and etched into my cracked heart. We had not talked in weeks since the truth of Rose was revealed. Obviously, he had a thousand excuses of why he kept the truth from both of us.

The music from the other room disrupted my thoughts, as Moby's song *Porcelain* played. His haunting lyrics seeped through the walls and into the steam of the bath. My heart needed this flow of tears.

In my dreams I'm dying all the time

Then I wake its kaleidoscopic mind

I never meant to hurt you

I never meant to lie

So this is goodbye… ©2000 Moby

**Soundcloud Playlist - Porcelain - Moby

I was suddenly brought back into my body in my hotel room.

The reality of it all was so unbearable, but I was a firm believer that I was doing what I was born to do, and that God would always provide. While sitting in that bath, I knew God had the answer and that all would be revealed. I had to hold onto my faith, as I felt that I was hanging onto the edge of a cliff.

The temperature of the bath water was becoming tepid, and my knees poking out from the water began to chill. The proverbial oxygen mask was slammed against my face. I gasped for air. Where was the oxygen?

I needed a reminder to breathe. I needed a sign to keep me going. I stepped out of the bath and wrapped a large, soft, white towel around me. I stumbled across the room and fell into bed. Trying to shake the doom of my day, I pulled my computer onto my lap. I wanted to be distracted from the pain, so I went through emails.

I opened an email from a friend, Gail Lynne Goodwin from *Inspire Me Today* who said that she was re-running an article that I wrote for her newsletter a few months back,

Now, I wrote this in 2009, long before many of the natural disasters and terrorist attacks. Gail's question was: *"If today were my last day on Earth and I could share 500 words of brilliance with the world, what are the important things I would want to pass along to others?"*

This came at perfect timing, as I needed this reminder of what I wrote many months before even going to Ghana and experiencing the heartbreak of Maxwell.

"What does it take to be inspired today, when stress is all around us due to the economy, environment, war, and more? To me, it is about being truly grateful on a daily basis and, sometimes a minute-by-minute basis on those days when you feel you just can't take one more step. Everywhere we turn there is continued devastation. Every minute there is a child raped, a person murdered, a rainforest dying, an iceberg melting.

But what if we looked at everything, good, bad, or indifferent and saw the magic? What if we saw things from a different perspective and knew that every experience was a gift to help us reach nirvana in our lifetime? What if we were able to see that through the dark, we saw the light?

I know that most of us already live by these principles, but what about when life is so overwhelming that we accidentally slip back into old, negative patterns of thinking and doing. It causes me to pause and remember what we have in this precious life is to usher in the light, come together as a community, lift each other up, and simply love one another as unconditionally as humanly possible; so that we can share the essence of our enlightenment.

To see at the end of a flood that devastates a waterfront town, there is a droplet of water on a leaf that sparkles in the sun and a whole new universe is opened. Or, at the end of a fire that destroys a forest, there is a chance for a new forest to grow. When Mother Earth shakes us so hard that a village crumbles to ground, gives us the opportunity to come together for those who have survived.

We all know on some level what is in store in the coming days and years, surrounded by much more devastation. It is a time when history is writing itself. However, we have the power to change those pages in life. We get to say LIFE GOES ON when we lose a loved one and have no other choice but to feel them in that intangible place in our hearts. We get to learn that LIFE GOES ON when we see our bank accounts drained, not knowing how we're going to feed our families. We get to feel that LIFE GOES ON even when the darkest night is all around us. We get to feel our power in faith and know there is a gift to give and receive with every encounter.

So I remind myself and invite all of us to BREATHE and to remain as calm and centered as possible during this transition time; so that we are beacons of light to ourselves, and, therefore, for each other.

Each of us are a blast of light, that when put together we cause a magical light storm so powerfully blinding, filled with faith, hope, compassion and above all love, that we only have the choice to live as one ... which to me, is the true meaning of life!"

Ahhh that is right. I was telling others to breathe, but I was forgetting that breathing was imperative to my own value and my own success.

"Victim to victorious, victim to victorious, victim to victorious" chanted in my mind, as I drifted off to sleep

I arrived back to Los Angeles, and in my usual fashion I moved mountains for the scientists' launch in Ghana. In a few short weeks, I lined up meetings with elected officials, celebrities, and corporations for a "Day of Health" and a Health Expo. All the work that I did while in Ghana for the Young Leaders was easily transferred over for this new endeavor.

After everything was lined up, the Scientist told her assistant that she was not ready to bring the product to marketplace and she took her offer off the table and headed for the hills. This was an abrupt change of plans without consideration or respect. I had no idea what happened. However, after years of feeling terrible and rejected I found out that the scientist and her husband were up to no good. They were forced to quit their endeavors and I believe they spent a bit of time in jail. Another instance in which I was shown that God always has a bigger and better plan, even when things look like they are not going in my favor. This was one of the most important lessons to learn in my life: the perspective of life can be changed with a slight twist of our minds. Is my glass half-empty, or half-full? I say that my glass is always overflowing, even in disturbed times.

And so I lost the Ghana opportunity, and Ann lost her job. We were both left vulnerable, with high rent and bills.

On my 50th birthday, the universe created my second move in four short months.

The doorbell rang. I was excited to answer the door, as my friend Coco was coming over to have my traditional birthday blueberries and champagne. I opened the door to see a delivery guy, not Coco. He handed me a bundle of papers and said, *"You've been served."* The paperwork was to pay rent or quit. We were not even late on the rent, but I figured it was a sign to move on.

Happy 50th Birthday to me! I did not feel that moving again was my favorite option, but it was time to simplify, move back on my own, and make things work.

I was sad to think that I had always envisioned my 50th birthday to be me bicycling through the countryside of Tuscany, with my love partner by my side.

"God has a plan!" I said with a tortured smile.

**Soundcloud Playlist - Fragile - Sting

Chapter 21

The Eagle and the Condor

Since 2000, I have traveled back and forth between Geneva Switzerland to do work at the United Nations. I was happy to be producing events, working with youth from around the world, and speaking at the United Nations on behalf of women and children.

Considering the fact that I was a producer in the technology arena, I spoke on many occasions on the future of technology and where our world would one day be an interconnected force. This would be the time where we could eventually see, speak, and feel one another through the power of technology.

I began this vision and passion in 1995, when I saw the forerunners of technology and what they said about where we were going in our world. I was happy to be alive to see these ideas come to fruition.

I feel it is important that the indigenous nations have their stories told, as there is so much wisdom in the rich history and lessons that have been passed down through the centuries. What better time than now to look to our ancestors and past history for answers? There is beauty in the lessons of simplicity and perhaps a roadmap to guide us in the world today.

During my visits to Geneva each year, I have had the opportunity to interview and get to know many of the wisdom keepers from around the world, during the Working Group of Indigenous Populations, held each August in Geneva, Switzerland.

I met tribal leaders from, Peru, Guatemala, Brazil, Mexico, Australia, New Zealand, Hawaii, and Alaska, to name a few. It was fascinating to see them all dressed in their traditional attire and watch them dance and drum. I have always been drawn to Indigenous traditions and the stories of their history.

Beginning in 2000, I continued to be a media-accredited journalist with the United Nations, which gave me the ability to go to the General Assembly rooms and film world leaders. I had the rare opportunity to witness the microcosm of the world inside this room, filled with global dignitaries fighting for the human rights of their respective countries. I had the opportunity to speak on many occasions in both Geneva and New York about the plight of abuses that were going on with women and children, as well as how technology was going to be a conduit to bring cultures together.

I interviewed medicine men, witch doctors, women leaders, child prophets, animal warriors, and I fell deep into the world of the Indigenous stories. One of my favorite prophecies from the Lakota tribe was a story that was shared by Sitting Bull to his tribes. Sitting Bull was a spiritual leader who gave the message of hope to all nations and he saw the white buffalo as a symbol of abundance and bringing all people together.

During my first visit to the United Nations in Geneva, in the year 2000, there was a white buffalo born in the United States. We all celebrated and danced on the lawn of the United Nations, feeling optimistic that the world could change for the better.

One of my other favorite prophecies is the one about the Eagle and the Condor.

Barry Fraser, from Heart of the Earth writes, *"Many of the indigenous cultures share a two-thousand year old prophecy from the*

Andes. The prophecy foretold an unbalance and tremendous conflict throughout the Americas from around 1500 to the year 2000. During this time the eagle, representing the mental and materialistic, has driven the condor, representing the spiritual and heart-centered, almost into extinction.

The eagle represents the modern, technological world, and the people of the eagle have developed the intellect at the expense of the heart. They have developed technology to an extraordinary level, bringing them material wealth beyond their wildest dreams. But they also find themselves spiritually impoverished to their peril.

The people of the condor represent the indigenous people of the world living close to the land, with the heart and wisdom that come from being attuned to the natural world.

They live from their heart and through their senses, and have an unparalleled depth of spirituality and wisdom that is an expression of their profound connection to nature.

These people are spiritually rich but materially impoverished. The forces of the developed world now threaten their environment that they depend on for their material and spiritual sustenance. They must understand and develop some of the intellectual skills of the eagle."

According to the prophecy of the eagle and condor, we are at the beginning of a time when the condor will rise again and will once again fly together wing to wing in the same space and same sky as the eagle and the world will come into balance. This is a time of partnership, love and healing, and a transition out of an era of conflict and turmoil into more sustainable and earth-honoring ways. This is also supposed to be a time of great transition but also with some dangers. The condor will not soon forget the domination of the eagle. The eagle must also change to help restore the balance.

Soundcloud Playlist - The Eagle and the Condor - Rodney Franklin

Our task now is to begin to return to the heart-wisdom ways of the condor; to individually begin to fulfill the prophecy. We need to come to our senses, and listen with our hearts to what the earth is trying to tell us. We need to begin to look at and understand how the individual choices we make every day not only perpetuate the destruction of the earth, but also contribute to our own sense of unhappiness, stress, and isolation from each other. We must begin now to help the condor soar.

In the nineties I attended many technology conferences and summits. I was able to hear what the leaders in the industry were saying and expecting for the future. I saw how the internet and technology offered us a way to stay connected to those from other parts of the world and that Internet TV (IPTV) would give us a place to produce content that would keep the stories and legends of our ancestors alive.

In 1995, I wrote a seventy-five page business plan that laid out a vision that I could see so clearly that it felt real at the time.

WTN (World Trust Network) was to be the exact culmination of the Native American vision of the "Eagle and the Condor" as it exemplified the technology arena: live-stream, original programming for social impact, virtual classroom, and the storytelling from the wisdom keepers from our indigenous cultures; combined with the heart of social impact to make the world a better place.

All indications pointed to a green light for go, but it was not my time. Thank God for the visionaries who laid the groundwork for what we have witnessed over the years in the technology arena, from the genius minds of those like Steve Jobs, Bill Gates,

Steve Wozniak, Larry Page & Sergey Brin, and, my personal favorites, Oprah Winfrey and Lucille Ball who set the stage for women-owned businesses in the entertainment industries to flourish.

I saw the importance of the eagle and the condor flying in the same sky. Now I just had to get my own wings.

Chapter 22

Wings of Love

I have had the honor of speaking at the United Nations since 2000. In 2000, I attended the *Commission of Human Rights* (CHR), which occurs every August in Geneva, Switzerland.

Before every CHR, there is the Working Group of Indigenous Populations, in which chiefs and activists gather to speak about human rights for our Indigenous peoples from all over the world. This has always been an eye-opening adventure for me, especially with my being able to interview these amazing and passionate activists.

Traveling to other countries always makes me feel as though I am walking across a bridge into another world. I do not take these assignments lightly. I feel this is my divine honor and privilege to take part in these global undertakings and I feel most alive while doing so.

Through my travels, I have learned about the different modalities to heal. Meditation and prayer became cornerstones in my path to forgiveness and self-love. In one meditation, I imagined I was soaring with the eagle and the condor. I dove in deep to take a closer look into my soul, looking for that pearl inside the oyster, that pearl of wisdom that could unlock the treasure chest of answers that had been locked up for so long.

I thought of a saying, *"The darker the mud, the more beautiful the lotus."* To me, the lotus flower represents mother earth, which is why I chose a lotus to be the logo of the World Trust Foundation, along with the name of the DVD, *Pink Lotus: Belly Dance for Girls of All Ages*. Over the years, I have held onto the image of the lotus flower emerging from the dark mud. I knew I was ready to emerge from my thick mud and burst forth with illuminating petals to reveal my treasures inside.

I traveled to various places around the world, mainly through the United Nations and Airline Ambassadors to work with youth and women. I was creating a television series called, *Wings of Love* where I filmed people from various countries, with their culture, food, and dance. It was my idea to highlight ordinary people, doing extraordinary things.

My first trip to the United Nations in Geneva Switzerland was cold. The weather was bone-chilling, and the snow capped mountains stood tall against the deep blue sky. I adore seeing the frozen tundra as I fly into Geneva, as there is always a clean and crisp feeling in the air.

Geneva is one of my favorite cities in the world. There is a grand mix of European cultures, as well as representatives from all over the world due to the United Nations.

I was attending the Commission for Human Rights with the delegation of Ms. Wilda Spalding, who is an heir to the famous industry of Spalding Sporting Goods. Wilda is eccentric, wise, and often misunderstood with her outgoing personality, boisterous laugh, and trying demeanor. She demanded excellence, which was fitting for her Fete d' Excellence (Festival of Excellence), an awards ceremony that honored those who were doing great work in the fields of education, environment, social justice, health, the arts, and more.

The festival and awards ceremony was held each August in Geneva. This medal was the same award that I was honored to receive in the category of Edutainment, and the same medal that I brought to my mother's bedside the day she passed. I was deeply moved and honored to be with the other recipients, including Wilda honoring the work of one of my heroes, Nelson Mandela.

Upon arriving at the airport my friend picked me up and brought me back to his house for a suitcase drop off, a shower, and a quick cup of European coffee to fuel my internal jet.

I had only moments to get ready and then dash to the United Nations for a lunch at the Delegate Dining Hall. I lunched with Ambassadors and their wives and began to make wonderful international connections. Nicola Furey was the wife to the Ambassador of Belize, and she had successes on her own accord as Vice President of Earth Focus. During my first time at the United Nations, most of the Ambassadors were men. I am happy to see that more women are being assigned to these roles, which is a dream of mine one day.

The flurry of activity inside the United Nations was breathtaking. I felt like I was inside the center of a beehive, with International laws getting ready to pass in honor of human rights. The fire in my belly began to ignite. I was finding my way to what I wanted to do in the world. When I arrived back in Los Angeles, I had a small window in which to create an Earth Heroes contest to identify youth who were passionate about the environment. This was March and Earth Day is April 22nd. I had to hurry with a lot of planning to complete. Since I was on the producing committee of Earth Day LA, it was a bit easier to add the contest onto the already planned Earth Heroes Awards Luncheon, where we honored activists, corporations, and youth for their service in the world.

I planned for the winner of this year to go with me to Geneva for the *Sub-Commission of Human Rights* in August of that same year. A passionate student, Annie Bird, won the contest. Through this experience, I realized the importance of helping to change the life of just one person and how simple actions could ripple far and wide by the lives we touch. During Annie's time in Geneva she won the Ralph Bunche Award for her speech while participating in the Youth Empowerment Summit (YES) through Wilda Spalding.

Annie was attending Santa Monica Community College at the time. She worked hard on her studies to then be transferred to Berkeley College the following year. She eventually went to work in Washington DC and, finally, began working internationally to follow her passion of social justice. I am so very proud of Annie and that we met during that Earth Day event, that changed both of our lives forever.

In 2001, I traveled back to Geneva for the *Commission for Human Rights* in March and the *Sub-Commission for Human Rights* in August.

Through the guidance of Wilda and other indigenous leaders, I explored the idea of holding a live-stream conference so that the leaders from North and South America could attend as a united force to the *World Conference Against Racism* that was being held in September, in Durban South Africa. Up until this time, all of the leaders from all the nations were working on separate tracks. I felt strongly that the power of technology could bring the leaders to unify their missions and their message for this global conference. This was an important gateway for me to see how technology was going to be an important path of merging my world of entertainment and philanthropy. Technology was quickly becoming my bridge to connect all of these worlds, and this was in 2001.

The First Nations from Canada sponsored the live-stream and the production of a video series. I was elated to produce this event, that could bring the leaders together for the first time in history. The plan was to connect the leaders who were attending the *Sub-Commission of Human Rights* in Geneva Switzerland, to the other leaders who were attending the *Indigenous Peoples Summit of the Americas* in Ottawa, Canada.

I began preparing for the live-stream event many months prior, so that we would be properly organized. I worked virtually from Los Angeles identifying the live-stream company, producing partners, crews in both locations, while also navigating a new terrain for the leaders from both summits to accomplish the task of a live-stream. This was an historic event, as well as the beginning of a new world for me.

We all held our breath throughout the two-hour live-stream, which went perfectly, and without technology hiccups. I was blessed to be able to witness the collaboration between the nations and they too felt that it was a successful event to prepare them for the upcoming conference.

Once the live-stream event was completed, we were just weeks away to the global conference, being held in Durban, South Africa - August 31 - September 8, 2001.

In the meantime, in my personal life, I was bitten by the bug to explore the world from behind my camera, to witness humanity through a global lens, to see how we are all connected as one. I held on tight to my camera and filmed everyone and everywhere that I could. Over the years that I have traveled, I strangely never edited the tapes, but I put them all in archived boxes. I had no idea what I would do with the footage, but I kept stashing them away for some rainy day.

I know now the time has come to share these messages with the world and to show a portion of my global travels. I had to open my eyes to different cultures, opinions, and passions. I was then able to open my heart and know that I was in the driver's seat for my own destiny. This trip to South Africa was the beginning of a beautiful, long road in my life and in my career.

**Soundcloud Playlist - Drive - Incubus

** Durban, South Africa

World Conference against Racism (WCAR)

I stepped off the plane at the Durban International Airport in South Africa, and instantly felt the heat and the passion.

There was a very strong military presence due to the world leaders and global dignitaries arriving in their private jets on an hourly basis.

This was my first time in South Africa. I felt strangely at home. I attended the WCAR as part of the First Nations delegation (Indigenous Peoples of Canada), and my duty during the conference was to film the leaders from North and South America as a follow-up to the live-stream conference in Geneva the month before. I wanted to film the progress of what they were able to accomplish.

The first day we arrived, there was a controversial global division, due to a tangled conflict that went deeper than this chapter will allow. More or less, there was political unrest when President George W. Bush and Israeli Prime Minister Ariel Sharon pulled out of the conference. This sent a ripple throughout the global community, as they were the only leaders in the world who did not attend the conference.

And so my first day filming in the field was snarled inside of a chaotic protest in which thousands of people gathered in the streets, carrying signs against President Bush and the United States administration. It was a very unnerving situation, so I had to keep calm and keep my journalism hat on. I needed to stay under the radar so that I could learn more about the underpinnings and backstory of this international disorder, rather than bringing attention to myself as an American.

The soldiers, guards, and military police stood before us like a wall, with stoic expressions on their faces. They held their rifles close to their chest, ready to push their guns at us if we got too close. Even though it was a peaceful protest, there was a lot of tension in the air.

I saw deep emotion in the eyes of the soldiers, as they seemed to have sympathetic tendencies towards the protest. I am sure that it was not long ago when they had to protest against apartheid and were actually on the other side of the battle. My heart was racing, knowing that at any time the crowds could turn against these uniformed men turning this into a full-blown riot.

President Mbeki was the leader of South Africa at the time. He had to rise to the occasion and subdue the tangled emotions of the other world leaders. This sort of diplomatic action was not a new situation in South Africa, but to us outsiders, the tension was an intense ride in and of itself.

One of the highlights of my lifetime was the first time I laid eye on Nelson Mandela. He had a fiercely strong and gentle presence. While I relished filming other world leaders, such as Secretary General of the United Nations Kofi Annan, Winnie Mandela, Angela Davis, and other world leaders of the day, no words could express how I felt when I saw Mandela.

There was an unusual sighting of Fidel Castro, but the journalist pit was too thick to get a great shot. Speaking of the press pit, I had to constantly battle this arena with tall, broad shouldered men who were mostly from European countries. I had to find clever ways to get a "head" above the rest, as I was one of the few women in the press pit filming. Sometimes, I stood on chairs to claim my territory so that I could get my shots.

The security was fierce, so getting into any of the larger summit rooms took the will of heaven. I did all that I could to carry my 80 pounds of camera equipment from the hotel through the streets, through security, into the rooms and then drop and roll at any given point to go back into the streets to cover a protest. I filmed on a tripod and by handheld, which took an extraordinary amount of balance and strength. I took the throbbing pain from my back, neck, and legs and pushed it down in my boots, so that the pain would not distract me.

Given my passion for youth empowerment, I found myself searching for the attendees of the youth summit. I walked into a large conference hall filled with youth from all over the world. I quietly walked up to a small group and asked them who would be the best one to interview. They all pointed to a young woman who was standing in front of the room, passionately articulating her message with an authoritative voice and wild hand gestures. Melody Botya became my "first African daughter" in my role of Mama Tess. I asked her if she would like to be mentored to do on-camera interviews. Her reply, *"Yes...that would be perfect. I want to grow up and become the South African Oprah."* I loved her spunk, tenacity, and clarity. She and I were attached at the hip for the duration of the conference, and she is still near and dear to my heart to this day.

Melody interviewed other youth from their delegation, including youth who represented Israel and Palestine. From their perspective, they did not want to have the conflict between each of their nations as their ancestors set it. Each of them talked about what they were taught in school, about how they wanted to be friends with those from the "other side" of their war-torn history. These youth just wanted to move beyond the pain and create space for peace.

This was a heart-warming and heart-breaking interview that opened my eyes to realize the importance of finding ways to mentor youth and my passion to create a platform to showcase cultures from around the world. I had never met anyone from Palestine and while I honor my Jewish friends, I always hoped that they all could find peace.

While in South Africa I filmed the Indigenous leaders from the live stream event. I also took Melody around to fulfill her dream of becoming the South African Oprah, while we did interviews with H.E. Mary Robinson, Harry Belafonte, and other celebrities and dignitaries from Sri Lanka, Nigeria, India, Tibet, and more.

One of the main agendas of the First Nation was to accomplish being recognized by the governments as Indigenous People(s) rather than Indigenous People (without the "s" at the end). This simple "s" at the end of the word represented an entire objective to a complex situation regarding human rights, which to this point had been ignored by the United Nations. Their fight had gone on for over twenty-five years, containing the sovereignty and the pride of their peoples. The history that is attached to this conversation runs deep and is well worth the dive to research, if you are so inclined. This was the very reason it was important for the live-stream in August, so that they could be unified as a force.

The process of the United Nations can be just as astounding and productive, as well as mainly inefficient. Governments step in for a specific agenda, while the heart of any matter turns into a skeleton of oppression and long-debated discussions, with seldom any successful outcome. This is totally frustrating to watch and know that there has to be a better way.

The global delegations of this conference represented every culture in the world and the topics ranged from racism, racial discrimination, xenophobia and other related intolerances. Back in this year, I had not yet learned about the atrocities of early child marriage, sex trafficking, or female genital mutilation.

Each province and country spent anywhere from days to a lifetime to make changes for the rights of being human. The huge machine behind these endeavors most of the time moves like a sloth sitting in a tree.

During the WCAR the world felt topsy turvy and the United States was constantly being describe as the "belly of the beast." I felt so sad about it all. Why could we not see that we all belong on this tiny planet together and just get along?

My refuge during this time was my hotel room. I woke every morning and threw open the balcony french doors. My room faced the Indian ocean. This was the break of day where this giant orb of a sun rose up in front of my face. Every morning I started my day in gratitude and meditation and blasted U2's song *Beautiful Day* as loud as my speakers would go. I danced on the balcony with wild abandon while watching the surfers heading out to the water's edge. This ritual was the only way I could make it through the day.

**Soundcloud Playlist - Beautiful Day - U2

Late one afternoon, I needed a break from the madness, so I took an afternoon walk on the beach near my hotel. I saw a group of young men doing Gumboot dancing. When I was told the origin of this dance I was mesmerized. The dance started during the mining of gold in South Africa. This particular dance was their way to communicate with one another, as they were not allowed to talk. The dance steps became their secret code, and they communicated through their percussive dance moves and by the stomping of their feet.

On the next corner, I saw a group of young Zulu dancers entertaining the crowds outside of a restaurant. The group leader was a gentle and kind man by the name of Bongami. He was excited to meet an American producer, as he wanted to get his dancers to America. I wish I could have taken all the dancers home with me. They ended up inviting me and another women from our delegation to visit their village. We were to meet at this same place the following day. And, what an adventure it turned out to be.

The next afternoon we climbed into a small van filled to the brim with twelve dancers, the driver, Bongami and us two American women. They drummed and sang for the hour long bumpy ride into their quaint village, which happened to be in the middle of the bush. We were greeted by a group of school children who sang and danced their tribal songs, dressed in their cultural dance costumes. I loved that the teachers kept their traditions alive.

We traveled back to Durban later that day. The sun was setting and our beachfront hotel had a beautiful full-moon glow. We ran into a few people from our delegation in the hotel lobby. They asked if we wanted to go to dinner.

After dinner we headed to the ocean to enjoy the energy of the full moon. Before we knew it, all of us had our shoes off and our feet glided between the waves. This North American delegation filled with Native Americans decided to anoint the Indian Ocean. They began to chant and pray, as the chill of the ocean breeze enveloped us with love. This felt like an initiation, a blessing, and a baptism all at the same time.

On September 6, 2001, I realized that I had not yet fully experienced all that I wanted in South Africa, so I extended my trip.

I was one of the only accredited journalists ever invited to attend a special ceremony in Zulu-land, where dancers from each Zulu tribe danced for King Goodwill. I had filmed King Goodwill speaking at the WCAR, but this was going to be an inside look into their culture and his kingdom.

I was told that I would not be able to film unless I followed their tribal rules. I was given the option to either be part of their tribal tradition of being topless, or be required to wear a dress that covered my shoulders. I was not sure how to differentiate the two choices, but I chose to cover my shoulders.

The conference ended and I was ready to go. We hired a driver and headed to a two-day excursion to Leopard Mountain for a safari retreat.

Leopard Mountain Lodge was between Huluwea and Mkuze game reserves. The family who owned the lodge was white, but they spoke fluent Zulu, which came in handy while driving through the rural areas.

Leopard Mountain was exquisite in every aspect of weather, landscape, and animal sightings. We took to the wild, and photographed what we could. Along our safari, we saw nature at its finest. The safari owners had built an enclosed hut with a view right on top of a watering hole, which allowed us to get less than ten feet away from the animals. I got close-up shots that would normally not be possible.

We saw warthogs, baboons, zebra, ynari, water buffalo, and all kinds of elk who came to get their supply of water. For some reason the giraffe were being aloof that day, while the leopards and lions rested out of sight, saving their energy for their prey-filled hunt of the night.

After the safari, our Durban-based driver picked us up and we continued into the Zulu kingdom. We arrived early Saturday morning, which was the opening day of the traditional Reed Dance. Driving through the bush was like driving through a postcard. The amber streaks of sunrise mixed with the clouds that intertwined with the sun made me feel like I could reach out and touch the sky.

While watching the vast landscape of beauty, I decided on my objective for the weekend. Due to the high-level event, I wanted everything to be just right; from clothing to camera.

We planned to stay until Monday, which would give us two full days to film the festivities. We were not allowed to wear pants, so I packed my best sarongs and a pretty pink Indian dress. I left the rest of my luggage at the hotel in Durban, figuring I could pick things up on the way back through the city to the airport.

Our driver was instructed to take us to the general feed store in the center of this quaint village. There was a farmer's market that consisted of booths filled with brightly colored tapestries, jewelry, headdresses, masks, and home-grown vegetables. I was in heaven.

While at the WCAR, I met two family members from the Zulu royal family; Princess Sibu, and one of her brothers, a Prince. They were to be our point of contact for this event, so we planned to stay close to them during our stay. There were too many opportunities to accidentally break a rule or tradition, and make the royal family upset.

The Prince and Princess were discrete as they arrived with quiet fanfare to the general market. We switched cars from our driver to the royals. Without pomp or circumstance we were whisked away to the castle of their mother, the second Queen.

Along the way the Princess and the Prince shared the story of their mother and their father, King Goodwill Zwelithini. As I remember what was told to me about their relationship, this was far from what I ever witnessed growing up in the cornfields of Iowa.

It was explained to me that King Goodwill believed in having wives who were educated and strong business women. Rather than using the Reed Dance as a way to find new brides as it was traditionally used, the King preferred to use the eight day ceremony as a way to educate the tribes to abstain from sexual activities and lower their risk of HIV/AIDS.

The traditional story of the Reed Dance (Umhlanga Ceremony) was created in 1940 in Swaziland. King Goodwill introduced this to South Africa in 1991, just ten years prior to my attending. I believe this might have been the first year they were letting any media into the event, so I was truly honored, especially to be the only woman journalist allowed.

Upon arriving to the castle of the Second Queen, we were greeted by their staff. When one uses the word "castle" one could conjure up the image of Buckingham Palace, or a castle in the mountains in a quaint European township overlooking the ocean. However, these castles were one-storied, humble, and sweetly, designed compounds.

We were guided to the room where we were to stay for the weekend. I dropped my luggage off in my room and prepared my camera for the shoot. I put on my Indian pink dress and we were driven to the event.

We were taken to a very remote area called Nongoma, which was where the King's castle was located. The weather was very windy and extremely hot. Sweat beads formed all over my body as I tried to focus on getting my camera set up in time.

I was still carrying my 80-pound camera gear, but instead of being surrounded by government officials and armed guards, I was surrounded by Zulu warriors in front of the castle where the Reed Dance would begin.

I was brought to the center of the circle where the Zulu warriors gathered. I was thrilled to be the only woman in the circle of journalists at the time, all on the same playing ground rather than in a press pit.

I put my camera on the tripod and focused all of my energy into becoming invisible. I wanted to melt into the majesty of my surroundings, so that I could purely witness the King and his Kingdom.

I barely recognized King Goodwill, as when I filmed him at the WCAR he was dressed in a suit and royal sash. On this special day he was dressed in the most spectacular traditional warrior attire. His headdress, staff, and sword matched the off-white groin covering, and arm and leg bands. I was in awe!

King Goodwill and his tribe were mostly made up of his brothers and cousins. They all stood around waiting for the festivities to begin, looking stoic, strong, and somber. The backdrop was a thirty-foot tall castle wall, with double-thick, arched, wooden doors.

I put my head down, eyes into the lens, and filmed my surroundings. At one point I looked up to see that the other journalists had been moved out of the circle. I was alone in the center, suddenly panicking that I was in the wrong place. I looked to the family attorney who was standing not far from the King. She nodded and motioned for me to stay where I was. I looked to the King and he also nodded his approval to stay where I was. I was less than fifteen feet from the King and his warriors. I had to pinch myself to make sure that I was not dreaming.

I had no idea what to expect. I know that the young women came from every tribe in Zululand dressed in their own unique tribal costume to dance for the King. In preparation for this day, each of the girls had to be tested by their village doctor to make sure that they were still virgins to participate. Every girl had their different tribal skirts, headdresses, bells on ankles, but the only commonality to their costume was that all of them had to be topless.

The drums began to roar. I shifted my camera angle to see the magnificent sight. The procession of girls began at the bottom of the mountain. Every girl carried a reed that was about twenty feet tall, hence the name Reed Dance. The tradition states that if a reed breaks during their walk then that particular girl is considered to be already sexually active.

This particular year had a record-breaking number of girls. Twenty-five thousand virgin dancers proceeding up the mountain road. From my point of view, I only saw a sea of twenty-five thousand reeds climbing the mountain.

The entire procession took about thirty-minutes. By tradition, each year a different Princess is chosen to lead the procession. This particular year's leader was the eldest daughter of the First

Queen. At this time, the King had five wives; all educated, strong business women. The lead daughter carried the reed directly to her father. They kiss on cheek and then the King takes the reed from her and breaks in on the door of his palace. He then sticks it in the door and the next stage of the procession begins.

All the maidens their reed leaning on the fence, representing the new year of prosperity for the King.

Even though the girls had traditional Zulu colors of red, orange, yellow, and white, their different patterns in their skirts, their beads, headdresses, and sashes uniquely represented each tribe.

Once I saw this part of the procession was coming to an end, I realized that I needed to get to the next shot. The King's attorney waved me to an open dirt road, *"Run down this road and stop in front of the stadium. You will capture the warriors running to take their place for the next part of the ceremony."*

Without hesitation, I ran as fast as I could with camera equipment draped off of my back and shoulders. I had no idea what to expect, but I set my tripod in the center of the road just as the attorney had told me to do.

I heard a thundering sound and tribal howls. Drums sounded louder and the ground began to vibrate. I raised my head to see the Zulu warriors racing down the path from the castle, running straight at me. I squeezed myself as small as I could, inhaled all my breath, and braced myself against my tripod. I think I might have screamed loudly as the warriors pounded past me.

They seemed to not even notice me or my camera, even though they parted ways like the red sea as they ran past me. I never had seen such a magnificent experience, even to date. I felt like I was in a National Geographic movie.

Once they settled into the stadium, the virgin maidens lined up to dance for the King and his court. I settled in to film in the hottest sun imaginable for eight straight hours. I never felt such heat and wind. I was parched and sweating but I was elated to have this experience.

One tribe after the next danced. Most girls had a look of shyness and respect. However, every once in a while there was a rebellious girl who wanted to make the crowd cheer and get a rise of applause and laughter. They wiggled a bit too much and let their short skirt dip below their hips. In a few situations, a skirt would accidentally fall completely to the ground. The crowd roared.

King Goodwill got up a few times during the day and spoke to his people. I did not understand the language of course, but when translated it was the message of hope and dignity. He encouraged the men to respect the women and for the women to respect themselves. He educated his people about safe sex, hoping that his voice would reach the masses and that the cases of HIV/AIDS would be decreased, or even eliminated for good. South Africa had been gravely impacted by HIV/AIDS over the years leaving children orphaned and villages devastated.

Tribe after tribe got up, continuing the ritual of music and dance.

Later that evening we attended a grand celebration in honor of the King. We ate wonderful food and danced the night away. However, I could not help to look over my shoulder for any potential dangerous situation.

That night we were all exhausted. However, before heading to bed the Princess shared stories about this particular castle and her mother, the Second Queen.

I noticed when I met the Princess that she had a long scar on her face, but I never really paid much attention, as her beauty far surpassed this mark. That night she told us the story of when her family and castle had been under siege by rebels and how they were all brutally attacked. Her scar came from a sword. I believe there were a few who died, and one Auntie who had her tongue cut out. I do not remember the details of which tribe, what year, and why, as I was suddenly thrown into a bit of a curve wondering if we were safe. We were way out in the bush and far away from any civilization. My family and friends did not even know where I was. I was far off the grid with no reception.

Needless to say I did not sleep well that night as I stared at the ceiling waiting for the sun to rise. I must have drifted off at some point, as the next morning I was awakened by a familiar African sound, the shouting of the rooster.

I heard a faint knock at my door. *"Come in."* I said.

I saw the door open slowly but I did not see a person enter. There was a small couch that was in front of the door that blocked my view. However, I saw a head bobbing from behind the couch. I wiped the sleep from my eyes. Perhaps I was having an illusion.

Within a few steps an older woman turned the corner of the couch and became fully visible. She was walking on her knees. She carried a tray with a teapot and cup, which explained her slow entrance. My mouth dropped as I saw her inch her way towards the bed. Her eyes averted to the other side of the room, to make sure no eye contact was made.

"Please… please stand up!" I could not fathom the idea of her walking to me on her knees. I respect other cultures and obviously this was their tradition, but I wanted her to know my gratitude of her bringing me tea. She smiled with eyes still averted. She placed the tray on the table next to my bed and swiftly exited.

I got up and walked into the large open room. I had not had a chance to really take in my surroundings, as the day before we only had time to drop our bags and run to the ceremony.

There was a long table against the wall. The early morning sun was streaming into the room. I walked over to the table and saw the most exquisite banquet of breakfast foods, all covered with this thin gossamer-type white netting to keep away the mosquitoes. I gently lifted the edge of the netting and took bites of tasty treats.

Princess Sibu walked into the room. This day was her birthday. This reminded me of her mentioning a few times the night before that she liked my dress, so I folded it up and ceremoniously bowed to give her my dress as an offering of gratitude. We hugged and proceeded to the final day of events.

Even though this event goes on for eight days, I was only going to be there for two days. My second day was filled with filming more girls dancing for the King and more speeches from the King.

I love being behind the lens of a camera, watching the world from an insular perspective. The camera allows me to form art in motion, as these dancers from each tribe showed their moves. Thousands of young virgins lined up row after row, bringing their passion to the crowd. Feet pounded, bells jingled, scarves waved, arms and legs danced in unison to their rhythm of their song. The tribes of drummers and musicians lined the stadium filling the air with heart-pounding music. This was a cultural feast of which I was far from being satiated. However, the high heat of the African sun created a great amount of sweat, and I felt faint from lack of water

The wind whisked the dirt through the air and I knew my camera and every inch of me had grains of sand in crevices that might take months to get out.

Our driver picked us up the next day and drove us back to our hotel in Durban. My one quest going back to the city was finding the maker of the amazing blanket that was on my bed at the castle. I was directed downtown to a district of blanket stores and searched high and low to find a blanket that still warms me to this day.

The energy in Durban was significantly different upon our return. The lack of police and military presence was definitely felt. We had to walk a bit faster, turn our heads more often, and keep an eye on our purses, our backs, and each other. The town was turned back over to the locals and the surfing tourists.

I was ready to go back to Los Angeles. I went to the post office to send a box of belongings back home, so that I would not have to pay extra for baggage on the airplane. I placed my African blanket, the United Nations materials, and business cards inside the box.

I made sure that my footage was safely placed in my carry-on bag. I made a solemn promise to Princess Sibu that I would not use the footage of their tradition and dance until I was given permission. I was granted permission a few years later, but to this day I have yet to share the footage of my experience. All of my footage has remained sacred in a box after all these years. I have realized while writing this book that the time has come to share this footage so that the story of these people from all over the world can be brought to life.

The first leg of my journey took twelve hours to London, along with a twelve hour layover at Heathrow Airport. I wanted to reach out to my friend Hiroshi who lived in London, but I realized that all of my business cards were in a box heading to Los Angeles. I walked around the airport from place to place, until finally I was tucked away in the silver-tubed airplane for a long journey back home.

Five or so hours into the flight I was awakened by the sound of the pilot's voice. *"Good morning ladies and gentlemen, I am sorry to disturb you, but I am sure that some of you have noticed that we have turned the plane around and are heading back to London Heathrow Airport."*

"What" I looked around and rubbed my eyes awake.

As he continued, I noticed that the flight attendants were standing stoically in the aisles, with forced smiles. *"Since the airspace above Los Angeles has been closed for any landing, we had no other choice but to turn around. We will keep you posted as we learn more. In the meantime, sit back and relax and we'll take care of the rest."*

"Excuse me... Miss...." I stated to the nearby attendant. *"Am I missing something? Last time I was in the United States there are hundreds of other airports to land between here and Los Angeles."*

"I'm sorry"...she said quietly and calmly, *"I have no other information other than what the pilot just shared with us. I'm sure everything will be alright."*

So I tried my best to stay distracted, and I watched the movie, *Shrek* over and over again until we landed back in London.

By the time we landed, it was dark. I looked out the tiny airplane window next to my seat and saw that Heathrow Airport looked like an airplane graveyard. We were the last plane to land for the evening, so stacks of planes were haphazardly scattered all over the tarmac.

As we pulled into the gate, I was in full view of all the action. I watched with exhausted curiosity as the following steps unfolded.

The jet bridge moved to connect us to the terminal. The flight attendants were standing at the airplane door as the final connection was in place. I will never forget seeing three uniformed people who pushed their faces up against the window, waiting to come on board. The door swiftly opened and without words they scurried up the stairs to the cockpit, while the attendants lowered the door to seal us back into the plane. I noticed that one person was carrying a piece of paper.

No landing instructions, we were just left in silence, waiting. I was trying to read the emotions of the flight attendants, but they were professional and emotionless.

Captain's voice came over the PA system. *"Ladies and gentlemen, we are sorry for any delay in getting you to your destination. As you may have noticed, there were uniformed guards who entered the plane to make sure that we do all procedures correctly. We have landed back in Heathrow due to an unfortunate tragedy that took place in the United States this morning. We do not know all of the details yet, but there was a bombing that took the World Trade Center down and many innocent persons died. If you live locally in the London area, we recommend that you proceed immediately to your home. If you are from another country we will do our best to accommodate you, but right now it seems that all hotels in the surrounding area are booked, as we are the last plane to land. The British Red Cross is on site to give out bottles of water and blankets if you do not have a place to stay. Again, we are sorry for any inconvenience. You can safely proceed to baggage claim and get your bags."*

9/11 - London Refugee

Like zombies we all proceeded out of the plane and into the baggage area. I had two enormous bags, along with my camera equipment. How was I going to sleep on the airport floor with all my equipment? *"This is not going to go down like this!"* I whispered to myself.

The Virgin Airline employees were sensitive and gracious. They explained what they could share, but we were all still very confused. Since they were a UK-based airline we had to come back to London. Otherwise, we would have been sent to another country. The only thing we knew was that the entire air space over the United States was off limits until further notice.

I got to the Virgin Airlines office, which was situated next to baggage claim area. I asked to use their phone. I was panicked as all of my business cards, including Hiroshi's number were in the box heading back to Los Angeles. I asked if there was a number for information. Somehow my angels whispered the name of Hiroshi's company in my ear. Thank God the number worked and there was one employee left to answer the phone, as it was after hours. He told me Hiroshi's cell phone number, I called to tell Hiroshi that I was stranded in London.

"Get a pen and write down my address. Have a cab take you to my home. My wife, Kate, is making up the guest room for you."

Hiroshi and Kate live in a lovely cottage-filled town about an hour outside of London. By the time I arrived safely to their home it was after 10:00 in the evening. The news was blasting the story for the hundredth time of the day, but it was the very first time I was seeing the devastating footage. Hiroshi and Kate were well informed of the story and they were shocked that I knew nothing.

I calculated the time of our original departure from Heathrow to the time of our turn-around in the sky and realized that we must have been right over the airspace of New York City at the time of the bombing. Hiroshi and Kate welcomed me with open arms. The following morning as I was coming down the stairs I overheard a conversation that Kate was having on the phone. *"Yes,…I know…so sad. I have a refugee in my home right now."*

I realized she was talking about me. I had never been referred to as a refugee. Refugees were people shifted out of their country because of a pending war, or disaster. Oh right…that was me!

Even though I was exhausted from Africa and I had promised myself to put my camera down for a few weeks to rest, I could not pass up this opportunity to film the aftermath of 9/11.

I grabbed my camera and tried my best to clean out the African dust from the lens and camera devices. I packed my backpack and jumped on the tube to head into London.

I sent emails to my family and friends as often as I could to let them know where I was and that I was still okay.

It was extremely somber in London. The news coverage was on all the time and everyone on the tube was reading the newspaper about the destruction.

There were thousands of people who poured into the streets in front of the palace for a very special changing of the guards. They hung all flags at half-mast all over the city and they even had a special performance with the changing of the guards, when they played the American National Anthem. It was quite moving to see people from all cultures come together for this historic event. I got the best footage that I could considering the circumstance.

I decided to take the afternoon and tour London. The feeling of this city overwhelmed me, with the sounds of Big Ben in the distance.

On my journey I ended up befriending a guy from Australia, a woman from New Jersey, and a guy from Germany. We all hung onto each other like one would expect after this sort of disaster, much like a codependent group of survivors.

The airlines took days to get back online. I did not have the proper clothing as the wet, brisk air was forming in the September dampness. I mostly had summer attire for Africa, so I was anxious to get back home.

I finally got on a plane almost two weeks later. I am truly grateful for Hiroshi and Kate who took me in. Otherwise, I would have had to sleep on the airport floor all that time.

I was grateful to the ones I met on my London path, who gave me hope that all is not lost and that humankind must be heading to a new place of kindness and love. At least that was what I was praying for at the time. None of us knew what would transpire over the following years, but I could hold on to hope.

I figure I have a choice everyday to be filled with deep gratitude. Life has little opportunity for a re-do, so I decide to take every minute as a tick-tock on the clock.

When I arrived back in Los Angeles, I went outside and kissed the ground. When I got back home, I opened the tattered, traveled box from Durban. I pulled out the cozy, African blanket and curled up on my bed, wrapped up in that vision of hope.

** 2002 Johannesburg, South Africa World Summit on Sustainable Development (WSSD)

The following year, in 2002, was my second trip to South Africa as a media-accredited journalist through the United Nations.

This time, we traveled to Johannesburg for the *World Summit on Sustainable Development* (WSSD). This time I was smart and brought a camera person with me, so that I would have double the angles and a travel buddy. Robert and I had just met, but I knew that becoming lifetime friends was inevitable.

Within the first 72-hours, I got sick with one of the worst bugs in my life. I barely moved out of bed. Once I got back on my feet, Robert and I worked together on everything from "running and gunning," to tripod standing during conference sessions. We covered the VIP event for the World Water Council and got up close to see Nelson Mandela speak, along with the United States Secretary of State, Colin Powell.

At the WSSD, environmental activists traveled from all over the world to see how we could secure our future with regard to global warming, climate change, and all the environmental protocols that the United Nations and World Leaders put forth on their agenda.

Los Angeles based artist John Quigley, or JQ, was also in attendance. JQ is famous for creating aerial art in which hundreds of people come together to form a shape that gives a social impact message when viewed from the air. I have participated in a few of these events over the years, and they are always powerful and exciting.

JQ brought a dance troupe called *Bandaloop* to perform on the famous Soweto water tower. The dancers suspended themselves from cables and danced on the side of the water tower to advocate for peace and equality. The performance was so breathtaking that I could barely hold the camera to film. Tears streamed down my face, as I watched the dancers leap from the side of the water tower, spinning around one another with grace.

Soweto had become the forefront of the anti-apartheid struggle in 1976, when youth from the area began a riot in retaliation to the government trying to impose their power. The riots spread to other townships, and hundreds of people were killed in the name of equality. Along with international attention and pressure on the government, this cracked the egg to end apartheid.

By the time I got to Soweto in 2002, I still felt the result of their struggle that gave them the ability to become more progressive.

On the last day of the conference, we heard about an international protest in the township of Alexandria. I hired a driver to take us to the protest.

Robert and I geared up with our cameras. We ventured into the over-crowded bumpy road, as thousands of people marched in the streets.

Flags and signs were carried through the streets, and the sound of chanting, singing, and drumming accompanied the various tribes' their cries for equality and their right to have clean water.

Most messages written on the signs declared anger towards President George Bush, as he was the only world leader who did not attend the WSSD. However, the main message of this protest was a demand for the basic rights of these people in the Alexandria Township to potable drinking water.

As it stood at the time, the government allowed water to drip into the homes for only six minutes each day, the equivalent of a small bucket. This drip-drop supply was the entire water supply for a family to survive, including water for drinking, bathing, and cooking.

This would mean that the women and children would have no other choice than to retrieve water from the wells, which could take hours each day. They would have to carry large and heavy pails on their heads back to their village. This also prevented children from attending school, thus perpetuating the culture of insufficient education.

This protest was life changing for me. I saw the disparity between how these people were living and how I had been living in the United States. This made me feel even more strongly to bring these issues to the world. Seeing these protests made me begin to realize that all of us have the power to have our voices heard and to make a difference in the world.

Robert and I were driven in a safe, air-conditioned car through the protest. We saw poverty from our window, and it was devastating. Our driver, Andile, was a sweet, young man who drove part-time to put himself through college. Andile knew the township well, so he took Robert and I through the back roads to give us access to different camera angles. I carried two cameras, one on each hip, raising one camera to capture video and the other camera to get still-shots. Cameras were much different back in 2002. Robert captured the wide angles of the protest.

At one point we were on the main road driving inside of the protest. I felt the passion in the crowd. We were so close we could reach out and touch the hands of the children who were skipping down the street with us. Even though they were in horrible conditions, they continued to laugh and smile.

I will never forget the faces of all those beautiful people who lived in small shack-homes that lined the streets. I felt like I was part of the problem and prayed to be part of the solution.

We rolled down the windows and sat on the rim of the car door to get better angels of the peaceful, determined people. My elbows became the tripod on the roof of the car to steady myself. The people represented all races, cultures, ages. Everything seemed to go by in slow motion, and my mind still plays this scene like it was yesterday.

I learned from the previous year during my time in Zululand to travel with water. I wanted to make sure that we were properly hydrated, so I stashed a supply of bottled water in the car. This day was a typical scorching, hot African day.

By mere habit, I reached into the car and pulled out a large bottle of water. Without thinking, I twisted off the cap and downed the precious gulps of water. Water spilled out of the corners of my mouth due to the bumpy road. As I regained my balance, my eyes met the eyes of the villagers who stared back at me. I felt this tsunami wave of guilt, as I realized I was sitting in an air-conditioned car, drinking water, while these people could literally be dying of thirst.

From that exact moment on, common phrases took on a new meaning to me. Whenever I hear someone say *"I'm starving to death"* or *"I'm dying of thirst"* my mind races back to Alexandria. Many people from privileged worlds use these phrases, but they have no idea what it is truly like to be without water or food.

We visited an orphanage in Soweto before we left Johannesburg. This special place is run by nuns who dedicate their lives to children orphaned by the AIDS crisis.

There is a wing in the orphanage for the mothers who are in process of dying. Even for the children who had not contracted the disease, it is a traumatizing experience for them to watch their moms and relatives die. And, even the other children die before their eyes.

My heart broke as I held these babies who were tiny beyond imagination. A small girl who was two years old was the size of a healthy six-month-old baby. I will never forget the feeling as I held her, as her lungs rattled with her labored breathing. Her pain vibrated through my hand and into my body. I wish I could have healed every one of these babies.

There was one boy who captured my heart. His name was Goodwin and he was up for a type of adoption called sponsored adoption in which someone elected to send money for his monthly medication fees. When they brought him out of the back room and told me his story, I wept. They asked all of us if anyone wanted to sign up for little Goodwin. Without hesitation, I raised my hand and picked him as my adopted son. I was not sure how I would come up with the monthly payment, but I would make it work. Goodwin sweetly smiled and took my hand. He looked up to me with these extra-large dark brown eyes. His heart and soul were beaming from his tiny, framed body. I bent over and received one of the most unforgettable hugs of my life.

Goodwin and I communicated through letters we sent back and forth between us. The nuns were saints to me, as they had no other life but this orphanage. They sent pictures and updates of Goodwin's progress, which, for a while, was mostly good. That was until the dreaded letter came stating that little Goodwin did not make it through his treatments. His poor body gave out and he passed while still at the orphanage. I still feel him as one of my spirit guides from the other side. Goodwin guides me through my days. A great name to have as an angel...Good-Win.

Soundcloud Playlist - In the Arms of the Angels - Sarah McLachlan

The last day in Johannesburg, a group of us traveled to Kruger National Park. One of our sponsors, Cody Kruger, was a member of the Kruger family. We hammered Cody with questions about the park and the importance of conservation and animal preservation. We were interested in finding ways to implement our passion about the hunting and poaching of rhinos and elephants. He avoided our tantrums, but hopefully our words stuck somehow. I have always, and continue to be a huge fan of elephants. We need to stop the madness of animal poaching, and collecting ivory, and let nature take its course.

We all ventured to Cape Town to experience the amazing sea-coast township. Cape Town reminded me of the French Riviera, mixed with the beauty of Africa. We took a tour of wine-country and did wine-tastings throughout the region.

We were finally able to exhale from the stressful conference and make a plan of action. We made a promise to one another to stay committed to taking care of our planet. And, to this day each of us has continued to do what we can to change the world through education, empowerment, and activism.

** BALI Global Peace Summit - Fall 2004

Bali is one of my favorite places that I have ever been. I was invited to attend a global peace conference and travel to the pure magical land of Bali. Upon arriving, I felt this gentle wave come over me like I had never felt before, as if the island enveloped me with love.

I settled into my hotel room and ventured out to the streets to explore the local culture.

I went to a local market on the main street in Ubud to get a bottle of water. In the short time that I was in the market, a gentle rain misted the air. I stood in the doorway contemplating which way to go. Left … or right?

Such a simple decision. Have you ever just stood still wondering which way to go? This is just like the sliding door theory, one way could lead you to a completely different story.

I chose to go right. The rain became more intense so I quickened my step. Coming around the corner was a young man who ran right into me. We exchanged apologies and polite comments, until he said, *"Who are you? What brought you to Bali?"*

I said, *"The hope and prayer of global peace."* He smiled and said, *"Can we sit for tea. I would like to hear more."*

We tucked ourselves away into a local tea cafe. Time slipped away without notice. He told me that his name was Rafi. Rafi told me about his ancestors and their wood-sculpting artistry that had been carried through the generations of family for the past 300 years. When it was time to leave, Rafi said, *"I'll pick you up at your hotel in three days and I will take you to my village to see my gallery."*

I agreed. Until then, I was immersed in attending the conference. On the first evening I met three other Americans who were also attending the conference alone. We quickly became the four musketeers.

We went on a tour of the famous Monkey Forest. There were signs everywhere that warn you to hide your camera, take off your hat and glasses and pretty much tie everything to your body, as these frisky tree-swinging adorable creatures have no fear to jump on you, take your belongings, and sit high in a tree wearing your hat, smiling all the while. They had no shame to fornicate, masturbate, urinate, and defecate for all eyes to see.

We took a hike in the rice fields and saw the local people harvest grains of rice. The scenery looked like a painting that had come to life. The multi-tiered emerald green slopes were neatly groomed, and the farmers wore their pointed straw hats to keep the sun off their faces. Some farmers used large, strange shaped wooden tools, while others carried double-barreled baskets. It was magical. I could only hear Sting's song Fields of Gold running through my mind as I soaked in the eye-candy of the land.

We took a cooking lesson in the middle of the rice field. It was an evening class so I was able to see the blooming of a lotus flower right at my feet. I watched this lotus poke out of the dark mud, while the pure white petals glistened in the reflection of the lights of our cooking area. I often see myself in the core of the lotus, rising out of the mud like the Phoenix out of the ashes.

Our instructor shared recipes and cooking techniques with local herbs and sauces. The food was tropical and fresh and I never wanted to leave.

The highlight of the conference was sitting by myself under the shade of a tree. Bishop Desmond Tutu and his lovely wife sat down beside me and we proceeded to have a lengthy conversation about my love for Africa and the work they were doing. I had a copy of *"Bella Wishes"* in my bag, so I gave Bishop Tutu the book to bring to his library in South Africa. I loved the idea that my beautiful Bella hippopotamus could bring joy to the children in his orphanage.

Three days flew by and the conference came to an end. Rafi arrived at the front of the hotel at the exact designated time. He had no idea that I would bring my three new best friends, but he welcomed us all. We climbed into his car to explore the countryside of paradise.

Upon entering his gallery and workshop, Rafi unveiled a large statue of a goddess that he was carving. He was not yet finished, but I instantly fell in love with the detail and beauty of his magnificent work. He told us that this goddess was named Dewi Sri, which is the goddess of fertility and prosperity, as well as she was the goddess of rice for the abundance of food for their families.

Rafi took me aside and told me that he wanted to share something very special with me. He walked me into the backroom of his workshop, as my friends continued to walk around his gallery. He had this small statue that was underneath a white cloth. Before he unveiled this piece, he shared that he wanted to thank me for our conversation the day we met. He said that he had been having a creative block for many months and that he had not been able to carve for that long. He was not able to remove this block until we had our conversation. He came home that night and began to carve a statue inspired by me. I was flabbergasted. How was that even possible?

Rafi lifted the veil to reveal an angel coming out of the crocodile wood. Tears came to my eyes; I had never seen anything so beautiful. I was speechless to hear that I had inspired him. This reminds me that we never know how we impact one another either in positive or negative ways.

I commissioned Rafi to complete a larger statue. I had both statues shipped to my house and they remain a constant reminder of the magic. Even while I was homeless, I kept these precious statues in a safe place with dear friends.

My last night in Bali I had a life-changing dream, which I still remember to this day. I was walking down a white dirt road. There was the deep, green forest to the right of me, and an open field with golden wheat to the left. I was following a baby elephant down the road. I had no idea where I was going, but I knew I was heading in the right direction. Suddenly, a group of people from all nationalities came out of the forest and they fell in line behind me and followed me, as I followed the baby elephant.

We ended up at the base of large stairs that led up to a shining, golden temple. I stopped at the base of the stairs, the people stopped behind me, and the baby elephant began to climb the stairs.

I felt the urge to climb the stairs and was encouraged to do so when the elephant turned his eyes towards me and invited me to follow.

The people stayed behind as I continued to climb. I noticed that with every step the elephant grew larger and larger. As he climbed, he began to grow to such huge proportions that he began to walk on his hind legs. The elephant got so big that the golden temple was hidden behind his large frame.

The elephant was now standing. He twisted his upper body and turned towards me. His front legs became arms that reached towards me and covered my hands which were now extended towards him. The elephant looked deep into my eyes and said, *"Yes, my dear, all obstacles have now been removed from your path. Now, is the time to live your purpose."*

I will never forget his piercing, loving eyes that penetrated my soul. I knew there was more that I needed to do in my life and that my journey had just begun.

I walked through the rice fields that turned gold from the setting sun. I saw a lotus rise out of the mud right before my eyes. The magic of Bali entered my soul, never to leave.

**Soundcloud Playlist - Fields of Gold - Sting

** SRI LANKA - DECEMBER 26, 2004

I was visiting my family for Christmas in 2004. News struck that one of the most devastating tsunamis of our lifetime hit the beaches of Thailand, Indonesia, India, Maldives, Malaysia, and Sri Lanka. This came as a shock to the world and to me, as I was just in those same waters when I was in Bali.

My friend Camille, who had been with me as part of the (YES! Youth Summit) in Geneva in 2001, called to say that she had a dear friend who was from Sri Lanka and that she wanted to help in the aftermath of the devastation that struck his country. Her friend, the Venerable Bhante Walpola Piyananda, had his dear countrymen in deep trouble from the horrific storm, and they needed help.

So Camille and I formed a group together under the World Trust Foundation called the Hollywood Artist Alliance. We raised money from our community in the entertainment industry and partnered with Bhante to build homes. Bhante, a sweet monk with a beautiful soul and big heart, is considered the Dalai Lama of Sri Lanka.

Our first trip to Sri Lanka was devastating to witness. We arrived only eight weeks after the tsunami, and the footage I captured paled in comparison to what we witnessed firsthand. Since Bhante is a highly revered leader of his country, we were able to move mountains in a short period of time, including meeting with one of Bhante's dearest friends, the Prime Minister Mahinda Rajapaksa. who was soon after named President of Sri Lanka.

On this trip our goals were to hire a contractor, architect, builders, and work with the media to get the word out about raising funds. We returned to Sri Lanka a second time to continue to spread the word of our building project. We also focused our message to help the orphanage that was attached to Bhante's monastery.

This experience fostered my passion for helping young girls and their need for education. In most of the world, girls are held in orphanages until they turn eighteen, at which point they are turned out into the streets without proper guidance or additional schooling. The girls inevitably fall into prostitution and/or sex trafficking. Camille and I did everything we could do prevent this from happening with the girls at Bhante's orphanage. With the help of Bhante, we opened a scholarship fund that offered eighty girls to continue their education once they turned eighteen. I often imagine what these young girls grew up to be.

By this second trip of ours, we had raised enough funds to built thirty-eight homes. I asked for Airline Ambassadors (AAI) to come with us. AAI was founded by a dear friend, Nancy Rivard, and it was composed of flight attendants and volunteers who traveled the world combining charity with tourism. I traveled with them as one of their filmmakers for a few years and loved every trip that I took.

For the Sri Lanka project, AAI brought the famous Dr. Patch Adams. Since the good doctor is famous for being the "clown doctor" bringing smiles to patients and orphans worldwide, all of the volunteers dressed like clowns to visit the villages.

One of my favorite parts about Sri Lankans was how graceful and peaceful they were. Even though they had lost their possessions, homes, and family members, they always had a smile on their face.

One of my sweetest memories was when we took thirty girls from the orphanage to buy shoes. They had never been to a shoe store before, and the only shoes they owned were either donated, or were hand-me-downs. The girls skipped out of the monastery, holding hands and giggling. We climbed onto the monastery bus. Their excitement was as thick as the scorching humidity that made my feet and hands swell. Everything about this day trip was special. They sang Christmas carols for us, as these were the only songs they knew in English. We laughed all the way to the shoe store, at the ho-ho-ho songs in the high-high-high heat.

Once we got there, it took time for the girls to understand the concept of a shoe store. They walked around looking at all the shoes lined up aisle after aisle. We noticed a few girls stopped to admire a certain pair of shoes. They shyly hesitated and then picked up the shoes. They were not sure how to try them on, as they did not want to hurt their friends' feelings if they wanted the same pair of shoes. They did not grasp the fact that there was a large room in the back of the store that had the same pair of shoes in all of their sizes. Their faces were precious when they realized that they could all have the same pair of shoes.

A few of the older girls gravitated to a shoe that had a small heel. I watched Bhante walk over to these girls and gently take the shoe out of their hand, placing it back on the shelf. He smiled and handed them a more appropriate shoe without a heel.

Camille and I beamed as we watched the girls skip back to the bus, each carrying a bag with their old shoes. Each girl wore her new shiny shoes and a smile on her face.

When the houses were built and ready to be given to the families, we had a ribbon-cutting ceremony and celebration. The First Lady of Sri Lanka came to cut the ribbon and speak to the people. We handed over the keys to each family. We bought bicycles for each family to have for transport from their home to the fishing village where they worked. They also received a welcome basket of soaps, lotions, supplies, and several toothbrushes and toothpastes generously donated by my brothers from the Iowa Dental Supply Company. It was the first time I asked my brothers to be involved with a volunteer donation and it was very special to me that they were a part of this event.

Airline Ambassadors had donated supplies as well for the grand opening of the homes. I loved working with AAI, as I continued to volunteer on their media team, on trips to orphanages to Cambodia, Thailand, Vietnam, and El Salvador. These adventures expanded my wings of love inside my heart, as well as footage that was captured for the series that needed a distribution platform. I continued to pitch to the networks in Los Angeles for feel-good content. The answer always came back,

"It's a little bit too soft." All the more reason I continued to fly, expand, and dream.

WINGS OF LOVE EXPAND

September 2016, I was in New York at the United Nations again, this time meeting at the Embassy for Zambia in preparation for the First Ladies Award Ceremony to honor the First Lady of Zambia and the women involved with the African Women Entrepreneurs Program (AWEP). AWEP is an offshoot of the African Growth Opportunity Act (AGOA), out of the State Department here in the United States. Through AWEP, African women are encouraged to become entrepreneurs and begin their own international businesses. This was a fantastic opportunity that I never knew existed. Why couldn't these sort of programs hit the news and inspire people to get involved?

In this meeting at the Zambian embassy, I realized that the rise of the African women was finally taking shape. I interviewed these AWEP women who had transformed their ancestral jobs of walking through the streets with large baskets on their heads, into export businesses selling the plentiful products from their respective regions in Africa. They were able to transform mangoes, tomatoes, and cassava into brilliantly packaged goods ready for global distribution. I was inspired to see a significant shift in the empowerment of these women and consequently of their families, villages, and countries. Finally, there was an innovative approach to empower these women and fortunately as well, offer an education to their girls.

The AWEP team gathered in the conference room at the embassy. The women seated themselves on one side of the table, while the men sat on the opposite side. I listened to their conversation, as it swelled into a heated debate.

A passionate roar grew from one wonderful woman, Eleni, who smiled through her powerful stance while she wagged her fingers at the men in the room. *"You African men need to step down and let us women take over from now on. You have held the power for the past fifty-years since our independence and you have done nothing, but push us into the ground and disallow us from advancing as a society, or as a country."* She pounded her fist on the table. *"Now is the time for us women!"*

I was not sure which way the conversation would go from there, as I watched the other women squirm in their chairs while the men slowly shifted from side to side.

Much to my surprise the men in the room were gracious and interested in approaching the topic respectfully. The men stated that they needed guidance on how to support their women as they became more empowered. These were African men... this was astonishing to me.

It reminded me of the beginning of this revolution of microcredit and microfinance, which started when the Bangladeshi social economist and banker, Muhammad Yunus, was awarded the Nobel Peace Prize in 2006 for founding the Grameen Bank. Yunus was a leader in helping to empower women from many developing countries through this system.

Even though the microfinance system had some struggles, due to the fact that there were men who were threatened by their women and their newfound empowerment. There were many reports of the rise in domestic violence. There had to be this balance between the masculine and the feminine to truly get to a place of success and progress. However, especially recently, I have been feeling the feminine rise on a global scale. I feel a birth emerging.

Understanding my journey of pain, healing, growth, and international exploration was the first step I took in giving birth to an international network to serve my purpose of healing the world through women. After reviewing the transformation that I had gone through, I was now finally emerging to give birth to GWEN.

This has been a stormy and surprising ride in life. I am hanging on for dear life: waiting, watching, wondering. I have become even more dedicated to build a network that could be a distribution platform for conscious programs, films, and series. Shining a spotlight on mentorship for building confidence, so that our past stories could reveal ourselves to heal. I found the need to make a difference by bringing experts and activists together to talk about communication, inspiration, financial literacy. I loved the thought of producing programs that would keep stories alive that were being held sacred through the wisdom-keepers from all over the world, while also embracing a new loving world. As I began to heal, I also began to uncover the concept that each and every one of us has a story to share, no matter the storms we have ridden.

Soundcloud Playlist - Riders on the Storm - The Doors

Chapter 23

The Birth of Gwen

As the title of Part 3 indicates, GWEN is Born: The Immaculate Perception, there is a birth to announce. Now is the time for the actual birth of GWEN, even though the inception in 2012 was not the full birth. I had to jump through fires, dive back into the caves and rabbit holes, to pull myself through the various stages of healing.

Today, June 3, 2018 is nearing the release of this story, realizing that there are many forms of giving birth and I could not do this without my faith, good friends, and those enemies that my mom warned me about, *"with friends like that you don't need enemies."* I believe life gives us the lessons through the people around us. If you do not believe this concept, then look up and look around. Who is around you giving you support, giving you a positive reflection, communicating from the heart? Then, look around and see who is being a time vampire, energy vampire, drama queen/king? When I say vampire, I am not describing a long-toothed demon ready to suck your neck for blood. These are the sort of friends, relatives, co-workers who want you to constantly stay in the drama of your life, rather than uplifting you.

This particular morning is a typical gloomy Los Angeles morning, that we call "June Gloom." This is the type of morning that grants us "Angeleans" a glimpse of what it must be like to live in Vancouver or Seattle. The typical California blue skies are filled with grey, and a spitting mist envelops our cars and lawns with gentle dew. There is a chill in the air that hints that summer is not quite upon us. Our Indian summers last late into October, so our spring starts late as well.

It has been seven years since January 21st, 2011 which was the day I had jumped into the metaphorical fire of homelessness. I am entering the final stages of launching this book and the GWEN platform with the true birth of GWEN. However, the last seven years has taken me into the fire and back out the other side. These past seven years has given me the appreciation and gratitude for my challenging times, as the saying goes, *"What doesn't kill you makes you stronger."*

I was seeing life in small circles symbolizing time frames and lessons learned. Somehow through the grapevine, JPM was back in the picture. Of course, most people are motivated by their own personal agenda and he is no different. This past February (2018) JPM approached Leontine to help him with his campaign, as "surprise" he was going to run for Congo president again, in the 2018 elections. Leontine spouted off to him that she would not help him, unless he paid me back after all these years. He agreed to get on a call with me and I was ecstatic to watch the flow of full circle and to get paid after all these years.

On April 25th he called from Congo, as he had supposedly moved from Belgium to Congo the year before. He knew about my book coming out, as Leontine forced this issue to see that he should make good on his past, so that the Congolese could support him. Our conversation began with a formal greeting. He tiptoed his way, trying to make light jokes about his wife and I having the Italian gene in common, seeing how I would react. He admitted that he owed money and that I had the most precious footage of his life in my possession. He crafted a dangled carrot, trying to lure me back into the hole, complimenting my nature and commitment. I waited for the other shoe to drop, as he mentioned several times that he had every intention of paying, but he would have to deliver a proposal to me the following week.

During our call I confronted him on some issues from our time on the road; including the alleged situation with the young journalist and his midnight entrance into her bedroom. Like all these Hollywood men who put the blame on the women, calling them liars, it was like he read from the same secret male society handbook of how to divert attention to get away from taking responsibility. I told him that my dream was to put an addendum to this book and give the readers a great update that he had come through in the end. No such luck! Instead, he boasted about him being assured that he would be the next President and that certainly anyone who said anything bad about him was also a liar.

However, as fate put serendipity into my life, at this same time I was introduced to another man running for President, alongside yet another candidate, Felix Tshisekedi, who was the guy I had dinner with back in 2010 while I was in Congo. It was his father who was going to run at that time. How strange that I would know three of the candidates who were running against one another for the race to become President of the Congo. Life has funny ways of showing up.

As I was preparing for my call with JPM, I was digging through my archives of correspondence over the years, I stumbled upon a very interesting email that I forgot about. In this email, JPM admitted of owing Kim, Rigo and me money, and he begged for our forgiveness.

JPM writes:

Dear Kim, Rigo and Tess,

Observing what's happening in my country today as well as in North Africa, I was bound to ask myself the following question: Why all this destruction?

I came to the simple answer: Lack of trust between human beings and especially amongst leaders that leads to fear of one another and finally to conflicts and deaths of the innocents.

My Second question was: Are you participating to peace or wars, as a leader?

My answer was: Right now I'm participating to peace as a political leader but to wars as an individual. Out of my weakness to have disappointed you for not paying you YET, I would like to ask for your forgiveness. Indeed, any moves that are being made right now are not from the campaign budget or even from my personal funds but from supporters ALONE. This is the simple truth and fact. Until this situation improves, I'm not in a position to pay you and will definitely do, once this parameter changes and it will.

Today, I feel sorry and not happy about the problems I've put you through and pray that better times will come when my heart will thank you in deeds for all you have done for this Tango Ekoki-Saa Inatimiya campaign.

All of this, I owe it to you and money cannot buy this input you have provided with your hearts and thoughts.

I've made lots of mistakes in my life and will make more but I've been sincere in my endeavors towards you. I have made commitments I have not been able to attend to yet and that's been also a learning curve for me and the ideals I wish to accomplish for my people. I would like to express though that I'm totally committed to the cause of justice and peace in my country and the rest of the world. My family has and continues to give me its fullest support in all my endeavors for the campaign.

I will be with the Pope this Wednesday in his office in the Vatican and ask all of you to forgive me for all my wrongs.

May my plea for forgiveness be heard and God have mercy on me?

Tango Ekoki-Saa Inatimiya

This email was sent in 2011, which for some reason he gave me the same excuses in 2018. He says he is known throughout his people for being a "brilliant and successful" businessman, so I am not sure how he can run for being President when he refuses to pay his obligations. How is he to run a country with billions of dollars at stake and to make sure his country is safe. However, I still hold out hope that we will get paid.

I believe that JPM made some valid points about leaders and people and fear and more. I feel this every day with our current situation in the United States. Even though this financial crisis in my life occurred while working for JPM and that was the tipping point of becoming homeless, I still know that God has a bigger plan.

Over the years I have mingled with superstars and rock stars, dined with Kings and Presidents. I have had the privilege of traveling to places that people only dream about, so I do feel that I have had many blessings.

During the time that I was without a home I had to rely heavily on my friends to be the refuge from my storm. I had to find places to live and places that could take my beloved animals. I knew that I was responsible for my situation, which only made matters worse.

I was deep inside the struggle, but I tried to stay on course with a positive attitude. I smiled a lot and practiced the art of surrender. I prayed to God and wondered when the pressure would let up. I knew there were lessons to be learned, but I had no way of knowing where or how to begin. I had to tear down the facade I presented to the world and show my real face of pain. But I was not ready for that yet. Through these past seven years I had to find a way to go underneath my ego and spit it out of my existence and know that I had to answer to myself and to God. Of course, ego is hidden in the deep pockets and it is not possible to get rid of it all, but I could at least try.

I headed into this storm thinking I was sailing towards healing waters. However, the back and forth throughout these years, was the exact lessons that I needed to have in order to fully do the work that I came here to do.

I thank God for the awareness that I have been given and to realize the change in the course for humanity. I had to learn how to keep my feet on the ground.

There were times when the turn on my road was so curvy that I was thrown off balance. Life tipped me so far that I was riding sideways on two wheels instead of four. The mountain's edge was looming. If I did not quickly grow wings to fly I would tumble down the mountainside, coming out a mangled mess. At that point I would end up being no good for anyone, not even myself.

During my time of homelessness, I never had to live in my car, in a shelter, or on the street. I was blessed to have loving people who needed me to be a house sitter, family chef, estate planner, dog walker, or garden tender. I did not fool myself into believing that they were happy that I was there, as I imagined the conversations they were having behind closed doors, when they whispered, *"When will she get it together? When will she get a break? When will she leave our house?"*

There were times that I felt that I did not belong anywhere in the world. These conflicted feelings were the most trying part of this experience, as I am a "Cancer" girl, a homebody and consummate hostess. I thrive on cooking for my friends and entertaining in my home, proudly displaying the artifacts and treasures that I have collected from my travels.

From the outside looking in, no one knew I was homeless. I dressed well, wore my best matching jewelry, trendy shoes, and a smile. However, beneath my smile and second-hand designer clothes, was a sadness that had been hidden for a very long time. I would drive near areas where homeless people lived in the streets, including Skid Row in Downtown Los Angeles, and look at these people living in tents on the street and I heard this voice in my head. *"Tess, you're not going to be in that place, but you are two steps away from being on the streets…so never forget. When you get on your feet, you will do everything you can to help those who are less fortunate than you."*

I looked up to heaven and I answered that voice, *"Yes…Yes…I am here to serve."* I dug down deep, dropped to my knees, and pleaded for the strength to keep on going. I had to rely on divine inspiration to keep me on my path, to keep me from going into depression. I had to strive to become better than I could ever imagine, as only then would the years of abuse make sense.

•• The Labor Pains of Birth

Going back to January 2011, I was packing my boxes again to move into my leap of faith. Outside of becoming homeless, not everything was grim for me at the time, as the song I wrote, *Politics of Love* was nominated for Best World Song of the Hollywood Music in Media Awards (HMMA).

I was planning to move back to San Francisco as that seemed to be my happy place. However, God had another plan where I had to learn the beauty of surrender. Although I did not know it at the time, I found myself in a tangled web that brought a few key people into my life that led me to the breadcrumbs to my next chapter in life. I had no idea where I was going. I had to keep my faith. The HMMA's led me to Brenda Brown, which led me to John Vinestreet. Vinestreet led me to new girlfriends, Delbi, Anika, and Mama Sue, which led me to Michael. Michael was a semi-retired real estate guy, who came from a very successful real estate family. His parents, sister, and uncle had all passed, so he was probably feeling the same sort of ironic freedom that I felt when both my parents had passed. Michael was working with his friend Lynn on a t-shirt and song project for women. The three of us met and began going down the road of working together. The long and the short of it, we began to focus the ideas on how we could bring all of this to the marketplace, while utilizing my nonprofit background. Things shifted and twisted and we planted the seeds of Global Women's Empowerment Network (GWEN) which was a name that we chose out of a list of names that were thrown into the mix, inspired by Kim (same attorney from the Congo project).

During that time, I volunteered to go with the Jewish World Watch (JWW) to Capitol Hill to fight for the Congolese women and children. JWW was passionate this particular year to change the International laws for the processing of Coltan. I found out we, as the delegation, were set to talk to elected officials about Blood-Coltan and the human rights crisis. I felt this was a wink from God. Being that our delegation was from California, we had private meetings with Senator Barbara Boxer and Senator Dianne Feinstein's office, as well as Representative Howard Berman and a few more. I was asked to share my story of being in the Congo and the plight of the women and children. I felt that karma was on my side and even though the film for JPM would never be seen, I felt that my work was not in vain.

Our goal was to tell our personal stories to activate the passion for these elected officials to influence Mary Shapiro (Chairperson of the Securities and Exchanges Commission-SEC) to change international mining laws so that the people of Eastern Congo would be protected.

About a year after our trip I researched to find out the outcome. Even though it was not all that we expected, I was happy to see familiar names listed in the letter of those people who were taking a stand, including Representative, Howard Berman. They were committed to take a stand as a voice for the people. This represented to me that each one of us can make a difference with our voice and with our passion and most importantly, with our vote.

Global Women's Empowerment Network (GWEN) was officially founded in January 2012. April of this same year I found a lovely home to move into, so I was settled back on a salary, sharing the vision of my dream, and seemingly making it all work.

We were in growing stages, so there was an influx of energy thrown into the mix. This was a long journey of learning how women can often go against one another and how the feeling of being betrayed can take years to heal.

I had brought on three women for various jobs within GWEN. Long story short, they ended up ruining GWEN's chances for funding in 2014. I was devastated when this happened and it literally took me years to come out of my cave. I had to realize that God gave me this experience for the purpose of making a mandate for GWEN to uncover such stories, so that we can reveal to heal. I felt betrayed by these women, but mostly by my partner in the business, as he was privy to their plight and did nothing to stop them. He eventually realized his mistake and that he had been manipulated by these women too, but it was too late. Throughout the following years of 2014 to present, I got to see who was loyal, who stayed with me during this time, and who ran away when the money stopped.

Even though I felt tremendously betrayed, I had to somehow figure out how I betrayed myself. All roads lead back to ourselves. This was a hard pill to swallow and even though it was a swallowed pill, it wallowed in my stomach and heart for a very long time. This is why GWEN took a step to the side, even though the heart and spirit of "GWEN" and "me" was growing to a different level. I had to forgive myself of the self-judgment of what in the heck I was doing with my life.

Life got to a point where I was too traumatized to leave my house. I let myself be paralyzed and let the dream and vision of GWEN became stagnated.

When I began to heal and share my story to get through the pain, every woman I spoke to said, *"Me too"* which was before the #metoo movement, but every woman I spoke to had been betrayed by other women, for some reason or another. This has to be a innate insecurity that is either trained, or shown my example, for women to pit themselves against one another. How can we make this change and be a full stand for one another?

I had to maintain the vision of GWEN, but also allow GWEN to grow to the place where we are today. I had to take the high roads, low roads, mangled roads, just to get to the other side.

During this time, the co-founder of GWEN decided to move to Europe. I was happy that he went onward to explore his new life, but it caused a bevy of other challenges. Again, I had to look in the mirror to figure out why I was continuing to attract such experiences and why I continued to stay, cleaning up his messes, rather than walking away. I was like a dog on a bone to make sure that GWEN would not die, breathing life support into her soul without even having any breath in my own body. Again, the theme of oxygen mask continued.

I struggle to write about this experience, which also delayed the release of this book. However, when it came time to sit down about betrayal and unjust behavior, I had to deal with the embarrassment of it all and finally healing. I also thought the story would take up the majority of the book and that every painful detail would have had to be spelled out to feel fully expressed.

However, the joy of lessons learned is that one can move forward with freedom and most of all forgiveness. This has to be one of the most important lessons I had to learn during these years. A lesson in the beauty of forgiveness and how it leads to freedom.

"Forgive those who trespass against us" took on new meaning. I took the precious time to look at every corner of my life and forgive my parents, teachers, boyfriends, classmates, women, and abusers. I had to learn how to forgive myself for my past, my present, and even my future, so that I would no longer be a prisoner to myself any more. Everything is in our control, even if it is something that is not kind or wonderful. How we look at things and how we react to situations is what helps us move forward in life.

Just in case God did not think I was paying attention, I was given yet another example of how to succeed when people cross my path with ill intentions.

This was the Christmas season of 2016. I love the holidays and it was my intention to wake up early on Christmas morning, do my traditional rituals, and then lock myself away to write for the rest of the day.

I decided to break this book into a trilogy with the last section called, *GWEN is Born: The Immaculate Perception.* As we know from the bible stories, the "Immaculate Conception" refers to the virgin birth of Jesus by Mary. This concept is something a young Catholic girl never questioned. However, as an adult this concept often comes to mind. After researching several religious doctrines, the concept of the immaculate perception began to take on new meaning to me as a symbolic connection.

Catholics point to the conflict between the serpent and the woman, which is equal to the conflict between the serpent and the woman's offspring. Therefore, it was not that Mary was a "virgin" when she was pregnant with Jesus, but that God knew that Mary was "full of grace" so that she would be sinless to give birth to Jesus, as Jesus was the chosen Son of God to live on this earth without sin. They explain this by saying that Mary, must be as equally sinless as her offspring, Christ. *"Hail Mary, full of grace the Lord is with thee"* now made sense to me. I always had a special affinity for the stories of Mother Mary. I even traveled to the site of her final home and resting place in Mount Nightingale, outside of Ephesus, Turkey. I found it beautifully odd that her home is now a shrine for both Catholics and Muslims. Imagine the idea to truly know that there is a common ground between us all and that we could take great strides towards peace.

Mother Mary is a role model to me, as she prepared herself to give birth. I am in no way stating that I am the Mother Mary, but I feel that the maternal and feminine side of our world is starving to be birthed. Just like for many decades now, people have talked about having Christ- consciousness. This concept seemed no different to how I take my role in the birth of GWEN seriously, as giving birth to a global concept like GWEN, during this time in history means more to me now than ever before.

I feel that all of us have a calling and that each one of us are chosen by God to be here to take part in this planetary evolution either by the LIGHT (surrender, forgiveness, love) or the DARK (prejudice, hatred, fear). God chose Mary to bear His Son. God chooses us to bear the concept of love. I choose love!

I have become more committed to living a life of grace personified.

"Hail Mary full of grace, the Lord is with thee. Blessed art thou among women and blessed are the fruit of thy womb Jesus. Holy Mary, Mother of God pray for us sinners now and at the hour of our death. For thine is the kingdom and the power of glory."

This prayer, which has been embedded in my soul since childhood took on a new meaning in the world today. I work everyday to manifest a simple, peaceful, and loving life filled with grace. I have become more mindful of the interactions between myself and others. I had to find the balance of having empathy and being aware of others, while also taking care of myself. Life often throws us curves, so it has become relevant to keep on my toes and watch for the signs on the road. However, this is my "perception" of the immaculate, rather than the "conception" of the immaculate.

**Soundcloud Playlist – Nightengale Music - Delbi Smart Vocals

It is hard to witness the ways of the world today, covered with much darkness and racial injustice. Since I studied various religions growing up, I believed that everyone had the same underlying belief systems. This was something I talked about since I was a child, when I was taken to all those bible camps with my neighbors, while attending Catholic mass by myself. To me this was the underlying message of all religions is that everything comes down to how we treat others, as a reflection upon ourselves.

Christianity

In everything, do to others as you would have them do to you. For this is the law and the prophets.

Judaism

What is hateful to you, do not do to your neighbor. This is the whole Torah; all the rest is commentary.

Buddhism

Treat not others in ways that you yourself would find hurtful.

Hinduism

This is the sum of duty: do not do to others what would cause pain if done to you.

Taoism

Regard your neighbor's gain as your own gain, and your neighbor's loss as your own loss.

Islam

Not one of you truly believes until you wish for others what you wish for yourself.

Zoroastrianism

Do not do unto others whatever is injurious to yourself

Jainism

One should treat all creatures in the world as one would like to be treated.

Sikhism

I am a stranger to no one; and no one is a stranger to me. Indeed, I am a friend to all.

("Ayurveda," by Curejoy).

Christmas Eve in my neighborhood holds a tradition that has gone on for the past thirty years. This famous Christmas truck saunters from street to street, even down my street, right in front of my house. Thousands of white, twinkling lights adorn a huge semi-truck pulling a lit-up train filled with carolers singing, elves dancing, and Santa waving to the crowd. This event always brings out the child in me and our street feels like a small piece of Disneyland entering into our sleepy village.

The only rule I have during my open house party on Christmas Eve is to be light-hearted, have fun, and be filled with love. My party often goes late into the evening with jamming musicians and caroling carolers. However, this years' Christmas Eve was different from any other year and it became a breaking point and a lesson for me.

At the peak of the party there were about thirty people mingling at my house. By the end of the night the party was winding down to a few choice people. I cleaned the dishes and swept the floor to prepare for the end of the party. I was determined to wake up with clean dishes in the dishwasher, a clean floor, and all things prepared for my solo Christmas morning writing session. The last few people to leave the party were my dear friends, Australian sisters (Szilva and Cyn) and a lesbian couple who I did not know well. We planned to have a glass of wine and a cup of tea, to recap the night and relax.

Unbeknownst to me, one of the women had been tipping the bottle a bit too much. She was adamant to leave right at that moment. Her partner was someone I knew from business. She tried to calm the situation and asked to stay and chat with us all. A fight between the partners escalated to a full-on verbally and emotionally abusive fight. Her partner had no remorse to hide the verbal attacks in front of us strangers, which only quickened the ire in me. The words that were thrown around forced me to stand up for her girlfriend, for my home, and for our safety. I felt that I had to go "GWEN" on the situation.

All of our reactions started out reasonable and peaceful. However, we all know how hard it is to reason with an abusive or drunk person. The more we tried to calm the situation, the more this person escalated. At one point we began to feel faced with potential physical danger. This person continued to threaten my friend. The more the threats came, the more my friend realized that she needed to break up with her, as she proceeded to do in front of us all. We were caught up in their cycle which was long overdue to be completed. I suppose she needed the support of us other women to stand up with her.

Of course, there were the typical theatrical exits, followed by the pounding at the door demanding for more confrontation. The third and final attempt of the abusive one trying to come back in my home, came after her girlfriend tried again to calm the situation. I was inside when I heard a violent scuffle outside on the porch. One of the Aussie sisters was in between the two in what seemed to be a physical brawl. The triad of bodies magnetically joined in a silent dance of anger, fear, and fight. The other Aussie sister screamed to break it up. They all rushed back inside and got behind me. I stood at my door, confronted by this dark energy that faced me at my door. To this day I am still not sure where this voice came from out of my body and the fact that not one neighbor heard the scuffle at the early hour of 1:00 a.m.

However, from the bowels of my body came a roar *"You are not welcome in my home. This is a home of peace and grace and there is no fighting or abuse allowed. You are not welcome here, you must leave."* I felt something shift inside of me, from deep inside of me. All of the negative relationships I had brought into my life were facing me inside of this woman standing at my door. I was talking to my past, as well as to this present situation.

I slammed the door and locked the "serpent" outside of the house. The pounding on the door ensued. I stood against the door with my hands holding the dark energy out. My friends were screaming threats of calling the police through the window to encourage this person to leave. I had no idea where this demon energy came from, as I had never experienced a darkness that was not afraid of unleashing their negative abuse in front of strangers. I had only experienced abuse behind closed doors.

This fight between these two people symbolized to me as a reflection of what is going on in the world. How two people who were once in love could go to this depth of this behavior still shakes me to the core. I knew this all too well in my own life.

Their fight created a wave of energy that sliced the air like fists that burst shards of glass. It brought up too many old memories and it did not take long for me to feel extremely violated and vulnerable.

I had been living a simple and peaceful life and relished my quiet mind and graceful flow. I had been feeling very strong, committed, and firm for this long-awaited birth of GWEN. No one was going to take this away from me again, especially after the fight that I had gone through over the past years to get back on my feet after the betrayal of my friends and partner.

I held my hands firmly against the door and began to pray for this person to leave. There was a silence from the pounding at the door. It was quiet for only a split second before this person's hand smashed through the small window on the front door. Her hand pummeled through a wooden dowel and a thick pane of glass. If it were not for the lace curtain that hung, supported by slim curtain rods, my face would have been hit.

We all stood in shock. The person ran to their car and drove away. I had to take a stand, for all the times that I had not taken a stand in my past when I was abused. I called the police. They offered for me to come to the police station to file a report and assured me that it did not have to happen that night, or on Christmas Day for that matter.

We decided to stay in, as our nerves were shaken to the core. I offered various places for the girls to sleep, as everyone was too shaken to drive home. It was a sleepless night. We were all in serious shock.

The next morning, I woke to find my friend was awake and battling with her now ex-partner over social media. This person had posted a photo of her bloody bandaged hand, trying to get sympathy from her friends.

I walked towards the entry hallway towards the front door and noticed one of my precious statues that had been on a pedestal in my entryway, was now leaned up against the wall with her head decapitated. This statue was created by a Mexican artist and it was a modern depiction of Mother Mary holding a peace dove. When I saw this all I could do was to get down on the floor and cradle Mother Mary and her head in my lap and sob. Mumbling over and over again about the violation of my home, my peace, but symbolically about the violation of our humanity. This was the time for GWEN to be born! I sobbed as I glued Mother Mary's head back on her body. I had no idea when or how the statue fell and broke, but it was more symbolic than anything.

My plans for writing on Christmas Day turned into hosting the women for the day. The four of us sat in a circle in my living room. It was a special time of holding space for each of them to share their own stories of abuse. These were stories that none of them knew they were going to share. I held the space and witnessed an opening and an awakening of healing for each of them, which ended up being a healing for me. This was part of the surrender, the forgiveness, and the healing. A definite and forever bond for us to take with us.

They eventually all went home around 8:30 that night so that I could squeeze in a few hours of writing to symbolically represent my day of Christmas writing.

While drifting off to sleep that night, I thought about the disappointments in my life. I saw the word disappointment in my head. The strange part of this image was that two of the letters popped out in my mind as I visualized this word. It was the ME in disappointMEnt. It was so clear in my mind.

Disappointment. Why did I keep getting disappointed in ME? Disappointed about this man, or that job, or this person who misunderstood me. It was a vicious cycle that seemed to spiral into this image of the ME inside of IT.

I calmed my busy mind and began to breathe and release. Slowly I felt a calmness come over me.

I relished in the softness. I cherished the silence.

**Soundcloud Playlist - Silent Night - Lizzie Sider

The next day I shared the disappointment epiphany with my dear friend Paula who asked me, *"What is it that you are disappointed in yourself?"*

My answer, *"Well, let me count the ways."*

This is the time in my life where I choose to release my limited thinking and disappointment, and instead reach for the stars.

The title of my book, *Homeless to the White House* brings up the obvious question of the White House and me. In the past I had no interest in running for political office and obviously the White House indicates a political scenario. However, I believe in the power of the vote, the power to be involved in our communities, in our country, and in the global stage of activism. As far as running for office, well, I'll never say never.

After all these years, I feel that I am ready to hold the space for the birth of GWEN, which has to do with this book and my story. I feel grateful. Divine grace has its perfect timing and God's plan is divine. After many attempts and false starts throughout the many years, GWEN Studios is now being launched with all of our series, films, documentaries, live streams, and more. Hallelujah!

**Soundcloud Playlist - Hallelujah - Jeff Buckley

We Are One

As said, I often get asked about the White House part of my title. Due to my Capital Hill adventure for the Congolese people, I felt an urge to find ways to get involved with helping to bring awareness to situations for human rights that need advocacy for change. The family court system, early child marriage, sex trafficking, and a passion that is obviously near and dear to my heart, homelessness and abuse.

In May 2017, I traveled to Washington DC with my dear friend David Longoria, who created a movement based on a song that he wrote and produced called *We Are One*.

This song represents a prayer for everyone to come together to make a change. I was one of seven hundred artists that David brought together to sing this historical song. The Day of Prayer event was on the lawn of the White House, and it was the closest I had come to the White House so far, outside of being a tourist looking from the outside.

While standing on the lawn of the White House, singing *We Are One*, the White House was in the background. I felt a surge of emotion come over me, one that reminded me of the power that each one of us have to make a change!

I had invited my dear friend Jacob Foko, who is a photojournalist from Cameroon to come shoot for the day. He is the one who took the cover photo of my book. After the *We Are One* performance Jacob took another photo of me sitting in the grass on the back lawn of the White House. I sat on this cool, well-groomed grass looking over my shoulder to the White House and I prayed really hard for a world of peace.

This birth of GWEN was long overdue, while also being the perfect divine time.

**Soundcloud Playlist - We Are One - David Longoria

Chapter 24

The Sea Of Cortez

I am on this underwater journey, floating in the abyss. I can see just above the water's surface, and there is a seagull floating overhead watching me. I am waiting for the light on top of the surface to guide me upward to pure air. I see that the treasure chest that I have been searching for is my heart. My pure love for God, the world, and my life is real and my heart has always been an open vessel. I do know how to love and to love deeply. And for that I am grateful!

The synergy. The magic. The dance.

Within my journey of self-discovery, I hear a voice inside my head shout, *"Stop getting in my way!"* A great epiphany to realize that no one was holding me back all these years, but myself.

After tracing the steps of my beautifully, blessed life, I realized the shadow and the darkness were only reflections of myself holding my own self back. And that I was dancing with my shadows as well.

"Why have I done my life this way?" I plead to my angels who I know have been with me every step of the way.

It has taken me decades on this journey to get to the place of forgiveness and surrender. *"How did I end up on this magical shore, at the Sea of Cortez?"* I asked myself. I must have done something right.

On my first morning walk on the beach I watched the rising sun. I sat on the sand to do a prayer, take a deep breath, and meditate.

I heard the ancient indigenous peoples, the mystics, shamans, seers, and doers calling my name between the sounds of the waves that gently caressed the sandy shore.

I opened my eyes and saw life in a different way. A seabird flew gracefully over my head, waving to me with her wings. I saw beautiful shells that had washed up in the sand. Memories of clam digging in Cape Cod with my "Handsome Hemingway" lingered in my mind. The sharp-edged shells peeked up from the grains of sand, reminding me of the shards of my broken heart that I knew now had been healed. I know that all my relationships were for a bigger reason, and I had to let go of self-judgment and let go of the question *"Why did I take this long to realize that I had it all, all along?"*

I stood on the edge of the wet sand, waiting with anticipation for a wave to rinse over my feet, like a baptism to cleanse my sins. The water kept teasing me to get into the ocean, *"Come closer, my dear... it's just me... the ocean."* I heard a gentle, deep laugh as if I would believe that this enormous body of water did not have the power to decide at any moment to swell up and swallow me whole.

I watched the rhythm and the gentleness of her waves. Could the sea be my friend? I stood firm, toes digging into the sand, forcing my feet to wait for the waves to reach me. I had done all that I would do in my compromise dance of not going too far into the cold December, winter water. I heard the voice of my friend Marlene say, *"Missy, the ocean has a rhythm. You just have to wait three times and then go with the flow."*

I waited... and waited... and there it was, just the wave I needed to rinse my feet and baptize me with the freezing sea. The exact and perfect wave that shocked my system into receiving the healing that I needed on this day. I am apprehensive and in awe of the ocean. I danced between the rhythm of the waves, until finally tranquility set into my breathing.

**Soundcloud Playlist - My Heart Knows the Way - Kimberly Haynes

Here I was at the Sea of Cortez, December 2017. Just shy of a year since the Christmas Eve where that guest at my party put her fist through my window. So much had happened in the span of a year.

Tracing back to how I ended up in Mexico, I only had to trace back to early November. This gal Nadya contacted me through LinkedIn, introducing herself and the foundation she worked for, Women Like Us (WLU). Now, that caught my attention...women like us!

Nadya introduced me to the founder, Linda Rendleman, who had started WLU over ten years ago. I got on a call with Linda, and we spoke for over an hour about the similarities and passions we shared.

Linda invited me to their annual fundraiser in Beverly Hills. I did not know what to expect, but upon arriving I felt like I had met a tribe of long-lost sisters. All of us on the same path, heading in the same direction, working to empower women through all adversities in life. This group of women, along with many others, were banding together in many ways; like the recent #Metoo #TimesUp and the GWEN campaign #Reveal2Heal which are movements to empower women and give us all a voice.

I met amazing people at this event and I felt like I finally found sisters to forge ahead in the area of empowerment, so that as women we could take our rightful place in the world.

I always say, *"We do GWEN with the men"* as it is only with the true balance of masculine and feminine that we are able to succeed in the arc of healing humanity.

One of the gals from the *Women Like Us* event, Eden, hosted a toy-drive for Planet Hope the following week. The event took place at her jazz restaurant, *Vibrato*, inspired by her famous father, a music-industry giant, Herb Alpert. Eden and I had been Facebook friends for over eight years, but this was the first time meeting in person. Our similar mission of helping women who have survived domestic violence was the backbone of our mutual paths.

I brought a large, velvet holiday bag filled with stuffed animals for the toy drive. Eden graciously moved around the bar introducing me to one wonderful person after another.

There was a sweet, familiar looking woman sitting at the end of the bar sipping a glass of wine. I had met Terry the week before, at the *Women Like Us* fundraiser. Terry is on the WLU National Board and she is an avid humanitarian with similar stories of travel and adventures, like myself.

She cheerfully greeted me and invited me to sit at the bar with her. As our divine assignment unraveled we discovered that Terry did not come for the toy drive, but to meet her girlfriends for dinner. She invited me to join them. I went back and forth whether to intrude on their dinner plans. But my newfound "yes to life" took over me and before I knew it I was sitting at a table with these fabulous women, dining on Italian food and drinking wonderful wine.

During dinner Terry announced to the group that she was going to her home in Mexico and asked if anyone wanted to join her. Without thinking twice I shouted out, *"I want to go!"* I surprised myself and I am sure even the others, as I did not even ask if she was referring to me. I was the new girl on the block and these women were long time friends.

Certainly I had no idea where in Mexico this would be, I just trusted the opportunity. Terry responded sweetly, with a look of surprise on her face. After expressing interest to go, I was not even sure how I would manifest the trip with all the pending things that needed to be done to get GWEN funded. I simply had to trust that if it was meant to be then it would happen.

Before I knew it, Terry and I crossed the border and we were in the Tijuana airport getting ready to board a flight to La Paz. I had traveled to Rosarito Beach in Baja California many times over the years, but this was my first time going further south in Mexico.

We landed in paradise. We drove through La Paz, which is the capital of Baja Sur. This is a truly authentic Mexican town, not really flushed with many tourists. I watched the mountains in the distance preparing for the pending sunset. We got into our rental car. Terry mastered the winding dirt roads, as she grew up in these parts and she was used to navigating the culture, language, and environment. Her home is in a tiny village about an hour outside of La Paz, called La Ventana, which translates to "the window." I felt this was an appropriate place to write, as the window represented the window to my soul. Terry had much to do to manage her properties, so she was fine with me planning to be a hermit most of the days to write my book.

As we drove through the mountain, Terry shared tales of her childhood. Her father was a well-known athlete and deep-sea diver. After losing her mom at the age of nine, Terry became an avid athlete and diver following in her father's footsteps. I could only imagine what it must have been like to grow up diving deep in the ocean with my father to catch fish and lobster by hand.

It was amazing to imagine this young girl swimming in the underwater wild, searching for the "hunt of the day." My last name, Cacciatore, translates to the hunter (for the hunt of the day) her given name is Terry, but she is called Teresa in Mexico. My given name is Theresa but everyone calls me Tess. We are both humanitarians and passionate about healthy living. This just seemed right.

I found it fascinating to learn how one dives for lobsters, as lobsters tend to hide in caves that are shared with eels. Terry told me the story that if one were to reach into the hole of the cave to take out a lobster, an eel could bite your hand and swell their body so big that you could not take your hand out of the hole. It would appear as though the eel was protecting the lobster from being taken, but the truth is that if the lobster gets injured then the eel can eat the lobster. What an odd pair of sea friends … the lobster and the eel.

Terry continued to bump along the dirt road through the mountain to get us to her home. The terrain was reminiscent of Africa, A car on the opposite side of the road blinked their lights at us, giving us a signal that something was coming up on the road ahead. *"Most likely a herd of cattle"* Terry murmured under her breath. Sure enough, as we winded the corner of the road, there was a herd of cows and a few young calves Their heads faced forward, as their eyes glanced sideways, fixated on me, as if to say, *"I'm watching you lady. Don't get any wild ideas to jump out of the car and come after me."* The two little calves at the end of the herd looked directly at me. One of them seemingly winked in my direction. Probably just a fly in its eye, but nonetheless I was elated.

Terry pointed out the ancient cactus forest. I had just began growing my own little cactus garden, so to see these monstrous-sized giants with outstretched prickly arms pointing to the sky was awe-inspiring. These cacti had to have been over three-hundred years old.

We wound our way through the village, stopping off at the local markets and a fish shop to get everything we needed for the next few days. Fresh caught fish, organic produce, large prep kitchen, view of the ocean, handmade margaritas, great company... I must have done something right.

The first evening Terry had a dear friend, Mike, come to town to help her with tasks for her properties. We all relaxed after a home-cooked meal, which I happily prepared.

Staring up at the star-filled sky, I excitedly looked for my main man. And, there he was tried and true, ever-present ... Orion. He came to greet me once again in the winter sky, whether he calmed me while in Ghana with Maxwell, or here in Mexico under more peaceful times, Orion always held for me a sign. He is my strongest constellation with his hunter bow out and the three stars that make up his belt.

The ocean was tranquil and the night sky was dark in the absence of a moon. I asked, "What body of water was in front of us? Mike replied, *"The sea of Cortez."*

I almost fell out of my chair. *"Of course it was,"* I thought.

**Soundcloud Playlist - Under the Milky Way - The Church

I felt completely filled with emotion and on the verge of tears. This was the place where some of the greatest writers of all time had drafted their most iconic works of literature. I could actually visualize Hemingway out on the sea. In my imagination, he sat on the deck of his boat and stared at the same lighthouses and stars that I could see right then, guided by perhaps the same muses who had inspired me.

From Hemingway to Steinbeck, I relished in the thought that this must be the reason for my being here. I had been waiting and praying for this for the past eight years, as every turn of the road felt like the turn of the page that was not yet complete.

I felt the ancient energy and took in the inspiration from the stars. I knew this was my marker for the ending of my book and the beginning of a new life. This felt like all the betrayal, confusion, and abuse simply vanished into the sea air offering me a healing and a new beginning for GWEN to be truly born.

Part Three of this book is titled; *GWEN is Born: The Immaculate Perception.* I came up with this title long before I gave any thought to the meaning. I just liked the sound of it, given my Catholic upbringing.

Now it became clear to me that the perception of myself had to be changed from the inside out before anything could be reflected from the outside to the in. This was the true symbiotic dance of the yin/yang. The inside healing was then reflected to what was now appearing to me on the outside. Healthy living, healthy relationships, flowing funding, right divine timing. It all related to the healing from the inside to the outer world. I am trying not to self-judge here, but why in the hell did it take me this long?

The stars were twinkling strong in the sky with no moon in sight. We decided to all settle in for the night. The village is so remote with no city lights that it gets very dark, very early. Often, 8:00 p.m. is referred to as "Mexican Midnight." Terry offered me a choice of one of the bedrooms inside the main house, or the casita with my own view of the ocean. Obviously, I joyously chose the casita. My favorite part of this charming cottage was the small glass-top table that was placed near the front window that faced the beach, the sea, the sea birds, and the wind surfers. It was a perfect perch for me to send out the signal to my muses that I had arrived and it was time to get to work.

After the evening conversation that I had with Mike and Terry, I climbed into bed with my laptop and feverishly researched the history of the area.

Upon reflection, I found it fascinating that my book begins in Kinshasa, Democratic Republic of Congo, as an undercover documentarian who was faced at gunpoint, to then end my book at the Sea of Cortez. I was now on the edge of tranquil waters, healed and empowered, ready to take on new meaning in life.

From Congo to Mexico the coincidence did not escape me when I connected the historical dots. Both places shared the same devastating story of European colonialism.

One of the tribes in this region of La Paz is a tribe called Pericú and they are best known for their harvesting of sea life and the hunting of small game. The Pericú were one of the few aboriginal groups that crafted with balsa wood to build rafts and paddles.

Looking out the window of my casita, I visualized the colonies of indigenous tribes with their campfires cooking their hand-caught seafood, while younger boys and girls played with handmade drums that echoed heartbeat rhythms across the sea. I leaned out my window to hear the chants of their ancient songs just as if I was there at that time.

I drifted off to sleep with the sound of waves luring me on a tranquility ride. *"Sweet dreams"* the ocean whispered. I fell into a deep slumber that was a deeper sleep than I had in a very long time.

That night I had a funny dream. A very tall man came up to me at a party. I felt like I knew him, but I could not place where I knew him from. I asked his name. He said,

"My name is Will." *"Nice to meet you."* I said. *"What is your last name? You look familiar to me."*

He spelled out his name, *"Finnish...spelled like F-i-n-n-i-s-h."* I wondered if this was his actual name, or was he from Finland?

I woke up laughing that I dreamt a pun, as I put his name together to be Will Finnish...as in will finish...as in *"I will finish my book."*

I looked out my window and saw a bright, intense sunrise that reminded me of being in Durban, South Africa on the Indian Ocean. The ocean called me down to the water's edge, where I began collecting seashells down by the seashore.

For the next five days, I sat at the tiny table in the casita with my makeshift altar of shells, incense and my computer. I watched the snowy egret birds fly in formation above my head. I watched the kite surfers fly around the sea on the breeze. I meditated and rested and exhaled to truly integrate the destiny that is about to take shape with the birth of GWEN.

Everything is full circle. The rats were off my ship. I put the men in my life inside the forgiveness box and sent them off to sea to make room for my true partner to come into my life.

What had to be "immaculate" inside of my "perception" for the birth of GWEN was the alignment of God, universe, angels, and other like-minded people who are truly dedicated to making the world better. The dark side will always exist, but it is the perception of how we allow (or not allow) the darkness into our lives.

Inside my mind, I unpacked the reasons that all things happened in my life and realized the cold hard fact that I am the only one who held me back. I am the one who chose the relationships that came into my life. I was the one who decided to go on the road with the band, rather than pursue my own recording contract. I was the one who chose the life I did, so that I could reach my destiny that was planned for me, by me, before I could be re-born in this lifetime.

While watching the waves on the Sea of Cortez I realized that GWEN is born. The immaculate "perception" I placed upon myself, the belief that everything had to be in place, perfect, and in line, was not a reality.

GWEN is born with the perception that life will always have its turns in the road, but along the way God is always watching. GWEN is the gift for me and now for the world to experience.

GWEN is outside of me now and in the world. It is here to inspire all of us to know that our voice is worthy of being heard and our stories are important to share. This is the time for the #Reveal2Heal campaign, so that we can make a difference in our lives and the ones we love. This is the time to break the cycles of abuse, by understanding and releasing our blueprint that was given to us in our childhood. We need to forgive ourselves most of all and know that we all truly have a divine purpose and passion. And, to find those things in our reality gives us the true meaning in life.

Let our dreams fall into line and our passions be realized. As today, I rise and I am free.

Written and Performed in New York March 2017 by Tess Cacciatore

I Rise!!

I am not free - as I carry the bondage of chains, ropes, robes that cover, smother, and suffocate the innocent slaves throughout history.

War torn, infernal murder, hot oil strikes the face and melts the skin beyond recognition.Falsely led from the sublime by the slime throughout time into the fire like a lamb into the slaughter house - we go I am wanting to be free - as the rise of the feminine meets the rise of the masculine to create to perfect symbiotic, symbolic, structure of the black and white ying yang spinning hope to find the balance.It is the divine right time to fall in line OR to fall out of line to mess up the crooked straight lines that box us in

It is time to wake up It is time to rise up to have the infinite intimate relationship with ME with YOU My soul is to **LISTEN** for my calling and to **FEEL** the better understanding that in every shadow there is a ray of light that cuts through the darkness like a hot sword cutting butter on a cold winter's night.

Rise up to be up now is the time to have a clear understanding within my mind - that thoughts are not just fleeting words of nothingness containing grocery lists and check off duties, but in these moments I choose what ultimately goes into my mouth to nourish my cells to keep my body clean of chem-trails and mind-obsessed disarray. Cleanse my garden with rich soil inside of my mind, my body, my earth. MOTHER EARTH

Cleanse the dark thoughts that lead to gossip and fear all tongue-tied to one thing called insecurity. Release the mind-clatter that chains me to my programmed self from long ago when I was an innocent babe inside my mothers' womb creating a tomb of rebirth all through my life - it is time to RISE!

Share the love towards my brothers and sisters in the HUMAN race, so that I can pace peace and harmony realizing disharmony of borders simply draws the line in the sand from MAN calling claim to a territory for greed, power, and lust. This is unjust - What if there were no lines in the sand - could the rivers of my tears wash the lines away - OR are the lines here to stay? KNOWING that every negative thought that flutters into my confused A.D.D. mind has a chance to be re-attached to a positive thought - as I put the jumper cables on the brain conductors and flush out the dark.

Bursting forth the pimple that is filled with dark puss of misconception - forcing the clear flowing liquid pumping through my veins - connecting me to every other race - because we all have the same color blood.

Be rid of my sorrow and blame it is a crying shame to not forgive those who trespass against us - as in forgiveness we find FREEDOM. be awakened to rise up in my feminine powers as it is within the feminine that I seek out my highest self to wake up wake up wake up and rise. the feminine in me celebrates a re-birth - the masculine in me re-calibrates and the dance begins

Light Only Visualizes Evolution

Light Only Visualizes Evolution

Light Only Visualizes Evolution ... There it is.... L O V E

Hail Mary - so full of grace, Gaia, Mother Earth, Quan Yin, the immaculate perception of the conception - the consummate giver of breath, of life - Give birth with a reason - without treason - with my full duty to future generations and the commitment to myself. DARK dances to share the light - light dances to end the fight. I Rise Up! I Rise Up! I Rise up! Now... I am free!

**Soundcloud Playlists - Today, I Rise - Tess Cacciatore

About the Author

Tess Cacciatore is co-founder and CEO of GWEN (Global Women's Empowerment Network), established in 2012. The award-winning producer, videographer, journalist, keynote speaker, storyteller, social entrepreneur – and now published author – has dedicated her life to advocating for peace, justice and equality around the globe.

Recognizing that everyone's story has value, Tess provides support for those who struggle to find their voice. She is a connector using entertainment, technology, and philanthropy to bridge people and cultures worldwide. Throughout the years, Tess has participated in various international forums, including the United Nations (Geneva and New York), speaking on behalf of women and children. Today, she continues her quest to advance humanity and enhance life quality with her inspiring memoir and the ongoing #Reveal2Heal grassroots, cultural movement. Tess advocates for human rights and has dedicated her life to social issues, homelessness, domestic violence, sex trafficking, and to offer a safe place for voices to be heard.

About GWEN

The Global Women's Empowerment Network (GWEN) utilizes the power of media and technology to enable people to share their stories and transform their lives. By design, GWEN is led by women and to be joined by all. Through live-stream events, online-curriculum, and in-person workshops, GWEN offers a safe place for people from all cultures and all ages, to reveal their story so that healing can begin.

With our 501c3 not-for-profit status, gifts and donations to GWEN programs and initiatives are tax-deductible. www.GlobalWomensEmpowermentNetwork.org

Have Your Story Published!

PSA's | Short Films

Our lives are full of experiences that shape the blueprint of who we become. Parents, teachers, siblings, co-workers, partners, can either make a positive or negative influence on our self-esteem and confidence. I feel that it is important to take charge of our lives and uncover the scars that keep us tied to our past, rather than having a new start. It is important to find a safe place to share your story, and GWEN is that safe place.

I can ensure you that your story is amazing and that you are not alone! By sharing your experiences, you could touch the heart of another. Your story could be the "Reveal to Heal" that a reader is searching for, to give them the strength to uncover their pwn story to a new life. The ripple effect of love can take our lives to a place of self-realization, self-empowerment, and self-love.

Visit this link today at
www.GlobalWomensEmpowermentNetwork.org

and apply NOW for our #Reveal2Heal movement. Upon successful application, your story with be published and you will have the opportunity to join us in a powerful moment and become a published author. We have every intention to heal other's through the power of words and every intention of taking you to that best sellers list!

We all have a story to share...
What's your Story?

Visit us today at:
GlobalWomensEmpowermentNetwork.org

Check out GWEN Studios for impactful content:
Films, Series and Music on www.GWEN.Live

92204628R00194

Made in the USA
Middletown, DE
06 October 2018